Yankee No!

Yankee No!

Anti-Americanism in
U.S.–Latin American Relations

Alan McPherson

HARVARD UNIVERSITY PRESS
Cambridge, Massachusetts
London, England
2003

Library of Congress Cataloging-in-Publication Data

McPherson, Alan L.
  Yankee no! : anti-Americanism in U.S.–Latin American relations /
Alan McPherson.
     p.   cm.
  Includes bibliographical references and index.
  ISBN 0-674-01184-8 (alk. paper)
  1. Latin America—Relations—United States.   2. United States—Relations—
Latin America.   3. Anti-Americanism—Latin America.   4. Dominican
Republic—History—1961– 5. Panama—History—1946–1981. 6. Cuba—
History—1959– 7. Venezuela—History—1935–1958.   I. Title.

F1418.M373 2003
327.7308—dc21   2003051118

To my parents, all three of them:
Marie Guindon McPherson, James McPherson,
and Arthur Selin.
Each gave me something irreplaceable.

Contents

Illustrations

Yankee No!

Introduction
Anti-Americanism as Historical Problem

Any criticism of the Americans to our north should always be accompanied, as in the case of any worthy opponent, with the chivalrous salute that precedes civilized combat. And I make that bow sincerely. But to ignore a North American's defects would seem to me as senseless as to deny his good qualities.
—*José Enrique Rodó, Ariel (1900)*

The deaths of thousands on September 11, 2001, and in the war on terrorism that followed propelled to the foreground of public discourse a word—"anti-Americanism"—that has cried out for decades to be taken seriously by historians.[1] Although the victims of the World Trade Center and the Pentagon included citizens from dozens of nations, observers immediately labeled the attacks there "anti-American." Soon enough, "anti-American" also denoted the suspects, Osama bin Laden and the al Qaeda network. The societies in which they lived were allegedly also "anti-American." In newspapers and magazines, the word appeared roughly five times more often after September 11 than it had before. The apparent sudden prominence of anti-U.S. hostility around the world at once outraged and perplexed U.S. citizens. Many longed to understand the roots of resentment and hatred against the United States. President George W. Bush himself asked Congress on September 20, "Why do they hate us?"[2]

The alarm, anger, and soul-searching that followed September 11 stirred familiar ghosts. In the decade or so starting in the mid-1950s, U.S. readers had surely felt similar emotions as they read the following headlines: "How Deep 'Hate-America,'" "Why Is America Misunderstood?" "Anti-Americanism Sweeps World," "Do They Like Us?" and "Why Do They *Hate* Us?"[3] Headlines had fed on an increase in criticism and attacks against U.S. institutions, policies, and citizens abroad. In the first half of the 1960s, there were more assaults on U.S. embassies and libraries abroad—one measure of anti-Americanism—than in the previous sixty years combined.[4] There was an odd simplicity to these U.S. headlines, one that suggested timeless themes. For one thing, there were substantial assumptions—first, that foreigners liked, loved, or hated U.S. citizens, but that they were not indifferent; second, that foreigners did not discriminate much between U.S. citizens and the U.S. government. U.S. citizens also seemed comforted by the duality of "us" and "them," by the fact that a sharp line separated those who lived in the United States from those who did not. In a nutshell, the U.S. response to anti-Americanism revealed U.S. national identity: idealist, universalist, and exceptionalist. It suggested a uniquely Yankee way of approaching negative foreign public opinion. Anti-Americanism and U.S. responses to it exhibited then, as they do now, recurring patterns that went to the heart of U.S. relations with the outside world.

One of the us-versus-them combinations was, as another headline proposed, "Yankees versus Latins."[5] Most "Latins" who expressed their discontent in the 1950s and 1960s lived in the Caribbean, the area of the world where U.S. influence was historically most pronounced. Spanish Caribbean images of the United States were long-standing and complex, and their vividness and political implications ebbed and flowed depending on the level of U.S. penetration in the region and also on larger Latin American political trends. In the late 1940s, for instance, U.S. military and economic power was focused less on expanding into the rest of the Western Hemisphere than on rebuilding Europe and containing the Soviet Union. This tended to minimize anti-Americanism in Latin America but also to leave the political field open to dictators who exploited U.S. neglect and anti-communist fears. From the mid-1950s to the mid-1960s, as U.S. military training in Latin America expanded, as the region integrated further into global commerce, and as the Cold War heated up everywhere in the developing world, fluid and sometimes inchoate Spanish Caribbean images from the first half of the century solidified into political structures and strategies. Elites, masses, and emerging middle groups articulated similar arguments, and for the first time they formed alliances with one another against U.S. influences. There had been waves of anti-U.S. violence before—notably against U.S. occupations in the Caribbean in the early century—but this cross-class momentum of the postwar era was new. As a result, anti-U.S. events grew not only more numerous in the world as a whole but also more concentrated in the Western Hemisphere: one study found that from 1956 to 1965, 65 out of 171 "anti-American demonstrations, riots, and terrorist attacks" in the world took place in Latin America.[6]

This book suggests the broader meanings and workings of anti-Americanism by focusing on its prominence in inter-American diplomacy roughly from 1958 to 1966. It opens with the physical attack on Vice President Richard Nixon in Caracas and continues with deeper case studies of events in Cuba, Panama, and the Dominican Republic. After Caracas jump-started U.S. worries about anti-Americanism as a distinct phenomenon in Latin America, Fidel Castro's revolution in 1959 redefined Cuban identity as anti-U.S. and turned U.S. worries into a fear that mass-based hostility might spread to the rest of the hemisphere, perhaps even the world. By 1964, however, when Panamanians rioted for the apparently symbolic right to plant their flag in the U.S.-controlled Canal Zone, U.S. policymakers learned to approach each case of anti-Americanism on its own terms. A year and a half later, the Dominican Republic erupted into a civil conflict only mildly concerned with U.S. power. Washington's overwhelming gunboat response showed that it still had a lot to learn about anti-U.S. sentiment and strategy. It did so to a degree that satisfied U.S. policymakers—perhaps too easily—by 1966. After that year, anti-Americanism did not disappear from Latin America, and may even have intensified, but the Vietnam War monopolized U.S. attention. These events—the Cuban Revolution, the Panama Riots, and the Dominican Intervention—together made up one of the most fascinating anti-U.S. sagas in the history of U.S. foreign relations. These crises greatly concerned Washington because each was a mass-based, cross-class, verbally or physically violent rejection of U.S. power that spoke to others in the developing world who seethed with similar resentments. Each is a milestone in the history of anti-Americanism.

Despite its persistence in Latin America and elsewhere, anti-Americanism has received little attention as a historical issue. Perhaps this is because it sometimes seems too nebulous yet also too fraught with specific assumptions. Anti-Americanism is, *prima facie*, nowhere and everywhere, evasive yet pervasive. We may not know what it is, but we know when we see it. So how do we avoid its pitfalls, and how do we think about it usefully?

First, we should not be too hasty to define anti-Americanism. Scholars certainly have been unable to agree on a central noun that would anchor a definition. Is anti-Americanism an "ideology," an "attitude," a "stance," or a "tendency"? One author used six different nouns—"mindset," "attitude," "sense," "predisposition," "sentiment," "type of bias"—within a few pages to characterize it.[7] Anti-Americanism could also be considered, as one Dominican scholar and critic of U.S. policy said, as simply "part of other ideologies" such as nationalism, anti-imperialism, socialism, or conservatism.[8] Still others have made valiant efforts to quantify anti-Americanism, but the variety of methods—including "attitude scales," "individual-level structural variables," and "multiple regression analysis"—only suggested the slipperiness of the concept.[9]

Second, anti-Americanism is an extremely politicized concept, leading at least one scholar to call for a cease-fire in the volleys of "emotionally charged code words" that surround it.[10] The political and intellectual right has done the most to sabotage serious thinking about anti-U.S. sentiment by overusing the term and exploiting its inherent negativity. Some have dismissed anti-Americanism for its "emotional" content—its envy, especially—or for its historical dependence on Europe for misplaced socialist theories and highbrow superiority. Others have characterized it merely as a reservoir of stereotypes akin to racism, sexism, and anti-Semitism.[11] Witness Paul Hollander's use of almost clinical language to paint anti-Americanism as a pathology: "Anti-Americanism is a metaphor that stands for alienation, estrangement, radical social criticism, or an adversarial view of American society and culture; it usually entails the misperception and exaggeration of the flaws and failings of American institutions and values; it also leads or amounts to an unrealistic and inflated view of the responsibility that the (American) social system has for the problems and difficulties of particular groups and individuals."[12]

The left, meanwhile, has preferred to speak of anti-imperialism rather than anti-Americanism, under the assumption that resistance to U.S. power is and has been a perfectly reasonable response to systematic intervention and exploitation.[13] True, resistance has been often called for, even required, and the concern that "anti-Americanism" is a fuzzy concept is warranted. Yet the term is impossible to ignore: it has proven its durability and its ability to shape international relations. There is room to speak of anti-imperialism and anti-Americanism as partly overlapping yet distinct phenomena. Otherwise, treating U.S. power as just one more manifestation of a worldwide pattern of empire neglects the specificity of anti-U.S. protests. Opening up the scholarship on international relations to include studies of anti-Americanism invites questions about resisters' political ideologies, economic grievances, and cultural backgrounds, and it compels scholars to make connections among the three. By doing so, we may begin to understand why there seems to have been no comparable "anti-Britishism," "anti-Russianism," or "anti-Chinesism" despite the substantial resistance to those empires. And speaking of anti-Americanism goes beyond anti-imperialism because it calls on scholars to examine how Washington (in contrast to, say, London or Beijing) responded to critics.

Finally, we need to study anti-Americanism as a sentiment and strategy for and by ordinary people. Scholars have for too long emphasized the anti-Americanism of a few intellectuals. This is understandable. Those trained to survey published sources would naturally turn to the "great texts" of anti-U.S. resistance early in the development of anti-Americanist studies.[14] Moreover, intellectuals in Latin America have long enjoyed greater prestige in political circles than have those in the United States, and they led several mass-based anti-U.S. movements and often placed themselves in harm's way. Besides, the lack of polls in Latin America before the 1950s made the description of mass anti-U.S. feeling even more difficult than it always is.[15] But to permit intellectuals' words to define anti-Americanism exaggerates their resonance, especially in largely illiterate societies. As we will see in the chapters that follow, when mass-based political groups came into their own they often ignored intellectual traditions and venues and used strategies more attuned to street-level sensibilities—and more dangerous, in Washington's view.

This book defines anti-Americanism in broad, intuitive terms, as the expression of a disposition against U.S. influence abroad. This definition does two things. First, it aims for political balance: as does the right, it includes dispositions against any U.S. influence—cultural, political, economic—but, in accord with the left, it does not assume that one disposition implies another. In fact, individuals who harbored limitless resentment toward all U.S. citizens and opposed any and all contact with the United States have been extremely rare, in Latin America as else-where, and at best they have been marginal to anti-Americanism. Anti-U.S. sentiment more typically has existed side-by-side with *pro*-Ameri-canism within individuals or groups. Yet even for supposedly more "ra-tional" critics who compartmentalized their opposition, it has proved extremely difficult to escape generalities about the United States—that all of its foreign policies were unilateral, that all its companies were ex-ploitative, that all its culture was vulgar, and so on. In addition, catego-ries of dispositions have tended to seep into one another. Opponents of the U.S. embargo on Cuba, for instance, might oppose the policy and ad-mire the U.S. political system, but they might also think, "What kind of democracy sustains a policy that most voters do not support?" To take another example of seeping generalities, critics of Hollywood may de-ride its supposedly trashy content because of a deeper resentment of the oligopoly that leads to U.S. domination of world cinema, as do U.S. oli-gopolies in many other industries. Economic, cultural, political, and other criticisms cannot help influencing one another every once in a while. In fact, the interconnectedness of anti-Americanism suggests that it has been an idealistic but confused resistance to idealistic but con-fused U.S. foreign policies.[16]

The second thing this broad definition does is imply real-world activ-ism, and so it values the *how* as much as the *why* of anti-Americanism. Voting, legislating, speech making, pamphlet writing, rallying around a party, and rock throwing: anti-Americanism in all its diversity and even its anarchy has been both thought and action, sentiment and strategy, each component calling on the other to form an ideological whole that exposed the alleged negative nature of U.S. power and justified specific means of resistance. Looking at the strategy of anti-Americanism also al-lows for a more manageable historical narrative that focuses on the ef-fectiveness of anti-Americanism rather than on its morality.

Three features of anti-Americanism best explain how sentiment trans-lated into strategy. The first of these features is *variability*. The cases un-der review in this book demonstrate that a dominant variant of anti-Americanism emerged in each nation—revolutionary in Cuba, conser-vative in Panama, and episodic in the Dominican Republic. This study examines the social structures, political traditions, and national, ethnic, gender, and racial identities along with the type of U.S. hegemony in each country that together shaped the rise of mass-based anti-U.S. strategies by the late 1950s. Anti-Americanism was variable in the most complex of senses: capacious, not capricious; shifting, not shifty.

A second feature of anti-Americanism has been *ambivalence*—the relatively clear-headed espousal of contradictory feelings or beliefs—and not ambiguity, which is more akin to uncertainty. This book asks how ambivalence toward the United States affected the outcomes of diplomatic crises. In normal times, Latin American leaders, even fervent nationalists, juggled a variety of positive and negative perceptions of the United States. Crises tended to intensify these perceptions, highlight their incompatibility, and test cultural and political loyalties to the United States. Crises also regularly brought together strange bedfellows, who tended to warm up to each other against more radical anti-U.S. groups. Often, however, the return of stability weakened political resolve and shattered these unions. Also, the bottom of anti-Americanism often seemed to fall out as crises revealed that Latin American public opinion was more supportive of U.S. policies than elites on one end and revolutionaries on the other said it was. Polls, public outpourings of friendship, and countless private moments all showed that ordinary people expressed significant pro-U.S. sentiment even as their governments did not. A subtle semantic dissonance expressed this ambivalence: in crisis after crisis, Caribbean peoples used the more pejorative words *gringos* and *yanquis* as well as the neutral or positive term *americanos*. *Americanos* created jobs for Latin Americans, for instance, but *gringos* took their land. *America* presented diplomatic credentials, but *el yanqui* landed Marines.

Finally, an essential third feature of anti-Americanism is the *resilience* of the U.S. response to it. "Anti-Americanism is generally perceived as a cultural or sociological phenomenon," the CIA's former deputy director Richard Bissell once said. "At some point during its accumulation, its impact on the conduct of U.S. foreign policy has to be recognized."[17] The crises in this book made anti-Americanism not only a household word but a priority for U.S. presidents and their aides, top members of Congress, and other opinion leaders. An anti-Americanism that emerged from the masses offered a challenge to the U.S. idea that ordinary people were kept from expressing pro-U.S. sentiment by corrupt foreign leaders. It forced the highest policymakers in Washington to reexamine their rationales for world leadership. The U.S. response to anti-Americanism, therefore, did not rest merely on power. Against small Caribbean countries, the White House and others could have responded to hostility only with force. It did, at times, use force. But generally, the U.S. policy-making establishment displayed a surprisingly robust ideological consistency across the political spectrum, U.S. public opinion included. U.S. responses to anti-Americanism often appeared naïve, but in reality they concealed a great reservoir of self-confidence that helped U.S. decision-makers bounce back and even get further involved in world affairs. Interestingly, the adjective "anti-American" first appeared in 1773, along with the nation itself, to qualify a "doctrine" held by the British parliament and its colonial representatives.[18] As an ideological outgrowth and a political strategy, anti-Americanism had to cope not only with its own ambivalence but also with a lack of ambivalence in the U.S. government. Anti-U.S. sentiment, then as now, grabbed the headlines, but anti-U.S. strategy rarely followed through.

1

The Road to Caracas
Or, Richard Nixon Must Get Stoned

On May 13, 1958, it may have seemed to many people that Latin Americans just did not like the United States anymore. That afternoon, Vice President Richard Nixon, while on a good will mission to South America, headed a motorcade into Caracas, Venezuela's capital. When the cars slowed down, onlookers rushed to gather around them. For twelve minutes, the crowd rocked the vehicles, bashed them with sticks and iron bars, spat on the windows, and shouted at the passengers. The U.S. delegates and their Venezuelan escorts feared for their lives, and barely escaped. The incident brought a climax to protests that marred every stop on Nixon's itinerary. Whatever else this was, most witnesses agreed, it was anti-Americanism—unbridled hostility toward "the United States." Costa Rican president José Figueres, like others, tried to define the problem narrowly: "People cannot spit on a foreign policy which is what they meant to do." Others feared a tide of revolution. As one aide told Secretary of State John Foster Dulles, "The preponderance of U.S. influence in Latin America is being challenged." Among shaken U.S. diplomats, the general consensus was at least that "real violence" against U.S. representatives was "something new," a qualitative leap in boldness stemming from resentment against nearly every aspect of U.S. influence in Latin America.[1]

The symbolic and sometimes literal stoning of Nixon— protesters threw rocks at him in Peru—did at least signal the readiness of mass-based groups to express hostility directly at the U.S. government. Anti-Americanism, to be sure, had a long history in Latin America. But before the late 1950s critics in the region were poor, disunited, or powerless to

9

challenge the U.S. government or military. By 1958, however, the right conditions lined up to transform widespread anti-U.S. sentiment into a compelling political strategy. The protesters represented a new social mixture, for one. Nixon's detractors were literate youths led by adult university students or Communist Party cadres, unemployed dwellers of poor neighborhoods, and leftist editorialists and cartoonists. These groups, also, had accumulated a vast repertoire of anti-U.S. imagery over decades—the predatory eagle, the omnipresent octopus, greedy Wall Street tycoons, the impersonal boots of U.S. Marines, and so on. In books that stirred the public imagination with the simple morality of fables, former Guatemalan president Juan José Arévalo denounced the slyness and voraciousness of the U.S. "shark" against Latin American "sardines."[2] It was no coincidence that Caracans called Nixon a "shark" when he came to visit. There were still other reasons. Anti-American groups had better financing than ever before, sometimes from populists or liberal democrats, sometimes from Moscow. And they enjoyed significant political clout in incipient democratic regimes increasingly run by middle groups bitter at the lingering power of dictators supported by the United States and looking for fairer trade agreements. In 1957–1958, finally, a sudden drop in world prices for many raw materials from Latin America triggered a recession that drove many into the cities—and into the streets. In this environment, anti-U.S. movements gained momentum, internal coherence, and international prestige.

The Caracas episode also set a precedent in the response it elicited from Washington. The few shapers of public opinion in the United States who paid any attention to Latin America had often wondered whether and how to predict, prevent, appease, placate, or destroy anti-American groups. Prior to 1958, however, the U.S. response to foreign critics largely denied the existence of a Caribbean empire. Such a denial implied that criticism of U.S. influence was *a priori* misguided, malicious, or controlled by extra-hemispheric powers. Rarely did an anti-U.S. critique strike Washington as reasonable, sincere, or disinterested. The near-death experience of Nixon, however, set in motion an effort to rethink Washington's breezy attitude toward the grievances of ordinary Latin Americans. Reliving the biblical tale of Saul (who becomes Paul) on the road to Damascus, "poor Richard"—as the operation to rescue Nixon dubbed him—declared Caracas to be a flash of light, blinding him at first, but then awakening him to long-ignored criticism. The vice president's own metaphor was that "Caracas was a much-needed shock treatment which jolted us out of dangerous complacency."[3]

Rising Resentment in Latin America

From the days of independence to the middle of the twentieth century, anti-U.S. sentiment touched every major social group in Latin America, especially in the Caribbean. Peasants, workers, and members of the middle class and the elite all resented being exploited or disdained by the United States at some point. Yet social divisions and ambivalence largely inhibited cross-class alliances among Latin Americans, who were left to resist U.S. imperialism in atomized, isolated groups. Eventually the U.S. government spread its influence even further. As a result, anti-Americanism seeped down from literary and other elites into the political consciousness of ordinary people as it also percolated up from the poor to shape mainstream politics.

Revealing ambivalence from the outset,[4] anti-U.S. sentiment in the early nineteenth century resulted from the shattering of hopes that elite Latin Americans had invested in collaborating with the United States following independence from Spain. From the 1820s to the end of the nineteenth century, Latin America's creoles repeatedly professed admiration for the Founding Fathers, Lincoln, Emerson, Thoreau, and the U.S. Constitution, and they conveniently overlooked the iniquity of slavery and the brutality of pre–Mexican War westward expansion.

Domingo Faustino Sarmiento was perhaps the most famous of Latin Americans to beseech his countrymen to emulate U.S. society. As a young man, Sarmiento left his native Argentina for a six-month tour of the United States. When it was over he wrote, "I leave [the United States] sad, pensive, pleased, and astonished; half my illusions lost or worn, while others struggle against reason." Sarmiento saw boundless possibilities in the physical greatness, economic development, and political creativity of the United States. Individuals were *simpático* and fairly honest, he thought, if a little superficial.[5] Twenty years later Sarmiento was back, as ambassador from 1864 to 1868. He now expressed even greater awe at the post–Civil War juggernaut. Like many of his peers, he foresaw an invigorating competition between the "Latin" and "Saxon" "races." He praised the latter's order, industriousness, cleanliness, high levels of education, social egalitarianism, and secularism. As president of Argentina toward the end of the century, Sarmiento called upon his compatriots to pursue a model of industrial development and an open immigration policy explicitly modeled on those of the United States: "Let us emulate the United States. Let us be America, as the sea is the ocean. Let us be the United States!"[6]

Such professions of admiration met with disappointing U.S. responses, which ranged from self-satisfaction to racist expansionism. Those who appropriated the name "Americans" seemed largely oblivious to the rest of the hemisphere. U.S. leaders sympathized in theory with the struggle against Spain, but kept their distance because of geographic separation and because of what they thought to be the political, racial, and religious inferiority of Latins. "I wished well to their cause," recalled John Quincy Adams of the post-independence leaders of Latin America, "but I had seen and yet see no prospect that they would establish free or liberal institutions of government." His father, John Adams, had been even less sympathetic: "The people of South America are the most ignorant, the most bigoted, the most superstitious of all the Roman Catholics in Christendom." Such prejudices gave ideological impetus to the U.S. war against Mexico in the 1840s and the filibustering of William Walker in Central America in the 1850s, events that dealt final blows to the idea of a hemisphere-wide confederation.[7]

Latin American elites considered the superior attitude of U.S. citizens disheartening and unwarranted. To the Mexican minister in Washington in 1822, for instance, U.S. racism and greed reinforced each other in the plunder of Latin America. "The arrogance of these republicans does not permit them to see us as equals, but as inferiors," he wrote back to Mexico. "They have a profound love for our money, not for us, and they are unable to enter into a treaty of alliance or commerce except as it suits them, without any thought of reciprocity." Latin America's leading creole, Simón Bolívar, lamented that "the United States seem destined by providence to plague America with miseries in the name of liberty." Even the success of the north only seemed to make the political divisions and social stagnation of Latin America stand out in contrast. Chilean José Victorino Lastarria characterized Latin countries as the "Dis-United States of America." His compatriot Francisco Bilbao in 1856 reproached the Sarmientos of Latin America for their love of the foreign: "Is there so little conscience in ourselves, so little faith in the intelligence of the Latin American race, that we must wait for a foreign will, a different intellect, to organize us and defend our fate?"[8]

At the turn of the twentieth century, anti-Americanism deepened when a powerful current of disdain for U.S. society and culture swept educated Latin Americans. Named after Uruguayan literature professor José Enrique Rodó's book *Ariel*, Arielism challenged positivist thinkers infatuated with Western notions of progress and order. It proposed that the United States was not an exemplar of these values, but rather an inferior Other. Rodó personified Latin America and the United States as two characters from Shakespeare's play *The Tempest*: Ariel and Caliban, respectively. The former—Latin America—was the quintessence of virtue and taste, heir to the highest European standards of dignity and spirituality. Caliban—the United States—was a reckless materialist: crude and self-absorbed, sumptuous and vacuous.[9] Finding itself now armed with a romantic but authentic identity for Latin America, the literary elite embraced Arielism and developed it into a full-blown continental shift in sensibilities that had a profound and lasting impact on education, scholarship, literature, and statesmanship. Acting on these impulses, for example, Manuel Ugarte of Argentina coined the popular term "the colossus of the north" to describe the United States.[10] All Arielists grasped the implication: not only did great power corrupt greatly, but powerlessness equaled virtue. The label stuck.

Yet Arielism, like almost all anti-U.S. movements, had its ambivalences. Rodó himself admitted to contradictory feelings about the United States: "Although I do not love them, I admire them." Progress, utilitarianism, egalitarianism, Madisonian republicanism, meritocracy, hard work, a sense of mission, curiosity, inventiveness, optimism, and self-confidence: these were all worthy U.S. traits, explained Rodó; the problem was that egotistical U.S. citizens too often marshaled them for the sake of productivity and delayed gratification rather than the enjoyment of life in the present. Rodó, in fact, had little personal experience on which to base either claim. He wrote *Ariel* in his twenties, when he had never been to the United States, and apparently he did not speak English well.[11]

Nicaragua's Rubén Darío was also of two minds. One of Arielism's few Caribbean representatives, and a competitor with Rodó in being "the poet of America," Darío lived most of his life outside Nicaragua to escape its provincialism and met other anti-U.S. writers mostly in New York and Europe. In "The Triumph of Caliban" he ridiculed Yankees as people who "eat, eat, calculate, drink whiskey, and make millions," and in 1904 he penned a sarcastic "Ode to [Theodore] Roosevelt." Yet only two years later he produced a "Salute to the Eagle," which sincerely expressed the hope that Nicaragua's delegation to the Pan American conference in Río de Janeiro would be met by a U.S. olive branch.[12]

Darío's cautious optimism proved misplaced. In the first third of the twentieth century, the United States made the Caribbean Sea its immediate outpost of world power. By challenging Britain in Venezuela in 1895 and then driving Spain out of Cuba and Puerto Rico in 1898, the United States cast its military and economic net over the whole of the Caribbean, securing it through bases such as Guantánamo in Cuba and commercial throughways such as the Panama Canal. The U.S. presence in Latin America now went far beyond trade and the occasional landing of Marines, both of which had increased in the late nineteenth century. Free from much European competition after 1898, U.S. landowners moved in on the heels of military occupations to buy up farms and concentrate land ownership. Capitalists mechanized plantations and built railroads and telegraph systems to connect those plantations to U.S. trade routes. Makers of finished goods also found ready markets in Latin America. One measure of new U.S. control in the Caribbean: from 1897 to 1908, U.S. investment grew from $200 million to $672 million in Mexico and from $49 million to $225 million in Cuba.[13]

Before World War I, elite Latin American animosity against such expansion—primed by Arielism to focus on the cultural—was far from linking up with the more grounded resentment of the masses. Anti-U.S. sentiment still faced a gulf separating social groups. Those who wished to organize, say, against U.S. copper companies in Chile or banana plantation owners in Honduras did so largely in isolation from each other, and certainly without much support from diplomats, who were busy defending the "Calvo Doctrine" or the "Drago Doctrine" against increasing U.S. investment. One Latin American called this a period of "micro" resistance, when pockets of workers could rarely hope to ally with governments or even with each other at the national or international level. The image of the United States as an octopus, popular at this time, effectively conveyed the fatalism of disjointed Latin American protesters before an omnipotent power to the north. Oppression in various areas seemed connected to a single system—centralized often around "Wall Street"—but its tentacles appeared too numerous to be cut off.[14]

World War I sparked a new type of opposition to the United States based on grass-roots identities and programs. Several factors caused the refashioning of anti-U.S. groups. The self-destructiveness of European imperialism made the continent's cultural underpinnings much less attractive to Latin Americans. The Russian Revolution popularized Leninist arguments about the "inevitability" of capitalist imperialism. And, closer to home, the ongoing Mexican Revolution revealed the power of mass organization and the imminence of radical social change. Into this unstable situation barreled the ambitious United States, fueled by the twin desires to protect itself from perceived German aggression and to increase its dominance over Caribbean resources and markets.[15] The U.S. armed forces began a decades-long period of occupations in Nicaragua, Haiti, and the Dominican Republic, while continuing more short-lived interventions in Cuba, Mexico, Panama, and other countries. In response, Latin Americans added to Arielism four more overlapping resistance movements: indigenism, Sandinism, communism, and what could be called populist developmentalism.

Indigenism was, like Arielism, a search for a positive identity for Latin America that used U.S. culture as a foil. Unlike Arielists, however, indigenists based their identity on race—in its modern conception, not its "Latin" or "Saxon" incarnation. Indigenists were a more expanded social group than Arielists. They included educators, painters, artists, and indigenous leaders as well as the expected poets and novelists. They united in glorifying the mixed heritage of Latin America and in foreseeing a showdown between *la raza* ("the race") and the "color line" Saxons doomed to cultural sterility. Indigenism's most representative text was perhaps José Vasconcelos' book *La raza cósmica* (The Cosmic Race; 1925), a mixed-race manifesto if there ever was one. It claimed, in response to social Darwinism, that mestizos and other mixed groups would not only be fit enough to survive but would flourish in the coming "Spiritual Age" or "Aesthetic Age." The book offered at times a sprawling, breathless millennialism, but its anti-Americanism was consistent. Vasconcelos once admitted he resented much of what came from the United States—not only its racism but its mechanization, Protestantism, anti-intellectualism, liberated women, even its food. As Mexico's minister of education, Vasconcelos reformed the school system to celebrate the country's indigenous past and educate the poor, and he devised a new motto for the National University: "The Spirit shall speak through my race." His work eventually inspired the Chicano movement La Raza.[16] Indigenism appeared to resolve the ambivalence of anti-Americanism, partly because U.S. racism's absolutism and brutality made Latin America's pale in comparison. Yet social divisions remained in indigenism, and mitigated its political potential. Only an educated minority, after all, wrote and read indigenist texts. Vasconcelos himself lost his bid for the presidency, and he achieved little in the fight against U.S. imperialism.[17]

The more than thirty landings by U.S. troops in Central America and the Caribbean from 1898 to 1933 gave birth to a second major movement, Sandinism. Its namesake, Augusto Sandino, spent his early adult days in Mexico, where anti-Americanism was more pervasive than anywhere else in Latin America. During the Mexican Revolution, U.S. representatives reported that "anti-American sentiment is almost universal among rich and poor alike"; "this district is 95 percent anti-American, and that is a most conservative estimate for I have yet to meet a Mexican who has any love for the people of the United States as a whole"; and "the great masses of the population hate Americans with an intensity that is awful to contemplate."[18] When the U.S. government occupied Nicaragua for a second time starting in 1926, Sandino left Mexico to return to his country, joined the resistance, and refused to surrender.

Sandino's anti-Americanism was ardent and thorough. He fully demonized U.S. Marines. To him they were "barbarians," "invaders," "blond beasts," and "piratical assassins" sent by "Wall Street magnates." He portrayed them as lustful, violent morphine addicts. He wrote to friends in 1927, "We must fight without respite until we are free from Yankee imperialism, because it and its government are the enemies of our race and our language; they are fearful and cowardly, underhanded and treacherous highwaymen, greedy and perverted pirates, with dark and despicable passions. . . . Wherever you find the North American, you will find perfidy and treason. They are egotists and gluttons! In the name of love, virtue, and piety, they will enter your home; they will take it over, control your wife, and be a despot to your children."[19] The United States was the ultimate enemy, making its way even into Sandino's hymn:

> We are giving our lives
> against the Yankee and the traitor [Nicaraguan guard]
> Here are the *guerrilleros*
> nightmare of the filibusterers.

Sandino notably brought to anti-Americanism a revolution in martial arts. His loose-knit bands of *guerrilleros* gained worldwide notoriety for using their knowledge of the Segovia mountains of Nicaragua to ambush and evade U.S. Marines.[20] The cruelty with which they used their machetes was bloodcurdling. As punishment for minor offenses, for instance, one would receive a *corte de bloomers,* a slash across the back of the legs that severed tendons and exposed the bone behind the knee. Sandino boasted quite seriously that "all North Americans who fall into our hands have reached their end."[21] To reinforce the glory of these practices, his "crazy little army" minted a gold coin featuring what was most likely a Marine moments before decapitation at the hands of one of Sandino's men. For otherwise powerless Nicaraguans and for the millions who read about these feats, there was empowerment in killing the Yankee, reflected in gruesome fight songs:

> Exclaimed Sandino one time,
> wringing his hands:
> "For ten cents apiece I will sell
> the heads of Americans."[22]

As a leader of the revived Sandinistas of the 1970s explained, *antiyanquismo* "helped buttress morale and national pride" among Sandino's troops.[23]

Finally, by shrewdly blending millennialism and indigenism, ideologies that spoke to the dispossessed, with the more abstract nationalist and anti-imperialist sensibilities of the well-heeled, Sandino began the process of tying together anti-Americanism's constituencies. The Nicaraguan struggle enlisted thousands of peasants and rural workers who feared the loss of their land to U.S. owners and who associated the spread of rural guards and national systems of repression with U.S. military occupations. It also gained sympathy from intellectuals all over the Western Hemisphere, including Vasconcelos, Ugarte, and a certain bohemian and left-leaning intelligentsia in the United States.[24]

In a society as deeply split along class lines as Nicaragua's, the dénouement was predictable: local elites allied with the U.S. minister made Sandino pay for his integrity with his life. After years of military stalemate, Sandino agreed to lay down his arms, and the Marines left. But Anastasio Somoza, commander of the national guard, soon betrayed and killed Sandino and began a decades-long dictatorship with full U.S. support. A key State Department specialist on Latin America, Dana Munro, said in 1933, after the negotiations but before Sandino's death, that the five-and-half-year struggle had "increased the prevalent suspicion and dislike of the United States. . . . Commercial rivals and other elements interested in creating anti-American sentiment were prompt to seize upon the opportunity for hostile propaganda, and distorted and misrepresented the details of a policy which in any case was highly offensive to Latin American public opinion."[25]

Socialism formed the third important stream of anti-Americanism in the early twentieth century. Given prominence by the Mexican and Russian Revolutions, communist theory gave peasants and workers a blueprint for deliberate and permanent change. Socialism provided agency, inspiration, and mass organization techniques to the poor. Workers and peasants also now explained U.S. hegemony as a consequence not only of cultural determinism but also of rational economic motives. Opponents of the United States targeted international corporations as culprits and elaborated a new symbolic idiom, which Peter Smith called "cultural and rhetorical codes."[26] Vultures, snakes, crocodiles, and men in frock coats and top hats—these images of willful rapaciousness challenged the fatalism plaguing old views of the United States as an omnipotent octopus. The new images showed that imperialism was no accident but a desired result of the calculated greed of capitalism. This was the golden age of Mexican muralist Diego Rivera, who imbibed these currents and juxtaposed the faceless mechanization of empire onto the quiet suffering of Latin America's poor. Like Arielism, finally, socialism spawned significant scholarly output. Peru's José Carlos Mariátegui applied explicit Marxist analyses to social and racial inequalities as early as the 1920s, and declared Rodó's "spiritual opposition" to the United States "discredited." In the 1930s and 1940s, Enamorado Cuesta and Vicente Saenz led another wave of scathing indictments of capitalism.[27]

Like indigenism and Sandinism, however, socialism by the 1950s had largely run its course as a national or international unifying force. The Stalin-Trotsky dispute divided much of the socialist leadership, and the struggle between the United States and the Soviet Union distorted local socialism and highlighted the threat it posed to the wealthy in Latin America.[28] By the start of the Cold War, Latin America retained few ties to international socialist movements. From 1947 to 1952 membership in Communist parties shrank from 400,000 to 200,000, and those remaining were mostly from the radical middle class. Moreover, by this time also only about 5 percent of Latin America's trade was with communist countries.[29]

A fourth mass-based anti-U.S. trend in Latin America was the blend of populism and developmentalism adopted by nondictatorial political parties from the 1910s to the 1950s. These parties lacked the international brotherhood that united the communists, did not espouse an essentialist theory like indigenism, and did not celebrate decapitation as did Sandino. But their charismatic leaders did attract a mass base and middle sectors by promising to develop Latin America, end corruption, and promote nationalism. These modern political parties benefited from the growth of cities, of the state, of literacy, and of "fast" media such as television and radio. Leaders as diverse as Argentina's Juan Perón, Costa Rica's José Figueres, Guatemala's Jacobo Arbenz, and Venezuela's Rómulo Betancourt rejected any political economy to the right of Franklin Roosevelt's, and actively promoted land reform and public works.[30]

Populist developmentalists, however, were more ambivalent toward the United States than other movements. More often than not, they came to anti-Americanism through the realization that U.S. foreign policies did not produce the same wealth and peace in Latin America that they did in the United States. They resented such asymmetries, as well as the continuing haughtiness and racism of U.S. diplomats. Much of this implied that the United States remained the model society for many of these movements. Perón's successful public confrontation with U.S. ambassador Spruille Braden, for example, was a challenge to U.S. meddling in Argentine politics but also an explicit alignment with the politics of Roosevelt.[31] Populist developmentalists, moreover, unlike Sandinists or socialists, realized that they were sorely tempted by U.S. capitalism. "Do I hate the Yankee? No!" exclaimed Chile's popular poet Gabriela Mistral. "Let us hate what is in us that makes us vulnerable to his steel and gold nail, to his will and to his opulence."[32] Anti-Americanism grew even more ambivalent as wealthier groups joined these new parties and U.S. troops pulled out of the Caribbean region in the 1920s and 1930s. Populist developmentalism's only cross-national movement of consequence was the Caribbean Legion, a loose organization mostly active in the late 1940s that focused its energies on largely unsuccessful attempts to unseat dictators.[33]

The career of Peru's Víctor Raúl Haya de la Torre underwent a shift to the center that was representative of this generation. Haya cut his teeth on the continent-wide movement for student reform, which swept Lima in 1919. He then wove together several strands of anti-U.S. discourse into his political message: he spoke of "spiritualism" and of the racial uniqueness of "Indo-America"; he supported Sandino; he promoted a "soft" socialist political economy compatible with democracy; and for decades he ended much of his correspondence with the salutation, "Against Yankee imperialism, through the unity of the peoples of Indo-America, for the achievement of social justice." Politically, Haya came into his own by forming the American Popular Revolutionary Alliance in 1924. APRA was initially an ambitious international organization— the words "Peru" and "party" did not figure in its name.[34] Haya, however, saw imperialism not as the last stage of capitalism in Latin America, but as the first—a wild imported beast to be tamed by a more balanced and humane civilization south of the United States. By the 1950s, Haya was striking a more accepting balance in the Cold War and with U.S. businesses. To many younger Latin Americans, he had lost much of his appeal.[35]

These four anti-U.S. movements formed only part of the growing momentum against U.S. power before the Nixon visit of 1958. Many Latin Americans loved or hated the United States not for ideological but for personal reasons. Especially in the Caribbean, daily life increasingly included brushes with U.S. power or arrogance (not to mention the cluttering of homes and public spaces with U.S. products and advertisements). One or two unfortunate run-ins with, say, boorish Ohio tourists or with a haughty manager from Boston could etch a solid prejudice in one's mind. "Many business connections between Latin and American firms are broken off for no more reason than some fancied slight to the Latin," a business student offered as an explanation in 1927, "which in all probability was entirely unintentional on the part of the American firm."[36] Confrontations with U.S. soldiers, notably, could range from relatively harmless bar brawls and rude sexual advances to rape, torture, and murder. And, as always, U.S. racism came back again and again to become what one scholar in 1950 called a "basic factor underlying Yankeephobia."[37] At this time, also, anti-U.S. leaders could draw from a collective memory imprinted with folktales about the evils committed by Marines during the occupations of the 1910s and 1920s. And some politically active Latin Americans simply found in anti-Americanism a good way to advance their careers and satisfy their desire for struggle and conquest. By the middle of the century, the balance between positive and negative images of the northern neighbor could easily tip to one side or the other. In this gathering storm, individual diplomats could be lightning rods.

"Do They Like Us?"

Before and after the Nixon trip, U.S. responses to foreign criticism entailed a basic contradiction. U.S. citizens longed to know, "Do they like us?" while simultaneously denying that "they" mattered. This was a dilemma that had long existed both in the U.S. public and among U.S. policymakers, but one that intensified after 1945 once the United States became a superpower. It was also a dilemma largely without resolution. While it sparked a widespread worry after the Caracas riots, it eventually produced relative inertia throughout the U.S. policymaking establishment.

The dilemma consisted of a tension between the momentous themes of democracy and power. On one hand, U.S. officials and others after 1945 were optimistic about their ability to tap into the democratic instincts of ordinary people the world over. They sincerely wished to take account of foreign public opinion in pursuing harmonious international relations. Imbued with a Wilsonian belief that foreign elites suppressed the goodness and common sense of the masses, policymakers longed to open a two-way channel of communication with world public opinion. As Samuel Huntington and others have argued, in matters of foreign policy, the United States has expected more from itself than Europe has from *itself*. Peregrine Worsthorne, a British correspondent to the United States, wrote in the 1950s that even "Europe accepts the idea that America is a country with a difference, from whom it is reasonable to demand an exceptionally altruistic standard of behavior." Buttressing this idealism was the assumption that not only were U.S. influences good for foreigners but that these foreigners *wanted* them. And so two fundamentals of U.S. national identity—the consent of the governed and the universal potential of U.S. civilization—were joined into a ready rebuttal to anti-Americanism. One scholar characterized the marriage as the "desire to be liked, coupled with the conviction that, as we become better known, we will become better liked."[38]

On the other hand, for all their idealism, U.S. officials by and large were safe in the knowledge that foreign public opinion had no legal mechanisms to influence their decisions. If even U.S. voters had little say, constitutionally speaking, in matters of foreign policy, how important could foreign public opinion be?[39] Besides, if there were "no votes in foreign policy," there were fewer still in appeasing anti-Americanism.

In the early Cold War, finally, the question of foreign public opinion was an even more distant priority. "Narcissus psychosis" is what Secretary of State Dean Acheson called the occasional U.S. concern with foreigners' views of the United States. As a result of such attitudes, remarked theologian Reinhold Niebuhr, Soviet and U.S. planners tended to face one another without much consultation with their citizens. Journalist James Reston observed that "the gap between our public pronouncements of equality [with other nations] and our private demands for authority equal to our power leaves us open to charges of hypocrisy."[40]

This postwar dilemma, pitting the universalism of democracy against the exceptionalism of superpowerdom, most clearly emerged in Europe. It was in Europe that one theme became clear: anti-Americanism as a particular phenomenon of allies. Moscow was obviously a source of foreign criticism after 1945, but to U.S. officials it was state-controlled and mind-numbingly formulaic and it did not constitute the core of what U.S. citizens considered anti-Americanism. In contrast, the opinions of both the elites and the masses in Europe mattered far more. Many ordinary Europeans were meeting U.S. citizens—GIs and tourists especially—for the first time after World War II. And because of their still-powerful intellectual resonance in former and remaining colonies, European politicians and media figures could influence much of the world if they turned virulently anti-American, as many in France had in the 1920s.[41] Most important, anti-Americanism in Europe directly affected the Cold War, argued the *New Republic*, "not because the aim of life is to be liked by others, but because the rise of anti-Americanism helps the Russians isolate the U.S. from its allies."[42] Apart from England, France, Italy, and West Germany, after all, few democracies and market economies were potentially strong U.S. allies. So if anti-Americanism could not be debunked or prevented there, it might not be defeated anywhere.

Paradoxically, these worries came about just as evidence indicated a widespread pro-Americanism in Europe. In 1957 *Life* magazine featured views from Europeans about U.S. tourists and GIs. It faithfully repeated criticisms of U.S. cultural insularity, boorishness, and arrogance. But its overall point was that U.S. tourists, as "envoys-ordinary," were still, after twelve years of peace, "winning foreign hearts" with their generosity, sincerity, optimism, and even religious devoutness. Europeans still remembered U.S. servicemen who had handed out food packages, built schools, and raised money for orphanages. Again and again, European descriptions of U.S. citizens expressed ambivalence through generous if paternalistic language: "just bighearted boys," "noisy but good-hearted children," and "delightfully adolescent" were common descriptions. One British editor concluded, "The more the Americans can visit here and work here, the better the effect will be on our relationship. Looking at the whole pattern, they unquestionably have been a success."[43]

In addition, starting in 1948 and continuing through the early 1950s, pathbreaking United Nations polls of foreign public opinion indicated that U.S. citizens *were* liked by ordinary Europeans. U.S. citizens were perhaps more "domineering" than, say, the Dutch, but overall, respondents thought them "generous" and "practical," a rating much better than the one given to the Soviets. Polls in the following decades consistently confirmed European goodwill both toward U.S. citizens and, to a lesser but still substantial extent, U.S. policies.[44] These results must have been a relief to U.S. officials unsure of what to make of the increased incidence of anti-U.S. demonstrations by small groups.[45]

Faced with this evidence of continuing small-scale protests despite general agreement with U.S. social and political leadership, many reflected on the passing of the torch of world leadership and the worldwide criticism that inevitably ran alongside it. As James Reston wrote, the United States would have to contend with the jealousies of Britain and France under any circumstances: "This is their century to be annoyed."[46] "We are out in front in the Great Cold Conflict," wrote the *Saturday Evening Post,* "and must expect to take the rotten eggs which John Bull used to get." The *Saturday Review* argued a more prescient but equally common theme—that Western European criticisms "are not specifically criticisms of or complaints about America. They are criticisms of the modern world."[47] This surrender to the apparent truism that along with great power comes great animosity typified a common U.S. response to anti-Americanism.

U.S. observers in and out of government, in other words, were making anti-Americanism a distinct issue. They understood that allies did have sincere grievances against the United States. Many also appreciated that anti-Americanism was not communism but at best a "counterpart" to it, as Reston said. Because anti-Americanism was a legitimate sentiment among allies, U.S. observers were hurt at the core of their national identity and could not help expressing dismay. "It irks us Americans to think that Europeans don't like us," admitted *America.* "We feel that anyone in his right mind ought to like us, or at least understand us. . . . After all, aren't we the most 'normal' people in the world?"[48] the *Catholic World* answered its own question, "Do they like us?" with resignation: "The Europeans do not love us. . . . The postwar illusion of European-American friendship has been dispelled."[49]

In the late 1950s, negative sentiment seemed to be spilling out from Europe and into two largely overlapping areas, the developing and decolonizing worlds. In 1956, for instance, a *Paris-Match* article alarmingly titled, "Why Are Americans Detested All Over the World?" focused on John Foster Dulles' frustrations with Indian neutralism. Next to a photo of the secretary of state sunbathing, the article portrayed him as complacently traveling from one hostile country to another "to make himself loved: an exact symbol of the policy America has followed desperately and disastrously for the last ten years."[50] That same month, *Newsweek* worried about "the new sweet reasonableness of Soviet propaganda"—which was disavowing Stalinism and courting newly independent nations such as India. It quoted one Indian official: "Five years ago America was loved. You are not hated now but distrusted. . . . The Russians still get the benefit of the doubt because they are new."[51] In the following years, when the Soviet launching of the Sputnik satellite into orbit suggested that the USSR might have gained a strategic advantage, U.S. anxiety about foreign public opinion also reached new heights. The simultaneous runaway success of *The Ugly American* (1958), a didactic indictment of U.S. paternalism toward the developing world that sold two and a half million copies, seemed to indicate that a broad-based response from the U.S. government was in order.[52]

That response took the shape of a Madison Avenue–type sales pitch. Especially since the 1920s, it was not elections but mass media advertising that had launched the public-opinion polling industry in the United States. Producers and advertisers wanted to know who was buying their products and why.[53] Now, with shapers of foreign policy craving similar feedback, evaluations of the "image" of the United States abroad took on added importance, and so did the desire to counter that image. The problem, many observed, was that a U.S. consumer culture driven by civil libertarianism had created too many voices expressing U.S. national identity abroad. In the opinion of *Newsweek*'s writers, these voices ranged "from Hollywood sound tracks to Congressional sounding boards." "A monument to the democratic process, this healthy Babel is often a hazard in presenting America to the world." Many thought that the opinion that foreign audiences had of Hollywood values—materialism, violence, licentiousness—often became the opinion they had of the United States as a whole.[54]

The irony of the Washington response to anti-Americanism in the 1950s was that, while policymakers regretted the Hollywood / Madison Avenue creation of simplistic or sensational images about the United States, they advocated the same approach to dispel those images. In a displacement of the consumer ethos into the realm of diplomacy, U.S. officials came to believe that if foreigners were "buying" the idea of U.S. benevolence, then that was good enough. A good product was a product that sold. Not incidentally, the language of movies and public relations pervaded discussions about anti-Americanism. The *Saturday Evening Post,* for instance, characterized "America's reputation abroad" as "our overseas box office." *Newsweek* warned that Soviet propaganda was "big business" and that "the U.S. must have its own public-relations office, so to speak."[55]

Despite scattered criticism of U.S. policies, soldiers, and tourists, there was relatively little organized mass hostility in the streets before 1958. While reporting on small protests against U.S. soldiers' behavior in Japan and Taiwan in 1957, *Commonweal* noted that there were "few incidents" like those. "The surprising thing is rather that the record of our troops abroad has been so good." At the same time, *Newsweek* provided a worldwide map of "the feeling about us" and concluded that in every region—save for East Asia, where hostility against U.S. bases had recently flared up—relations between foreigners and U.S. citizens abroad were either "better" or the "best ever."[56]

Newsweek's map from 1957 did not even include Latin America. The disdain with which the Eisenhower administration looked upon the region made it likely that, unless there were a crisis there, Washington would pay little attention to anti-Americanism in the region. Mostly, U.S. observers believed that Latin American statesmen who criticized U.S. policy were out of touch with popular opinion. While reporting Perón's repeated confrontations with U.S. power, for instance, U.S. magazines focused on the details of "hate-the-*yanquis*" campaigns through ambassadors, official press contacts, and labor unions rather than on the sympathetic reception of that propaganda among Argentines. When foreigners spoke of U.S. cultural mediocrity, U.S. observers were quick to retort. "It is hard to take the charge of illiteracy with equanimity," wrote one journalist who returned from Brazil in 1951, "from a nation in which countless millions, indeed a majority of the population, are still illiterate." He resurrected the anti-Arielist charge from earlier in the century, according to which Latin Americans were under the negative influence of European intellectual snobbery. "The French have been sending cultural ambassadors, professors, writers, and so on, to Brazil for nearly a hundred years. Brazilians have been going to France to study for that long. Culture is to Brazilians . . . synonymous with France, and to a lesser degree with England."[57] The cry of "Go home!" gathering steam in Latin America, others noted, was allegedly born in postwar Germany. And as for communists in the region, their propaganda also merely parroted that of the Soviet bloc in the eyes of many U.S. citizens. As a measure of Latin America's distant importance, in 1957, after the United States Information Agency (USIA) had already been taking worldwide polls of attitudes toward the United States for two years, an internal memorandum concluded that negative attitudes about the United States did of course exist there, but that it was unnecessary "to bring them up and make issues of them, even for purposes of refutation."[58]

Caracas

The riots against Vice President Nixon in Venezuela were, as one State Department official said days later, "the first time that minority groups have been able to exploit these issues [of resentment toward the United States] to incite actual violence against an important American representative. This is something new in Latin America."[59] Nixon's run-in with Latin American mobs did convey the impression that anti-Americanism enjoyed popular appeal in the hemisphere. Yet once again the dilemma of the U.S. response reemerged: recognizing Latin Americans' democratic right to rebel was one thing, but admitting anything akin to "U.S. imperialism" would place U.S. power in jeopardy. Caracas was mostly what Nixon said it was: a "shock treatment"—but a shock to the body rather than the mind. The ordeal triggered no deep questioning of the impact of U.S. influence in Latin America. Rather, it simply revitalized the public relations approach to anti-Americanism. The U.S. response, it seemed to Washington, had to be more culturally sensitive, more accurate, and more rapid.

"Of all the trips I made abroad as Vice President, the one I least wanted to take was my visit to South America in 1958 . . . because I thought it would be relatively unimportant and uninteresting." So began Nixon's memoirs of the trip, reflecting the complacency of the Eisenhower administration toward the hemisphere. Nixon grew more interested in his mission, however, when the trip's planners began to warn him that he would be beleaguered by protesters. A product of the middle class, the vice president seemed genuinely distressed by the deepening anti-Americanism among new social strata. He wished, he said, "to meet the opinion makers and people in all walks of life." But if we can judge from the "walks of life" he described, he really meant the new middle classes: the "university students, labor leaders, editors, and other opinion makers. . . . I was determined to meet and answer head on some of the attacks which were currently being made against the United States in Latin America."[60]

Before the stop in Caracas, the trip was generally safe and even pleasant at times. Pro-U.S. demonstrators usually outnumbered anti-U.S. elements, and foreign leaders seemed pleased to receive such a high dignitary. Protesters did show up in every country Nixon went to, but they consisted of small groups that did little more than burn photos of the vice president and hand out anti-imperialist pamphlets. In repressive Paraguay, students were arrested not for anti-Americanism but for shouting the anti-government slogan "Long live liberty!" Nixon the stern Quaker could even charm crowds when he really tried. In front of ten thousand Ecuadorians cheering "Viva Nixon!" he walked onto a *fútbol* field and practiced awkwardly with a ball, joking that he never could use his head.[61]

Privately, however, Nixon and aides noticed the growing visibility of anti-Americanism and disparaged it as a weakness in Latin American political culture. They were incensed at hecklers who called the vice president a "shark" and a "pirate." To Assistant Secretary of State for Inter-American Affairs Roy Rubottom, a first debate with students in Montevideo "began the beat of the drums all the way up the line for the rest of our trip."[62] Nixon personally showed little sympathy for counterparts who were trapped between their duty to protect him and their need to soothe the anger of the crowds. The chief of police in Lima, Peru, for instance, advised Nixon not to show up at the city's leftist San Marcos University, yet "at the same time said, in effect: please don't quote me—publicly." Nixon had to lay his head on his pillow one night while crowds outside his hotel chanted "Fuera Nixon! Fuera Nixon! Fuera Nixon!" (Get out, Nixon!). Stoned by students the following day, after he disregarded security warnings, Nixon wagged his finger at them and shouted back, "You are cowards, you are afraid of the truth! You are the worst kind of cowards!"[63]

Venezuela brought together many of the conditions that made Latin America so propitious for a mass-based anti-U.S. incident. First, Venezuelan democracy was uncertain in May 1958. The previous January, a military junta had taken power after the overthrow of dictator Marcos Pérez Jiménez, whom the Eisenhower administration had decorated and now harbored, and a legitimate government had yet to be elected. Second, the U.S. government imposed restrictions on crude oil imports from Venezuela, a move that contradicted its free-trade ideology and crippled Venezuela's comparative trade advantage.[64] Third, small groups of communists operated in a political atmosphere brimming with new-found freedom, and the martyrdom they carried over from the previous regime gave them a prestige far beyond their numbers.

Most immediately, however, security forces were ineffective. During the overthrow of Pérez Jiménez, Venezuelans had hunted down his secret police in the streets. In the months that followed, police officers became wary of keeping the peace in any situation, especially when called on to protect U.S. representatives. The Venezuelan junta oscillated between warning the U.S. delegation not to come and reassuring it that there would be no danger. Rubottom arranged to make Caracas the last stop on the trip because he knew "that there would be a critical security problem." Nixon, however, heightened his own peril by disregarding the CIA's warnings about assassination plots and refusing a police cordon along the seventeen-kilometer road from the airport to the city center.[65] The vice president's party even requested an open car. The response from Caracas: "Are you people out of your minds?"[66]

The Nixon delegation's experience in the capital on Tuesday the 13th—a day of bad luck, according to Latin American tradition—changed from insult to terror in a matter of minutes. As the vice president and his wife, Pat, emerged from the plane, one embassy staffer recalled, their "waves and broad smiles . . . quickly disappeared."[67] The banners on the tarmac and the balcony were less than welcoming: GO

HOME, NIXON! TRICKY DICK, GO HOME! GO AWAY, NIXON! OUT, DOG! The crowd that carried these banners—according to one journalist, a group of five hundred, about 90 percent of whom were teenagers—whistled and hooted to express their contempt. How deep the hostility ran became all too clear when the spitting began. "It was the damnedest thing I ever saw in my life," said one witness. "I thought it was a new trick," Nixon recalled, "someone busting water bags on us." "Where is this coming from?" thought a military attaché. "Then I saw the people from behind the [Venezuelan] soldiers. They had cocked their heads back and were spitting up into the air. They weren't spitting on the soldiers—they were spitting over them."[68]

Aides pushed the vice president into a car—one with a roof on it—as the Venezuelan foreign minister wiped spit off his guest's suit and face. "Don't bother," Nixon shot at him. "I am going to burn these clothes as soon as I can get out of them." The embarrassment was nothing compared to the upcoming terror. Nixon recalled the moment when, minutes later, his motorcade ground to a halt in the working-class suburb of Catia. "Out of the alleys and the side streets poured a screaming mob of two to three hundred, throwing rocks, brandishing sticks and pieces of steel pipe. . . . Those who had no weapons used their feet and bare fists to beat upon the car. The spit was flying so fast that the driver turned on his windshield wipers." "I saw the attack from a truck fifteen feet in front of Nixon's Cadillac," said one correspondent soon after. Even the "expressions of silent sidewalk onlookers—those who did not demonstrate—were icily hostile."[69] After what seemed an eternity to the passengers, the motorcade's Venezuelan drivers gunned their engines and pulled away from the crowds. By chance they avoided a planned visit to a sacred tomb, where six thousand protesters awaited, and headed straight for the U.S. embassy. The Nixon trip to South America was over. The violence had completely overshadowed its good will.

Once Nixon was back in Washington, many in the government refused to confront the possibility that the hostility displayed in Caracas could be widespread. They preferred to see anti-Americanism as a subset of communism, and not the other way around. J. Edgar Hoover of the FBI publicly fingered the small groups of communists who had printed propaganda and organized demonstrations against Nixon. "Red"-obsessed publications such as *U.S. News and World Report* subtly used a traditional anti-communist language of forethought and coordination. Protesters, said the magazine, supposedly used "clocklike precision," acted "as though on signal," and "methodically" ripped a U.S. flag from Nixon's car.[70]

Others recognized the popular nature of anti-Americanism, but refused to equate it with the will of the people. Charges of gunboat diplomacy left Secretary Dulles unruffled, and he supported Eisenhower's decision to put the U.S. fleet on alert. Dulles fell back on his patrician and paternalistic instincts and warned against "a tremendous surge in the direction of popular government by peoples who have practically no capacity for self-government and indeed are like children in facing this problem."[71] Still others concluded—more accurately, but still neglecting deeper issues—that the only problem had been the incompetence of Venezuela's security forces.[72]

For the U.S. public and policymakers as a whole, however, anti-Americanism was emerging as a distinct issue for three reasons. First, it simultaneously became a worldwide issue, which increased its visibility in the administration far beyond what Caracas alone would have done. The day of the Nixon disaster coincided with a burst of other anti-U.S. protests in Lebanon, Algeria, and Burma. "Another of the worst days of our lives," wrote Eisenhower's secretary in her diary once the sun mercifully set on May 13.[73] The anticolonial feel of many of the protests was too obvious to ignore. "Does the rest of the world hate the United States?" asked Newsweek. At the very least, the magazine now included Latin America in its world overviews of anti-U.S. hostility.[74]

Second, there was little evidence that international communists had orchestrated Caracas or any other South American protest. Aides did suggest to Nixon and Eisenhower that they should emphasize in public that "the abuse to which the Vice President and Mrs. Nixon were subjected was due solely to the organization and inspiration of an ugly international conspiracy."[75] But the same aides concurred in private that communist groups were small and clumsily dwelled on international issues rather than on more compelling national grievances. Protesters also lacked coordination, both between and within Latin American countries. Even local communist parties were "surprised by the virulence of the students' reaction."[76] In fact, many in the United States admitted, there seemed to be no conspiracy at all. One State Department official conceded to the Senate Foreign Relations Committee on May 19 that "there is no evidence at present of a Soviet effort to effect a coordinated worldwide demonstration of anti-Americanism coinciding with Vice President Nixon's visit to Latin America." Recalling not only South America but Algeria, Burma, and additional incidents in Lebanon and Indonesia, he found "no marked step-up in Moscow's propaganda immediately prior to the events in these areas."[77]

The third reason anti-Americanism took on sudden importance was that it altered domestic U.S. politics. Nixon was ever alert to his chances in the 1960 presidential election. He returned from Caracas eager to balance his vigorous defense of U.S. policies with his attempts to convince the common man in Latin America to embrace U.S. friendship rather than communism. "We must all take the line that this trip was a plus," Nixon urged Dulles. Eisenhower did his best. The president orchestrated a hero's welcome for him at the airport in Washington, and indeed U.S. citizens seemed to rally behind their beleaguered vice president. Nixon himself boasted in *Six Crises* that, one month after the trip, a "Gallup Poll showed me leading Adlai Stevenson for the first time, and running neck-and-neck against John F. Kennedy [both were contenders for the Democratic presidential nomination]. It was the high point of my political popularity up to that time."[78] Nixon also stifled rumors that the CIA and State Department were blaming each other for failing to predict the riots, thus avoiding a potential political embarrassment.[79] Yet trouble continued. Long-time Democrat Adolf Berle called it the "Venezuelan Waterloo." Immediately after Caracas, Senator Wayne Morse (Democrat from Oregon), a prominent figure in inter-American relations, called for hearings in Congress that came to little but annoyed the White House.[80]

As a result of anti-Americanism's new resonance, the press experimented with a tone of lofty open-mindedness. The *Des Moines Register* warned that "the anti-American demonstrations around the world cannot be passed off as just the unavoidable price of power and leadership. Americans need to be aware of the often justifiable causes of discontent with their policies and to try to adjust these policies accordingly." The *New York Times* called for calm while the United States faced "a test of maturity, statesmanship and common sense" Even the *Nation* was pleased that Hoover's reactionary anti-communism was in the minority and that "public opinion has not veered toward isolationism."[81]

1. "It ain't th' man, mac—it's th' uniform." After Vice President Nixon
   was attacked in Caracas, President Eisenhower ordered U.S. forces
   to move in close to Venezuela in case Nixon needed evacuation.
   This cartoon by Bill Mauldin expressed the desire of many U.S.
   citizens—and many Latin Americans—to explain anti-
   Americanism as a prejudice against representatives of the United
   States—"th' uniform"—and not necessarily against specific
   persons. It also suggested that U.S. citizens would jump to the
   defense of any compatriot attacked overseas. Reprinted by
   permission of Bill Mauldin and the Watkins/Loomis Agency.

Bouncing Back

Anti-Americanism, thus framed as a rite of passage for a democratic superpower, sparked a burst of activity. Eisenhower officials wondered how to showcase a fresh, smiling attitude while doing as little as possible to alter the asymmetries of U.S. power in Latin America. They abandoned their fondness for psychological warfare in the face of such a manifestly civilian discontent. The post-Caracas situation, rather, presented them with the opportunity to try out modern marketing metaphors to win what they considered a somewhat vapid but necessary world popularity contest.

The most basic change in the administration was one of attitude, not policy. Upon the vice president's return from Caracas, a reporter asked Nixon which "South American liberation movement" he preferred. Was it the rumba, the samba, or the cha-cha-cha? he joked. Nixon gently reproved the reporter for his levity.[82] The Operations Coordinating Board (OCB), which helped set the agenda of the National Security Council (NSC), similarly reported that "our failure to win understanding and support from the Latin Americans was due to our not being sufficiently mindful of Latin American interests, emotional prejudices and sensitivities." Even Eisenhower lamented the "superior attitude" of the United States and spoke of "the vital necessity to avoid giving rise to injured feelings by the other American Republics."[83]

This new premium placed on "attitudes," "feelings," and "sensitivities" may have sounded impalpable to some, but at the very least it opened the door to appreciating the emotional dualities of anti-Americanism. A National Intelligence Estimate, for instance, noted that "Latin American attitudes toward the U.S." were "ambivalent": Latin Americans expressed "envy by disparaging U.S. materialism"; they admired U.S. stability and democracy but were "keenly aware of imperfections"; they wanted hemispheric solidarity yet insisted on each country's uniqueness; they wanted U.S. protection without having to contribute.[84]

The Nixon trip reinvigorated the practice of drawing up lists of Latin American "grievances" and "attitudes" toward the United States.[85] These lists seemed to inform every other report that went through the White House for the next decade or so. While Nixon was still in Caracas, one Department of State memorandum drew up nineteen of these items, many of which were economic but some of which recognized the impor-

tance of emotional issues: "belief that the U.S. does not pay attention to Latin American problems," "feeling that Latin America is a step-child so far as the U.S. is concerned," "cultural and religious differences," "vestigial remembrances of U.S. military intervention," "the race question," and so on. Synthesizing the results of such lists, one official wrote Rubottom that "this nationalism is anti-American for various reasons, most of them irrational and unjustified. The problem it poses is primarily a psychological one, not to be measured in financial terms nor answered with dollars."[86]

The lists themselves suggested a lack of self-criticism and direction in Washington. The point of the oft-repeated exercise was unclear. Lists most likely served to train Foreign Service officers, Agency for International Development staff, and Peace Corps Volunteers to be sensitive to—or at least anticipate—certain lines of criticism. Otherwise, compiling lists seemed to offer reassurance that grievances could all be written down on a few pages and therefore circumscribed as a concern. Lists did not differentiate between the behaviors of U.S. civilians and those of military personnel or between criticisms of U.S. society and those of U.S. policy, and thus highlighted the U.S. tendency to define anti-Americanism as a sweeping prejudice. Just as anti-Americanism said as much about critics as it did about the United States, so lists said as much about list-makers as about anybody else.

Regardless, anti-Americanism had earned its right to be analyzed. And although, as *Newsweek* said, "anti-Americanism is bigger than any government agency," the USIA would take on much of the task. And what a task: the U.S. government's propaganda arm abroad already had a track record for not quieting anti-Americanism but, on the contrary, for bringing it out. In the decade before Caracas, more than fifty USIA centers or similar public diplomacy institutions in twenty-one countries had been bombed, burned, or sacked. Often presenting a literal façade of U.S. ideals and achievements behind their windowpanes, these centers made for tempting targets.[87] In the Eisenhower administration, the USIA also fought an uphill battle against aides such as Dulles, who figured that ambassadors should be unconcerned with mass opinion and simply deal with their diplomatic counterparts. Moreover, the USIA's ongoing "barometer reports" bypassed vocal minorities by consistently showing that "good" overall worldwide views of the United States far outweighed "bad" ones.[88]

After the Caracas trip, USIA director George Allen went around meeting rooms making a candid presentation titled "The Image of America." In it, he warned against abusing superpower status. "Our chief problem is to grow up psychologically. We continue to act like adolescents. We boast about our richness, our bigness, and our strength. We talk about our tall buildings, our motor cars, and our income. Nations, like people, who boast can expect others to cheer when they fail." He also made prescient observations. "There is considerable concern in many quarters lest they be swamped by American 'cultural imperialism'—by a way of life characterized by Coca Cola, cowboys and comics." Allen's recommendations, however, were a mix of the reassuring ("the U.S. Government and people should relax, not into complacency but into realism") and the petty ("if American tourists must chew gum, they should be told at least to chew it as inconspicuously as possible"). Eisenhower was not surprised. Turks, in his experience, resented U.S. soldiers for enjoying "all the women and all the wine." Nevertheless, he took Allen's presentation seriously and said the USIA needed to "know how we stand in the eyes of the world."[89]

Part of that knowledge would come from polls. By 1958, the USIA and other organizations had professional local pollsters who could query hundreds of people in a few days in major Latin American cities, all in Spanish, and supposedly without the appearance of working for the U.S. government.[90] The Nixon fiasco sparked a frenzy of poll-taking. A "flash" survey right after the affair indicated that Caracans' opinion of the United States had dropped by 21 percent. Worse, while negative opinions were still in the minority, Latin Americans were convinced that they were in the majority. Months later a more thorough poll concluded that "irritation at the United States . . . is very widespread. Large numbers say that their opinion of the U.S. has recently gone down." No previous data could confirm whether these opinions were indeed on the rise.[91] The Spanish-language edition of *Life* responded to the Nixon trip by conducting its very first survey. It found that Latin Americans were still greatly opposed to communism but also firmly on the side of neutralism. "The U.S. must conclude that the recent deterioration of its relations with the Latin American peoples may be even more serious than the Nixon affair indicated." Months later, according to more polls, levels of hostility remained high. Department of State pollsters warned gloomily that "during the next few years there is little prospect that Latin

American attitudes toward the United States will change substantially for the better."[92] Resorting to polls proved risky business, since the results could be undesired and unsettling.

Eisenhower officials, however, bounced back, confident about their ability to turn around Latin American public opinion. They knew they were walking a tightrope, partly strung by the polls themselves, which fostered an addictive need to improve the numbers for their own sake. Here the superpower's dilemma between democracy and power returned. If the Eisenhower administration "gave up" on being liked and did nothing, it appeared neglectful or complacent. Yet if it tried to "defeat" anti-Americanism through economic or military aid, it seemed a briber or a bully. Thankfully, polls, for all their alarm, also brought good news. *Life* observed "that the Latin American peoples still consider the United States a 'good neighbor.'" It also concluded, perhaps with not a little self-delusion, that "the Nixon tour did more good than harm."[93]

Whatever the poll results, Nixon and others had been long open to greater cultural exchanges and economic aid, and they were more so now. In meetings with the Cabinet and the NSC, Nixon reiterated his view that the "laboring classes" were now major political actors in Latin America. He indicated that some Latin American economic grievances, such as the one concerning U.S. resistance to commodity agreements and public funds, should be heard. Producers of raw materials were especially vulnerable to world recessions, after all. "Whenever we sneeze, they catch pneumonia," said Nixon. In the political field, he counseled giving dictators a firm handshake and democrats a warm embrace. Finally, he recommended that educational exchange programs should be "at least doubled."[94] Newly declassified portions of NSC meeting notes suggest that officials planned to "organize" pro-U.S. groups among students and intellectuals, who would then be "bought." Soon the administration took steps in all these directions. It also began lending an ear to presidents Juscelino Kubitschek of Brazil and Alberto Lleras Camargo of Colombia, who seized the moment and proposed a program of public investment that later became Operation Pan-America, the genesis of the Alliance for Progress.[95]

Overall, however, U.S. resilience carried the day in the face of foreign criticism. Throughout the Nixon trip and the frank White House debates and policy changes that followed, the denial of imperialism persisted. It characterized every government agency, Democrats and Republicans, officials and journalists, public and private comments. When a university official from Mexico wrote to Nixon in July 1958 to complain that the United States held Latin America "tied to its imperialist yoke," State Department officials called the suggestion "malicious." Foreign criticism created tension among U.S. observers, but not remorse. "Our failures are principally psychological," concluded Rubottom in August 1958. "We should not, through excessive reluctance to enter into the argument or a feeling of guilt, appear to accept the prevalent Latin American argument that it is entirely *our* fault that *they* have failed to solve *their* problem."[96]

The stoning of Richard Nixon and the anxiety it produced in the United States foreshadowed the coming decade of mass hostility. But rather than force the U.S. government into a brooding or reactionary stance, anti-Americanism in the Caribbean met with a relatively buoyant atmosphere in Washington, in which U.S. officials openly discussed others' perceptions of them. To pursue Nixon's metaphor of Caracas as a "shock treatment," U.S. policymakers were indeed stunned, and many responded with knee-jerk alarm. Yet they were also energized by a firm sense of U.S. national identity. The ambivalence of anti-Americanism, too, was already apparent to U.S. policymakers in 1958. Polls told them that Latin Americans were envious of U.S. standards of living and that they still looked to Washington for Cold War leadership. And if anything, Latin Americans had stoned Nixon because he represented the broken promises of U.S. free-market modernization—promises that they wanted realized as much as U.S. citizens did. Just as the political expression of anti-Americanism in Latin America had, in the course of more than a century, become increasingly popular, literate, and organized, so U.S. responses to it had solidified into a consensual, consistent, and coherent defense.

2

Cuba, 1959

Revolutionary Anti-Americanism and U.S. Panic

If the vitriol directed at Nixon in 1958 marked anti-Americanism as a distinct concern for Washington, the Cuban Revolution made it a national emergency. In Cuba, anti-U.S. sentiment was always potentially revolutionary—sweeping, transformative, and irreversible. This type of anti-Americanism aimed to abolish all social configurations linked to U.S. influence. In 1959 it became swift, intransigent, and thorough. The abruptness of revolutionary anti-Americanism contrasted sharply with the decades it had taken for Cubans to create a national identity infused with U.S. ways of life. The pendulum of anti-Americanism in Cuba suggested the deepest ambivalence to be found in Latin America: it had long been swinging from mainstream liberal democrats' moderate opposition to marginal revolutionaries' radical rejection. Up to 1959 Fidel Castro fused both tendencies into a subtle political strategy. That year, he took anti-Americanism and swung it violently to the latter tendency until it held there.

Washington's answer to Cuba's hostility, mirroring the swing in Cuba's pendulum, oscillated between near-paralysis and near-gunboat diplomacy. Oblivious to the deep roots of revolutionary discontent in Cuba, the U.S. government failed to foresee the rise of a major variant of anti-Americanism. Moreover, faced with Castro's rapid embrace of revolution over liberal democracy in 1959, U.S. policymakers acted too late to take advantage of Cuba's ambivalence. Perhaps they never had a chance. Whatever the case, they addressed the sources of revolutionary anti-Americanism elsewhere in Latin America with growing sophistication, all while throwing up their hands at Cuba itself.

The Deepest Ambivalence

At the heart of Cuban anti-Americanism was a paradox: Cuba incubated the conditions for revolutionary hostility precisely because it seemed to have no chance there. By the 1950s countless Cubans were leading thoroughly transnational lives, yet familiarity with things Yankee bred contempt for them. Because Cuba's national identity was pegged to U.S. influence, "in every Cuban . . . festered the humiliation of being—and of not being—*American*," observed Venezuelan Carlos Rangel.[1] As a result, two parallel anti-U.S. tendencies developed. The first, a liberal democratic resentment, was more widespread. The second, a revolutionary anti-Americanism, simmered among smaller political groups. When the liberal democratic order finally collapsed in the 1950s, Fidel Castro moved in with a strategy that balanced liberal and revolutionary styles and thoroughly confused U.S. observers.

Prior to 1959, liberal democratic Cubans maintained an ambivalence toward the United States that became less sustainable every time one of its two pillars—trade stability and representative democracy—showed signs of crumbling. Throughout Cuba's Republican Era (1902–1958), U.S. capital transformed the island's economy, far more than any other in the Caribbean, from merely an oversized colonial plantation into a paragon of capitalist agrarianism, a highly mechanized monoculture. Cubans—especially in cities—adopted U.S. cultural norms and standards of consumption as their own, and all aspects of Cuban society evolved under the shadow of U.S. models. As a consequence, many in Cuba lived and dreamed far beyond the means of a dependency.[2] Throughout this half-century, noncommunist anti-U.S. movements felt frustrated in their attempts to build a nation that could at once stand up to the United States yet live up to its standards.

The War of 1898 foreshadowed much of liberal democrats' disillusion toward the United States. U.S. intervention against Spain, they soon realized, curtailed their drive for freedom. The nation that had been Cuba's counterweight to its corrupt colonial masters was now not only its greatest trading partner but also a new enemy, one without counterweight and therefore impossible to best. In addition, although they were allied with U.S. troops, many Cubans balked at the indiscriminate racism of U.S. commanders and resisted the menial tasks assigned them. Was this what the future held? The arrogance of U.S. administrators and their utter refusal to treat Cubans with respect were endlessly humiliating to leader Máximo Gómez. "None of us thought that [the U.S. intervention] would be followed by a military occupation of the country by our allies, who treat us as a people incapable of acting for ourselves, and who have reduced us to obedience, to submission, and to a tutelage imposed by force of circumstance. This cannot be our ultimate fate after years of struggle."[3] Unlike other Caribbean nations (with the notable exception of Haiti), Cuba had achieved nationhood after an epic conflict. Yet, just like those other nations, it had to suffer the same theft of its sovereignty by a U.S. military occupation. As one historian has stated, whatever nationalism flourished on the field of battle found itself "weakened by the contradiction inherent in [Cuba's] opposition to the wartime ally, the partner in prosperity."[4]

Ambivalences toward U.S. power intensified as U.S.-Cuban ties grew more intricate and U.S. corporations turned out not to be at all a "partner in prosperity." Direct U.S. investment skyrocketed from $50 million in 1896 to $1.3 billion in 1924, and by the 1920s U.S. businesses were providing 75 percent of Cuba's imports.[5] Cuban workers, however, bore the brunt of economic dependence during the Great Depression, when the daily pay of cane workers fell sometimes by two-thirds. Even in 1957, when U.S. domination had receded a bit relative to that of other countries, U.S. moneys were more important in Cuba than in any other Latin American country except for Venezuela and Brazil.[6] Also because of this dependence, the ease with which Cubans could have access to the same clothes, cars, films, and other products as U.S. citizens created lasting habits of consumption, and urban dwellers, especially, needed the funds to satisfy their longings. A key ambivalence grew out of the impossibility of achieving the "good life" with the income of an underdeveloped nation. In 1957, Cuba's annual per capita income was $374, the second highest in Latin America but still a paltry sum compared even to that of Mississippi, the poorest U.S. state, whose per capita income stood at $1,000.[7] As Carlos Montaner wrote (with some exaggeration), U.S. economic penetration was "a more or less superficial development" compared to "the total and voluntary spiritual submission of the country to the United States." "In a way," he added, "being anti-Yankee is being anti-Cuban."[8]

Given this hobbling national identity, anti-Americanism among early noncommunists was largely a protest against the fact and style of intervention rather than against its effects. The source of much resentment was the Platt Amendment, a U.S.-engineered add-on to the Cuban constitution that gave the U.S. government the right to intervene in Cuba's affairs. Municipalities, civic organizations, and veterans' groups immediately protested the amendment when it passed in 1901. Intellectuals such as Manuel Sanguily, Enrique José Varona, and the members of the Anti-Plattist League criticized U.S. meddling in Cuban matters and the outright military interventions of 1906, 1912, and 1917. Others such as José Antonio Portuondo focused on the existence of a U.S. base at Guantánamo. The mere presence of the base, undercutting Cuban sovereignty, was cause for resentment, and those who knew of the goings on around the base further denounced it as a site of salacious transgression, sexual and otherwise.[9]

Picking up on concerns about "social imperialism," artists and intellectuals conveyed the hurt pride and the fear of cultural degeneration among Cubans. Starting in the 1920s and 1930s, poets met at the Café Martí in Havana, named after the leader of the insurgency against Spain, who was himself deeply ambivalent about the United States.[10] Poets, especially, elaborated an anti-U.S. imagery that was becoming pervasive among Latin Americans: the United States appeared often transmogrified into a vulture, a triton, a vampire, or an eagle. Artists decried the moral failings of the United States in Cuba—the materialism of Wall Street, repression by Marines, and the ruin of pristine tropics for the benefit of a few *gringos* living in luxury. A leading writer, Nicolás Guillén, illustrated in his poem "West Indies Ltd." the Americanization of Cuba by highlighting among other things the ubiquity of English expressions in Cuba's Spanish—terms such as "ferry boats," "all right," "Lucky Strike," "foxtrot," and "jazzband."[11] Guillén and his contemporaries regretted the way U.S. modernity was invading Cuba and despoiling its virtue with the sex-obsessed, money-mad ethos of soldiers, tourists, and capitalists.

Much of the resistance to U.S. influence turned inward and expressed disappointment that Cubans accepted their fate so readily. After all, though it had done so by only one vote, the Cuban constituent assembly had adopted the Platt Amendment—it had not been forced upon the country. To add to the embarrassment, both Cuban candidates to the 1905 elections called for U.S. intervention, and some Cubans referred to U.S. veterans of the War of 1898 as "our saviors." Others bemoaned the competition and favoritism in hiring by the government and armed forces that resulted from the fact that foreign owners and managers kept so many middle-class Cubans out of industry. Anti-U.S. authors denounced the "pessimists" who accommodated the U.S. presence, politically or culturally.[12] One Cuban historian, disheartened at the way well-to-do Cubans seemed to live half their lives in either Miami or Madrid, flatly concluded that "the Cuban bourgeoisie lacked all sense of class consciousness."[13]

Throughout the student reform movements and antidictatorial struggles from the 1920s to the 1950s, anti-Americanism remained on the back burner of Cuban political life. As dictatorship persisted and some students became quasi-gangsters in the service of political bosses, suddenly the role of the United States seemed less sordid in comparison. From 1934 (when the U.S. government rescinded the Platt Amendment but helped defeat a leftist revolution and usher in the overlordship of Fulgencio Batista) to 1958 (when Batista openly ruled Cuba but faced imminent defeat against Fidel Castro), Cuba was coping with its own demons, not the United States. As scholar Jorge Domínguez has written, "anti-Americanism was . . . not a politically productive plank in Cuba between roughly 1940 and 1959." Graft and favoritism plagued even the rule of the Auténticos and the Ortodoxos, liberal democratic parties that claimed to be purifying the political system. Batista's coup in 1952 only compounded Cubans' shame. It seemed to many to sanction the judgments that U.S. overseers had conferred upon them—that they were unfit for self-rule, ignorant of civic virtue, best ruled by violence, and in need of autocratic control.[14]

Partly out of disenchantment with liberal democratic anti-Americanism, a more radical Cuban variant emerged. To be sure, revolutionary Cubans were not purists who planned to exorcise *all* U.S. influences from Cuba. And politically, they remained far from power before the arrival of Fidel Castro. But the revolutionary variant of anti-Americanism showed early on that it was robust in Cuba. Two characteristics marked Cuban revolutionaries: first, a strong sense of cross-class collaboration, and second, a practical realization that, for the moment, one had to work within liberal democratic or even dictatorial rules of the game, if only to stay alive. One of Castro's closest advisers, Antonio Núñez Jiménez, summarized the sophistication of his colleagues: "One important characteristic of Cuban culture is, in politics, a pragmatism that does not sacrifice ideological principles."[15]

Before Castro, the few active revolutionaries there were in Cuba mostly sharpened the tone of anti-Plattist protests without threatening U.S. hegemony too seriously. In 1913, Julio César Gandarilla published *Contra el yanqui* (Against the Yankee), a short polemic that one historian called "probably the earliest attack on the United States and its policies by a Cuban Marxist."[16] Gandarilla grew up near the coast, in Manzanillo. Scandalized at the sight of U.S. lobster and shrimp boats fishing in Cuban waters, Gandarilla stirred up local sentiment by warning against threats from the "eagle" swooping down on Cuba. Subtitled *A Protest against the Platt Amendment and against North American Absorption and Machiavellianism*, Gandarilla's tract was unrestrained. "Pillage is an instinct of the Yankee," it declared. "Yankee History can be summarized in one word: looting; in one ideal: absorption; in one strategy to attain its ends: trickery, pain, and perfidy." He characterized U.S. entrepreneurs as "tragically insatiable octopuses" intent on dragging Cuba into a "satanic maelstrom."[17] It was the first time that Blas Roca, later to become Cuba's premier Marxist and a survivor of the Batista era, had ever heard of imperialism.[18] But Gandarilla's scathing rhetoric was mostly just that. He eschewed talk of worldwide revolution and foreign capital and focused instead on the Platt Amendment. Perhaps, in the end, name calling and local issues made for more compelling reading for the average literate Cuban than did Marx. One journalist, at least, remembered that *Contra el yanqui* "echoed like a permanent clarion call."[19] Gandarilla's words were energizing, but not daring.

Student leader Juan Antonio Mella, in contrast, was almost reckless in his defiance of U.S. power. Before Fidel Castro came along, Mella epitomized revolutionary anti-Americanism's vigor to the point where fellow student leader Raúl Roa dubbed him "the first Olympic athlete of the communist movement in Cuba."[20] Mella rejected the romanticism of Arielism and the moderation of university reforms. He wanted nothing less than full social justice, the death of imperialism, and proletarian dictatorship. Unlike Castro, he never concealed his true goals, and perhaps for that reason he died young. Behind many movements of the 1920s one could find Mella. While demonstrating against U.S. ambassador Enoch Crowder's embarrassing tutelage of Cuban president Alfredo Zayas, Mella called together the First Congress of Cuban Students and became secretary general of the Student Directorate (DFE). When student reform failed, he did not give up; he became more radical still and founded the short-lived Popular University José Martí, devoted to educating workers. With the backing of the Communist Party, he also formed the Anti-Imperialist League in 1925 and the Anti-Clerical Foundation, edited two magazines, and called together all of Cuba's communists to a congress (which failed to attract many of them). Mella suffered university expulsion, imprisonment, and exile, and was murdered in Mexico in 1929 by assassins allegedly under orders from the current dictator Gerardo Machado. He was twenty-six. Many assumed that Machado had the hyper-activist killed under orders from the U.S. government. It was an "ambush by Yankee imperialism," said Roa. Whatever the case, Mella's clear-mindedness and courage influenced Castro and his generation to reach out to workers in their struggle.[21] His early death, however, may have prompted Castro to be more tight-lipped about ulterior motives.

Fidel Castro's contribution to Cuba's anti-Americanism was to infuse it with an ambivalence so well balanced that he threw U.S. policymakers off guard. By the mid-1950s, revolutionary anti-Americanism lay in waiting. Completely reconfiguring society *and* flushing out ambivalences toward the United States was its proper domain, but seeing that commitment through took tremendous devotion, organization, and cunning. Castro had all that, and more. He mastered what Søren Kierkegaard called "doublemindedness," or the ability to "will [two things] completely and totally as opposed to halfheartedly."[22] The guerrilla leader espoused both liberal democratic and revolutionary anti-U.S. attitudes, and freely expressed both strong negative *and* positive dispositions toward the United States. By embodying the twin perceptions of many Cubans, he gained their support. Philip Wickham-Crowley has called Castro "*the* phenomenological virtuoso" for his ability to persuade people from different backgrounds that contradictory goals were all simultaneously attainable.[23] In response to doublemindedness, the Eisenhower administration and the embassy in Havana showed an absentmindedness toward Latin American aspirations typical of its pre-Caracas outlook. Washington was not ready for such a strategic unlimbering of ambivalence.

Castro's duality had deep personal roots. "In Castro there is a love-hate relationship towards the United States that reflects his love-hate relationship with his father," said one of his acquaintances.[24] Angel Castro was a bullying Galician landowner who fathered Fidel out of wedlock. A bit like the United States did with Cuba, Angel raised his son in privilege but treated him brutally. Yet he also sided with Spain during the war and hated the United States. In 1961 the CIA hypothesized that "Fidel may have been influenced by his father's anti-US attitude." However, it added, "he also may have been influenced in his attitudes against wealthy landlords by his father's property-grabbing behavior." Social injustice profoundly angered Castro, who at age thirteen reportedly organized strikes on his own father's plantation.[25]

Growing up, Castro seemed to identify with those in power yet longed to confront them. As a boy, he wrote to President Franklin Roosevelt:

> My good friend Roosevelt. I don't know very English, but I know as much as write to you. I like to hear the radio, and I am very happy, because I heard in it that you will be President for a new *(período)*. I am twelve years old. I am a boy but I think very much, but I do not think that I am writting to the President of the United States. If you like, give me a ten dollars bill green american, in the letter, because never, I have not seen a ten dollars bill green american and I would like to have one of them.

Rather than just money (he got a thank-you note from the White House, but no cash), Castro seemed to want a tangible connection with a man whom Latin Americans saw as the humanitarian who had ended U.S. military intervention in the Western Hemisphere. As Castro began life on his own and conceived of injustice on a national and then an international scale, his father's moral failings may have appeared less important next to those of the United States and of Batista. Castro also came to know the corrupting influences of U.S. gambling and tourism in Havana and traveled to other red light districts such as the one in Panama City.[26]

In March 1949, Castro happened upon the perfect opportunity to marry his belief in national dignity with his desire for personal power. One night, three U.S. Marines got drunk, climbed atop José Martí's statue in Havana's Parque Central, and proceeded to swing from its arm and urinate on the revered monument. Castro led protests against the Marines, forced the U.S. ambassador to offer a wreath and a formal apology, and for the first time his name figured prominently in the press, along with photographs of the vandals.[27]

In the years following the incident at the statue, many Cubans pledged allegiance to Castro because he was such an unusual landowner's son. Guillermo García Frías, for example, a *comandante* in Castro's guerrilla forces, needed little prodding to join him in the Sierra Maestra after 1956. García was born a campesino in the Sierra, and but for the United States he would have been a child of the city. His grandfather fought in the wars of 1868 and 1895, first against Spaniards, then against U.S. soldiers who chased him "into the heart of the mountains." García recalled that his grandfather "was an anti-American, a tremendous anti-imperialist, because he was among those veterans who had lost all their rights." Life in the Sierra was hard. Several children in García's family died of malnutrition. Yet there was strength in suffering. "We made up a sort of tribe and from there *we* emerged as a new generation, a third campesino generation." García naturally grew fond of Castro, who, in contrast to U.S. managers, spent time with campesinos, getting close, touching, listening. Such loyalty allowed Castro to confirm the legitimacy of anti-Americanism as part of his political strategy.[28]

It was during his difficult, uncertain years as a guerrilla leader from 1956 to 1958 that Castro most seemed to struggle to balance Cuban ambivalence. He juggled positive and negative perceptions of the United States in public and private, but his private statements became more hostile as the fighting intensified and he came closer to seizing the reins of power. After seeing Batista's U.S. weapons destroy a friend's home, Castro wrote to aide Celia Sánchez, "When I saw rockets firing at Mario's house, I swore to myself that the North Americans were going to pay dearly for what they are doing. When this war is over, a much wider and bigger war will commence for me: the war that I am going to wage against them. I am aware that this is my true destiny."[29] Whether Castro was serious about this "destiny" may never be known. Statements such as this were few and should not weigh too heavily in assessing Castro's pro- or anti-Americanism. More pertinent is how he calibrated his hostility to both attract moderate Cubans and keep U.S. observers guessing.

On one hand, Castro revealed little trace of revolutionary anti-Americanism in his statements or his actions. He refrained from talking about imperialism or any radical change. Instead, he kept a steady gaze on Batista. He also allied with those in the urban underground who, wrote scholar Julia Sweig, did much of the planning during the struggle and saw a bright future for a liberated Cuba reforming itself along New Deal lines.[30] Any hostility Castro directed toward the U.S. government was issue-specific, and much of it was in the past. He criticized U.S. arms shipments to Batista until Eisenhower finally cut them off in mid-1958.

Castro also focused on individual U.S. citizens: he ridiculed the anti-communist fury of U.S. ambassadors Arthur Gardner and E. T. Smith and pressured them to withdraw their support for Batista. Most important, Castro pledged not to nationalize or expropriate any foreign property if he came to power, even though he chided the U.S. government for protecting foreign investors. All these stances carried the classic liberal democratic implication that if Cuba were free from Batista, it would likewise be free from anti-Americanism. "You can be sure we have no animosity toward the United States and the American people," Castro told Herbert Matthews of the *New York Times* in 1957.[31]

The other side of Castro's ideological strategy, however, was to strike out against the United States in order to prove his independence. In the summer of 1958, rebels under the control—or temporarily beyond the control—of Fidel's brother, Raúl Castro, captured about fifty U.S. and Canadian citizens. U.S. officials knew that the hostages were meant as shields against Batista's bombs, and they could do little but protest. Castro's strategy worked in two ways. First, the bombings halted.[32] Second, the rebels treated the captives well and thus showed that they could distinguish between hostility toward the U.S. government on one side and consideration toward U.S. individuals on the other.[33] To keep U.S. officials on guard, however, rebels also burned canefields and sabotaged or looted U.S. farms and factories. They singled out for harassment the electric and telephone companies, both U.S. subsidiaries that charged high rates. As a result, in the first nine months of 1958, U.S. corporations reported a loss of over $2.25 million from rebel attacks. Castro seemed to do just enough to enrage but not to spark reprisals. He also kept everyone on edge by targeting U.S. property whether or not owners had contributed to his effort, and he levied "taxes" in exchange for protection.[34] (He allegedly also suspended his puritanical moral standards and protected growers of marijuana.)[35]

Up to the very last days of the guerrilla struggle in late 1958, the intense yet dual nature of Castro's movement baffled U.S. embassy and State Department officials. Partly, this surprise resulted from cultural conditioning. In Cuba, U.S. officials thought, the United States had come to mean many things to many people: some good, some bad, but nothing earth-shattering either way. As State Department officials wrote, Cubans were "influenced by a sense of inferiority which promotes exaggerated nationalism. . . . The Cubans tend to feel that the United States will bail them out before a collapse and this encourages irresponsibility."[36] Most U.S. citizens cared more about beaches, croupiers, and *mojitos* than about radical hostility. In August 1958, therefore, when faced with Castro's now menacing 26th of July Movement, State Department analysts expressed confusion about its apparently unprogrammatic hostility. "While on the one hand protesting [professing?] admiration and respect for the United States, most of the leaders of the 26th of July Movement have attacked U.S. policies. . . . The degree of bitterness expressed by the rebels varies and many of them have admitted their dependence upon U.S. friendship." The 26th of July, they noted, "appears to lack any significant ideology."[37] Homer Bigart of the *New York Times* agreed. He spent time with the rebels that year and noticed no anti-Americanism "among the people he talked to."[38]

U.S. officials in Washington, especially, failed to appreciate the cultural breadth and compelling politics of anti-Americanism because of their obsession with the Cold War. As historian Thomas Paterson has noted, Eisenhower officials "dwelled on the wrong question"—on communism rather than anti-Americanism.[39] As in Caracas, they were trained to see anti-Americanism as a minor offshoot of communism rather than the other way around. They spoke of anti-Americanism as a "soft sell" technique for concealing one's true socialist tendencies. Roy Rubottom, the assistant secretary of state for inter-American affairs, noted as particularly meaningful that the Cuban Communist Party in March 1958 publicly supported Castro's threat of "all-out war" against U.S. property.[40] But in reality, communist support for Castro was catching up with the struggle, and it had little influence on it when it did catch up. At the same time, neither the State Department, the CIA, nor the FBI was convinced of widespread communism among the rebels, and so all refrained from either supporting or opposing the Castro movement.

Inertia set in. U.S. intelligence in the field rarely communicated the seriousness of the war in Cuba to the now-ailing Secretary of State Dulles, his imminent replacement Christian Herter, or Eisenhower. The National Security Council (NSC) met twenty-six times between April and December 1958, and Cuba was never on the agenda.[41] Right before the long silence, CIA Director Allen Dulles (the secretary's brother) informed his NSC colleagues that he "had had a man with Castro's forces" but the spy learned nothing worth reporting. It was only two weeks before Batista's flight, then, before the NSC went on alert against a rapidly approaching Castro victory. On 18 December, Eisenhower expressed befuddlement (and perhaps felt envy) at the fact that Castro enjoyed a 95 percent approval rating among his people.[42]

Top Eisenhower advisors realized the power of anti-Americanism too late. In a recently declassified portion of a memorandum to the president, Herter on December 23 finally declared that "the [State] Department clearly does not want to see Castro succeed to the leadership of the Government." Herter brought up the kidnappings and the sabotage as evidence, "and there are other clear indications that irresponsibility and a degree of anti-American sentiment are characteristic of the Castro movement." Unfortunately, he added, Castro's distance from the communists made it impossible for the U.S. government to launch an expedition against him like the one it had mounted in Guatemala in 1954 against the regime of Jacobo Arbenz.[43] As the rebels closed in on Batista, Secretary Dulles said, "I don't know whether this is good for us or bad." On January 1, 1959, Batista fled Cuba, Cubans rejoiced in the streets, and Castro rode into Santiago like a messiah bearing the gifts of democracy and liberation. Partly because he had done so almost entirely without the help of the U.S. government, revolutionary anti-Americanism was ripe for becoming a major disposition of the new Cuba. Even children intuited the enmity toward the United States that hung in the air as decades of frustrated politics and years of war came to a close. Núñez Jiménez recalled playing with his infant daughter, when, confused by talk of *los yanquis,* she asked innocently, "Daddy, are the Yankees some kind of disease?"[44]

The Anti-Americanization of Cuba

Revolutionary resentment became the dominant variant of anti-Americanism in Cuba in 1959 because it allowed Fidel Castro's government to gradually purge Cuba of almost all of its ambivalence. An anti-Americanism that went to the root of Cuba's intimacy with the United States urged Cubans to admit how dependent they were on it for their very sense of themselves as a nation; reversing that dependence meant redefining "Cubanness" itself. That realization set a tone of staunch independence in foreign policy and garnered mass support for sweeping change at home.[45] By October 1959, revolutionary anti-Americanism was a full-blown ideological campaign, and dissent largely died down. Cubans maintained a certain affinity for U.S. social and cultural norms that they now considered their own, but increasingly they suspected all U.S. policies and even all U.S. citizens in Cuba.

The response of the Eisenhower and Kennedy administrations to this sudden anti-Americanization of Cuba was diplomatic rigor mortis. Diplomats in the field and U.S. business representatives, shocked at Castro's rhetoric, waited to see if Castro's policies would be as icy. They were. The speed and thoroughness of Cuba's attack on private property ran against the U.S. self-image as an agent of progress in Cuba. By the end of 1959, Eisenhower had hesitated too long. He could only respond to Castro's intransigence with intransigence of his own. He vowed to overthrow the Cuban leader.

In a first stage of anti-Americanization that lasted about four months, the Cuban government still contained many liberal democrats and attempted to preserve its ambivalence toward the United States by drawing distinctions between U.S. society and the U.S. government. According to a vision in which, as Castro said, "the average American is a nice guy," ordinary U.S. citizens were model reformists and supportive of the revolution while their government was hegemonic toward Cuba and disrespectful of Cuban dignity. U.S. observers in and out of government were skeptical that such a distinction could be made. Nevertheless, the lack of any significant attack on U.S. interests in Cuba made for a polite "honeymoon" in U.S.-Castro relations.[46]

In the euphoria of the early months of the Castro regime, liberal democratic Cubans celebrated the defeat of dictatorship and heralded the diversification of their economy as harbingers of U.S. levels of material comfort and political freedom. What U.S. citizens thought of the revolution was important in Cuba. It seemed that every comment on Cuba by a U.S. member of Congress, even letters of support from private U.S. citizens, found prominent placement in Cuban newspapers. Two U.S. soldiers of fortune who helped out during the struggle now joined the Rebel Army. Cuban leaders, especially, celebrated the lofty ideals they shared with U.S. citizens. Upon accepting credentials from the new U.S. ambassador, Philip Bonsal, President Manuel Urrutia assured the crowd that Cuba's decades of contacts with the United States had borne fruit. "Surely, the United States and Cuba share the same democratic, republican, and liberal ideology," he said.[47] Amid the nationalistic huzzahs, many Cubans still looked to the United States for a nod of approval.

In keeping with this initial soft stance, Castro's anti-U.S. actions in those early months were largely issue-specific. Either they fell in line with the reforms he had promised as a guerrilla leader, or they seemed reasonable given the bitter aftertaste of the U.S.-Batista partnership. Castro insisted, for example, on the departure of the U.S. military mission, which had provided arms to the dictator. He also investigated the rates charged by U.S.-owned utility companies and slashed rents by as much as half.[48] Minister of State Roberto Agramonte assured U.S. chargé Daniel Braddock that "Cubans had no complaints against [the] American people or [the] US government, but did have [some] against Ambassador [E. T.] Smith, [the] American press, and military missions."[49] How it could be that military missions and ambassadors were not part of the government was never clear.

Castro also distinguished good U.S. social and moral influences from bad ones. To keep funds inside Cuba after Batista had virtually emptied the government's coffers, Castro called on nationalists to "consume Cuban products" rather than the U.S. goods they were used to. "A Cuban should be ashamed to be seen smoking an American cigarette," he said.[50] More controversial was Castro's policy toward gambling establishments, many of which were owned by U.S. mobsters. In January, some rebels declared they were opposed to all games of chance; others were inclined to be more tolerant. Castro initially sided with the former and closed down all casinos because, he said, they debased moral character and funneled money out of the country. Within weeks, gambling bosses such as Meyer Lansky and Santo Trafficante had fled Cuba. Soon after, when laborers protested the loss of employment and the drop in hotel income, casinos reopened and juke boxes blared again. Castro had realized that what Cubans disliked was not so much the culture of U.S. citizens but the atmosphere of criminality that surrounded the mob. He justified his reversal saying that he could not allow the loss of so many jobs.[51]

Castro's unpredictability also paid off by concealing the darker side of his ambivalence with apparent hot-headedness. Most distressing for U.S. observers was his threat that there would be "200,000 dead gringos" on the streets of Havana if the U.S. government ever attempted an invasion. In hindsight this may seem like a slip of the tongue, and Castro brushed it off as "not for publication"; but at the time, the statement was a frighteningly violent one for a leader anywhere to make, especially in Cuba.[52] Such "errors" recurred, and similar apologies followed. After bringing up the memories of Hiroshima and Nagasaki in an enormous public rally on January 21, Castro reassured Braddock in a "sincere manner that he hoped we had received no hurt as he had intended none and that it was necessary in a public rally of that sort to express certain points of view."[53]

Apologies came most notably from liberal democrats, who, it turned out, spoke without the authority that they claimed. They reassured U.S. diplomats in Havana and Washington that anti-Americanism was for Castro a temporary rhetorical sop to the socialists and radicals who had helped him triumph. Felipe Pazos, president of the Cuban National Bank, told Braddock "that he was sure Castro did want friendly relations with the United States, but that it was good politics to have someone as a whipping boy." José Miró Cardona, who had just resigned as prime minister so that Castro could replace him, was also confident that Castro's public utterances "are purely for internal political purposes."[54]

Faced with conflicting messages, U.S. officials were left to doubt both the vituperation and the contrition of Cubans. One diplomat in Washington concluded that Castro's attitudes toward the United States were "still in the formative stage." Officials worried that anti-U.S. sentiment might be impossible to pin down. "Nearly every speech by a 26th of July official contains some at least implied criticism of the United States," reported a consul in Santiago. But "implied criticism" meant little; nobody belonged to an "Anti-American Party." Fights between U.S. and Cuban private school children increased, but what did that mean? For a wider sampling of opinions, Braddock drove fifteen hundred miles around Cuba in February. He reported only "some anti-Americanism . . . concentrated almost entirely among the educated civilians who participated in revolutionary activities, or who now claim to have done so." He added that "the feeling does not appear to be at all widespread among the lower ranks."[55]

Frustrated U.S. officials resorted to an attitude of passive watchfulness supported by traditional paternalistic images of Cubans as volatile, amateur diplomats. In a meeting of the NSC on February 12, CIA director Dulles "pointed out that the new Cuban officials had to be treated more or less like children. They had to be led rather than rebuffed. If they were rebuffed, like children, they were capable of doing almost anything." He and Eisenhower agreed on a "wait-and-see" policy.[56] Throughout Castro's unofficial eleven-day visit to North America in April, the White House kept relatively quiet but resented the Cuban's effort to go "over the heads" of officialdom and reach out to a U.S. public caught up in Castro's celebrity status.[57] A "Tentative Evaluation" prepared by the State Department and sent to Eisenhower concluded wryly that "the Castro who came to Washington was a man on his best behavior" and that public relations results were therefore "contrived." Christian Herter, the new secretary of state, described him as "a most interesting individual, very much like a child in many ways, quite immature regarding problems of government, and puzzled and confused by some of the practical difficulties now facing him."[58]

If Herter sought practicality from Castro, he got it—and then some— from the Agrarian Reform Law of 1959. The Cuban government abandoned much of its ambivalence and turned toward a more calculated anti-Americanism with a land reform program that swept away the material basis of U.S. hegemony in Cuba. To be sure, the rebel rhetoric around the Agrarian Reform Law still expressed shared ideals of modernization between U.S. citizens and Cubans. But its clandestine conception and its hurried implementation revealed deep and widespread animosity running in both directions. Further exorcising Cuba's pro-U.S. dispositions, the reform allowed Castro to recenter the revolution around the rural workers, perhaps the most "un-American" of Cubans. U.S. officials and landowners took notice of the threat, to say the least. But they hesitated to strike back at Castro because he continued to express ambivalence so skillfully that he stood just barely on the edge of the communist "abyss." In much of Washington, Castro remained a tolerably liberal democratic anti-American; any aggressive U.S. response against him would have brought more criticism to the United States, not less.

Poor rural Cubans were not naturally disposed against U.S. power. While they often lived in misery, they were not on the cusp of revolutionary upheaval. First, they were divided among themselves between *relatively* well-paid laborers, who cut and refined sugar—often for U.S. companies—and much poorer landless, independent, or "squatting" farmers. In addition, rural Cubans were not in the majority. Most Cubans lived in cities and enjoyed one of the highest standards of living in Latin America.[59] Although Juan Antonio Mella and other communists had long called for an "anti-imperialist and agrarian revolution," middle-class urban parties had considered such a thing unattainable. And by 1959 U.S. capitalists were less of a target for land reform: their 35 to 40 percent ownership of sugar interests was down from 65 percent, and the world price for sugar was more stable than it had been.[60] U.S. scholar Frank Tannenbaum in 1962 wrote that Castro "decided to make an agrarian revolution in a country that had no agrarian problem. . . . He mistakenly identified social reform with agrarian revolution." Scholar Lowry Nelson, to whom Castro looked for inspiration, predicted that rural Cubans would be "poor material for revolution." He characterized them as "abysmally ignorant, impoverished, and seemingly devoid of aspiration for something better." As if taking a cue from Nelson, rural Cubans rarely joined revolutionary movements. Only 180 out of Castro's Sierra Maestra force of 1,000 to 3,000 fighters were from the peasantry, and, as Ernesto Che Guevara himself explained, these were not wage laborers looking to overthrow their U.S. bosses but peasants hungry for any land at all.[61]

Nevertheless, Castro had good reasons for placing campesinos at the center of the revolution. Significant discontent did simmer among rural Cubans whether they worked for U.S. companies or not, and their voices were not heard. The wealth of the cities could eclipse the squalor of the *campo,* but it could also highlight it. *Revolución,* the 26th of July's daily, early in 1959 ran exposés on life in the plantations of the Boston-based United Fruit Company (UFCO). Unlike other urban publications that spoke for the countryside, *Revolución* quoted UFCO workers, supposedly the royalty of rural labor. Interestingly, these workers revealed, it was not poverty or the lack of land that most irked them, but rather the wage economy itself and the control that U.S. capitalists had over their lives: UFCO's workers often received their pay late, had to pay for medical care, lived in segregated neighborhoods, hated the aloofness of U.S. overseers, lacked freedom of movement, and had no control over water, land, or community life. U.S. employees' comparatively heavenly lives—polo fields, swimming pools, shops stocked with U.S. goods, and private security forces—aggravated anti-U.S. sentiment.[62] This was not simply underdevelopment, but subjugated development. There was plenty about it to resent.

The rebels saw in a reform of the lives of campesinos what one author called "a master lever with which to transform radically both Cuban society and its relations with the United States."[63] Strategically, campesinos were the ideal Trojan Horse of anti-Americanism. They had a just cause. They remained untainted by collaboration with U.S. politicians, consumption of U.S. goods, or adulation of U.S. culture. And there were millions of them. All in all, campesinos carried the moral and political weight to tilt the revolution out of its ambivalence and redefine Cubanness. As a character in the Cuban novel *Bertillón 166* said, "the principal force are the campesinos. They are the most whole and pure Cubans."[64]

The Agrarian Reform Law galvanized not just peasants but a broad range of Cubans, uniting heretofore alienated urban and rural groups. Shepherded by 26th of July rebels, peasants willingly filled plazas, held huge rallies, and worshiped Castro as he promised them land. On July 26, 1959, half a million made a pilgrimage to Havana, where Castro declared that the machete was now the symbol of the revolution. "Welcome, Brothers!" bellowed *Carteles* magazine as city and country, long alienated by U.S. power, mingled, and Havanans took campesinos into their homes. The starry-eyed visitors praised the coming changes as a gift from "God through Fidel."[65] Many urbanites, in turn, felt compelled to join the rural Cubans in their adulation. "We who have always lived in the capital often forget that the countryside exists," wrote a lifelong Havanan. "Yes, the revolution has made us feel guilty." Workers, too, rallied in support of the reform, and Castro requested voluntary contributions of 1 percent of their salaries.[66] Boxing matches, baseball games, and other traditional Cuban events raised funds for a law whose details remained unknown. Under the headline "And What Have *You* Done for the Agrarian Reform?" *Revolución* daily listed donations from peasants, municipal groups, schoolchildren, artists, bankers, and sports personalities: they gave a tractor, an ox, a few pesos. Even U.S. film distributors chipped in. Contributing to the reform became a mark of social acceptability in the new Cuba. The day before its signing, the Agrarian Reform Law had already gathered 75 million pesos from private sources.[67]

Agrarian reformers, meanwhile, placated U.S. property owners. They promised that the reform would compensate expropriated owners with Cuban bonds at a 4.5 percent rate over twenty years, which, they explained, was better even than what the U.S. occupants of postwar Japan had offered. Referring to that comparison, Che Guevara sardonically proposed that "a certain general of the Army of the United States [Douglas MacArthur, supreme commander of the Japanese occupation] has been more of a Communist than any of us." Castro also played down U.S. fears by offering Canada as a model of successful industrialization on the U.S. periphery.[68] Agrarian reform, he explained, would build an internal market for nascent Cuban industries. At a press conference in New York, Castro, in his broken English, called the Agrarian Reform Law "the base of our . . . economical program. Why? Because we need that the farmer have the money. When the farmer have the money, we will have an own industry with his own market, like happened here in the United States."[69] Castro and his aides even indulged in Lincoln-like phrasing. They characterized the reform as "de los humildes, por los humildes y para los humildes" ("of the poor, by the poor, and for the poor") and quoted the Great Emancipator's dictum that "whenever a conflict arises between human rights and property rights, human rights must prevail." Finally, grand religious rhetoric infused Cuban speeches on the Agrarian Reform. Castro used the Bible, not Marx or Lenin, to get through to peasants, and he played up the church's limited endorsement of his egalitarian goals.[70]

Behind the scenes, however, agrarian reformers designed a radical and deceptive law. They had in mind not the redistribution of land but rather its collectivization. They believed—ironically agreeing with U.S. policy-makers—that poor Cubans, if handed their own small plots, would sell them or lose them to unscrupulous speculators and that the cycle of property concentration would begin anew.[71] Thus, while a nominal bill underwent drafts in the government of President Urrutia, Castro and six radical advisers secretly drafted their own definitive—if slightly im-provised—text. As one member of this group recalled, "No one really grasped what had to be done in the countryside."[72] Castro knew, at least, that he should avoid appearing to create Soviet *kolkhozy* or Chinese communes. On the plane heading to the proclamation of the Agrarian Reform Law on May 17, 1959, he decided to speak of "property" when in fact he had in mind a system of cooperatives under the tutelage of the National Institute for Agrarian Reform (INRA). He chose his wording, he said, "so that our enemies cannot exploit it." "What we did was treat [U.S. businesses] with all the cunning that was necessary under the cir-cumstances," he later explained.[73] The law did not single out U.S. lands for expropriation, but it did bar foreigners from owning sugar planta-tions (they could still own sugar mills). The move was evidence of a far-reaching distrust of foreign capital. Although liberal Cabinet members opposed the law at a May 13 meeting, it was adopted without a vote.[74]

Proclamation ceremonies were fraught with subtle anti-U.S. symbolism. Castro signed the reform into law in the town of La Plata, in the wooden shack of a *guajiro,* a typical Cuban peasant. There, the brutality and poverty of life in the countryside were apparent to all. At the historic signing, when the press corps complained of hunger, Castro himself picked up a rifle and provided lunch by shooting some nearby cattle. The *Havana Post* described the episode as Castro's effort to open the eyes of U.S. citizens and urban Cubans to "the glorious mud and famine of the Sierra."[75]

Starting that summer, the implementation of the reform—the fastest ever in Latin America—unleashed much of the vindictiveness that Cuban revolutionaries had been holding in check. Rebels exaggerated campesinos' desire for these lands with gleeful disregard for U.S. standards of decorum, productivity, or law.[76] They "intervened" sugar mills and used the transitive verb to express the active, poetic reversal of the asymmetry of hegemony. Núñez Jiménez, newly appointed director of INRA, personally headed the taking of Preston, an UFCO company town, where he had grown up. Upon his arrival, he demanded access for workers to a U.S.-owned creek. He was turned down. "Months later," he proudly recalled in 1985, "I rode in on horseback accompanied by the Rebel Army and the people to implement nationalization. I didn't bother to see any manager. I *was* the Republic of Cuba at that moment, I was the Cuban people taking possession of its own country. That, the North American entrepreneurs could never understand."[77]

Expropriations proceeded with increasing arbitrariness. According to one count, from July to December 1959 Cubans "violated lands and/or property owned by U.S. citizens on over forty occasions."[78] It worked this way: Local representatives of the 26th of July would show up at the gates of, say, a sugar estate. With or without a written order, they would declare their intent to take over its management. (Cuban depictions usually end with this symbolic triumph.) Within days they would either pay workers to be idle, send them home temporarily, or otherwise upset production. Theodore Draper described such scenes as displays of spite and lawlessness: "Though the law says nothing about farm machinery or cattle, they also are appropriated. The whole transaction is completely informal; there are no hearings, no inventories, no receipts." A U.S. Information Service (USIS) officer reported that "one American, who will be stripped of roughly 40 percent of his land, was told by an INRA official to be content 'or we'll take more.'"[79]

Back in Havana, Castro realized that the Agrarian Reform Law, as radical as it was on paper, was nevertheless modest compared to the momentous shift in land ownership unfolding on the ground in the countryside. He encouraged the yawning gap between theory and practice. During a sixteen-hour meeting on August 4, he lost his patience with legalities and banged his fist on the table, shouting, "What we have to do is occupy *all* the lands!"[80]

Common sense suggests that the White House, identifying itself as the defender of U.S. private property, would have acted swiftly against such sweeping anti-Americanism. Herter and Eisenhower, after all, had close friends among the large landowners in Cuba, and these men of means did not hesitate to sound alarms in Washington about "interventions." Two days after the proclamation of the Agrarian Reform Law, the *New York Times* reported widespread "consternation in the American-owned sugar mills." Within another four days, representatives of thirty out of the thirty-four U.S. mills in Cuba had stormed the embassy to voice their panic.[81] "Confiscatory" and "absolutely disastrous," they called the reform. Sugar baron Rionda Braga argued that "it is only a sham that anybody [among poor Cubans] is getting land down there." By the end of May, wires between Washington and Havana were burning with demands for a swift rebuttal to the subversive law.[82]

But the apparent ideological incompatibility between U.S. and revolutionary economic visions confused U.S. officials and slowed their response. Reacting to anti-U.S. policies meant understanding the logic behind them, but in this case there seemed to be none. U.S. policymakers truly believed that U.S. ownership of Cuban means of production had been good for Cubans. One could only deduce, then, that rebel economics were either absurdly misdirected or dangerously subversive. Even in private meetings with Cubans, U.S. officials insisted that "American companies in Cuba . . . had a good record of treating their labor well, of paying their taxes, and of otherwise abiding by the laws."[83] Observers were convinced that a radical redistribution of land—even one that respected private property—would make Cuba's capital-intensive agriculture inefficient and would lower the standard of living of rural workers. "I'll have to admit," recalled Rubottom, "that I had a pretty heavy bias in my mind against Castro all the time, because his whole approach to development . . . is destructive." Not once did U.S. policymakers express doubts about the benefits of U.S. foreign investment to ordinary Cubans.

Not once did they suggest that owners who valued their land four or five times higher than their taxable amount were greedy. And not once did they concede the central claim of dependency theories about the exploitative nature of U.S. investment. The bottom line was baffling to them: "Castro and his Government are hostile to private enterprise."[84]

Another reason for the slow U.S. reaction was that some corporate giants agreed with the White House that too aggressive a rebuttal would stoke greater anti-U.S. sentiment and do further damage to their property. There still lingered, after Caracas, a fear of further alienating noncommunist critics abroad. For example, King Ranch executives (Eisenhower called their president, Robert Kleberg, "Bob") suggested as late as June 1959 that "we do not want to fall into the error of taking measures which would only make a martyr out of Castro."[85] The president of the American Chamber of Commerce in Havana likewise persuaded his colleagues "not to issue any statement on this law in the thought that any such action would have been considered provocative by the present [Castro] administration and would probably have been counter-productive to American interests."[86]

In the end, fear of anti-Americanism won out over the fear of radicalization in Cuba. U.S. officials drafted a polite and futile formal letter of protest to the Cuban government. Rubottom, rejecting unspecified "drastic" alternatives proposed by some furious landowners, convinced Eisenhower to cut his losses and salvage "a favorable attitude toward the U.S. position vis-à-vis the Castro administration throughout the Hemisphere and the Free World." U.S. taxpayers paid much of the $1 billion in losses, written off by U.S. landowners. As Rubottom summarized the lesson learned belatedly from the first summer of the Cuban Revolution, "we were dealing with a force that irrespective of its ideological base— that is, Communist or not—was so anti-US that we were going to have a serious problem on our hands."[87]

By the end of 1959, Castro would dramatically abandon ambivalence and develop revolutionary anti-Americanism far more consistently. The foil that would, as Núñez Jiménez said, "create the conditions" for completing the anti-Americanization of Cuba was the "bombing" of Havana. On October 21, 1959, Major Pedro Luis Díaz Lanz, the chief of the Air Force who the previous July had defected and testified in Congress about communist infiltration in Cuba, flew a small plane over Havana. While circling the capital, he dropped thousands of leaflets explaining the reasons for his desertion. The appearance of the plane, coming on the heels of firebombings of canefields the previous week, sparked what *Newsweek* called "a frenzy of anti-Americanism" among Cuban forces. Twenty minutes into the flyover, two persons were dead and forty-five wounded.[88]

Several facts emerged immediately. Díaz Lanz admitted flying out of Florida and over Havana, but denied he had fired on or bombed the city. U.S. Navy investigators reported that the wounded were victims of shrapnel and anti-aircraft fire, and therefore not of Díaz Lanz's plane. The U.S. government also examined the plane itself and concluded that it could not have carried a bomb of any size or even held a machine gun. (Nothing would have stopped the pilot from dropping grenades or firing pistols, however.) Most likely, as newspapers reported the day after the event, many of the wounded had been victims of men throwing grenades and shooting from passing cars. Only one witness thought he saw machine-gun fire coming from the plane, and still he could not be positive. Even the Cuban National Police on the day of the event confirmed that what had dropped from the sky were leaflets, not bombs.[89]

Castro's espousal of the unlikely "bombing" scenario showed a desire not only to fan the existing hatred against subversive exiles such as Díaz Lanz but also to spread it to the U.S. government. He refused to accept the most plausible explanation of the event—that it was the act of a single man or a small group of exiles acting independently from Washington. Castro insisted that there was no way U.S. officials did not control all planes leaving U.S. air space. He also refused to consider the State Department's evidence that Cuban armed forces may have wounded their own civilians, dismissing the argument as "matchless cynicism." Drawing on sensitive historical memories, Castro compared the attack to the sinking of the U.S. battleship *Maine* in 1898, an event that had precipitated U.S. intervention into Cuba's war for independence.[90] It was almost as if Castro welcomed further confrontations. "Imperialism wants to do battle, mobilize its nest of worms, promote subversion, it doesn't matter," he once said. "There is also virtue in this; it invigorates the revolutionary, it excites him, it quickens his fighting spirit."[91] The Ministry of State quickly published pamphlets such as *Havana's Pearl Harbor,* which featured an aircraft strafing Havana. Another pamphlet, titled *Cuba Denounces before the World!* and distributed in many countries at 100,000 copies, suggested that the event was part of a concerted attack on the island. It did not name the United States explicitly, but others did. *Sierra Maestra,* the 26th of July's voice in Oriente province, claimed that Díaz Lanz was "armed, protected, and sustained by the Caribbean tyrannies, their owners, American companies, and the Department of State." Striking the same theme, the communist *Noticias de hoy's* cartoonist por-

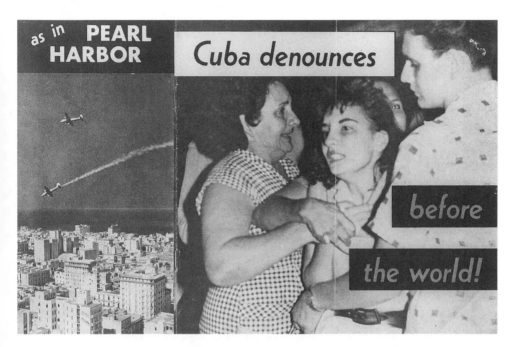

2. The Cuban Minister of State published this pamphlet in late 1959 after defector Major Pedro Luis Díaz Lanz flew a small plane out of Florida and dropped anticommunist flyers over Havana. Published in Spanish and English, the pamphlet suggested the incident was a Pearl Harbor–like sneak attack from the United States. Some of its claims were plausible—notably, that the flyover was linked to recent attacks against sugar mills. Yet the pamphlet also contained graphic photos of torture victims and bombed-out ruins, both the work of strongman Fulgencio Batista before he was ousted, not of the United States or of Cuban exiles. Moreover, the photo of two large planes over Havana—one of them veering toward the ground—was almost surely unrelated. Such inaccuracies helped to convince U.S. officials that Cuban anti-Americanism had now become a deliberate strategy of misinformation. *U.S. News and World Report,* 23 November 1959. Reprinted with permission of *U.S. News and World Report.*

trayed attacks on canefields as the work of "imperialism" in retaliation for the Agrarian Reform. Finally, the day after the flyover, the Cuban Revolution held its first demonstration in front of the U.S. embassy.[92]

U.S. observers were furious at what they saw as Castro's full-blown anti-Americanism. Herter deduced that Castro's campaign was "deliberate and concerted." "Under these circumstances," he wrote the embassy, "the U.S. Government cannot but view with shock and amazement efforts to imply that it countenanced the 'bombing' of Habana, assertions which can serve no purpose other than whip up unfriendly feelings between the two countries." "We cannot let Castro's charges and anti-American campaign go unanswered," he resolved. Bonsal surmised that Castro was using "Goebbels-type propaganda" to create "straw men and bogies."[93] Picking up on the Nazi analogy, one U.S. businessman living in Havana claimed, "We've become Castro's Jews. Hitler used to blame the Jews for everything that went wrong in Germany; Castro blames the U.S. You don't expect him to blame himself for that blood bath, do you?" Rubottom shared the discouragement and outrage. The State Department had done all it could, he thought, by recognizing the origin of the plane and pledging to do more to ground illegal flights. The FBI simply could not keep a constant eye on all the airfields—280 in Florida alone. Rubottom stormed into the Cuban embassy in Washington, called the *Cuba Denounces* pamphlet "a shocking compilation of half-truths, innuendos and insinuations," and demanded an explanation.[94] Cuban officials replied that the pamphlet said nothing about the United States and that therefore no explanation or apology was in order.

Such exchanges were mounting evidence that Castro no longer balanced his hostility with the populist bonhomie of early 1959 or even with the economic idealism of the Agrarian Reform. Ambivalence was collapsing. By the end of November 1959, U.S. officials had obtained from Castro no more than a commitment to speak of an "air incursion" rather than a bombing. It was weeks before the Cuban government admitted there was no evidence that the Díaz Lanz plane had dropped any live explosives. Around that time *Life en español* had exposed *Havana's Pearl Harbor* as a photo-montage.[95] For the moment, however, since the Cuban government was making no formal accusations or demands, there was little U.S. officials could do. As with the Agrarian Reform, they again sent a formal note of protest that had little impact in Havana.

"Here We Go Again!" headlined the *Times of Havana* as Castro called another million Cubans to Havana to rally against Díaz Lanz on October 26. He had summoned them first on television the day after the excursion, declaring that the cold war (it was not clear which one) was now a shooting war. Once more Castro hoped that a massive gathering would raise Cuban fervor against foreign domination to a fever pitch and consolidate his power.[96] Castro's speech at the rally dismayed Bonsal. The ambassador found it "as strongly anti-American as anything [Castro] has ever done. He listed virtually all local American interests as items which were not in the interests of Cuba. He talked of controlling utilities and of new mining and petroleum laws. He got approval from [the] audience for [the] re-establishment of revolutionary tribunals. . . . He repeatedly mentioned [the] Cuban people fighting to [the] last man in caves and tunnels if necessary to repel [a] foreign invasion." The "crowd was with him to the last man," sighed Bonsal.[97]

Castro made sure Cubans were with him by institutionalizing anti-Americanism. The *líder máximo* soon revealed the two political goals behind his abandonment of ambivalence: to neutralize possible turncoats and to approach the Soviet Union from a position of power. His first goal stemmed from the fact that Castro faced increasing opposition within Cuba, mostly from middle-class allies and Cuban property owners. Since Castro had engineered the downfall of President Urrutia in July, he was the sole wielder of any significant power in Cuba, yet he still operated in a nominally free political system. Previously loyal center-left rebels now began to criticize him. The most respected of these was Húber Matos. As military commander of Camagüey province, Matos had shown plenty of revolutionary zest in winning the war and "intervening" U.S. lands. In mid-October, however, Matos worried about the communization of Castro's forces. He offered his resignation. On the same day as the Díaz flyover, Castro arrested Matos on grounds of treason. Many U.S. observers reasoned that Castro was making an example out of Matos to foment a fear of internal subversion. Such fear would not only silence possible dissent, but it would allow Castro to ally more closely with Cuban communists—and through them, with the Soviets. Matos himself agreed, after spending the next twenty years in prison, that Castro was "seeking enemies" to gain Soviet support against them. In that endeavor, said Matos, anti-Americanism always proved "an easy sell."[98]

Castro had no intention of becoming a puppet of the Soviets. His second motivation for reacting so strongly to the "bombing" was to ally with the Soviet Union as an equal partner. As scholar Edward González has argued, the Matos and Díaz Lanz episodes went far beyond what even the local communists or even Moscow thought wise. Castro, in effect, presented them with what González called a revolutionary "fait accompli," clear evidence that he could single-handedly stand up to the United States and would ally with communists only if *they* were subordinates.[99] In a brilliant move, therefore, the madman gambit of anti-Americanism aimed to give Castro both support from the Soviet Union and independence from it.

It worked. After the October 26 rally, resignations from liberal democrats came in quick succession. Felipe Pazos, Faustino Pérez, Manolo Ray, and other prominent noncommunists were allowed a kinder fate than Matos: they fell silent from fear or else left the country. Castro then filled key positions with favorites: his brother Raúl gained control of the armed forces, and Che Guevara took over the direction of the National Bank. In addition, INRA, now more powerful than ever, quickened the pace of confiscation.[100] A few weeks after the leaflet incident, Castro announced that he would arm students, workers, and farmers to prevent training by "foreign instructors," a reference to U.S. military personnel who had trained Batista's forces.[101] In the following six months, purges affected not only land ownership and government but universities, professional associations, trade unions, and the media.

As long-time spectators of the political process who were now increasingly forced to choose sides, most Cubans were torn between their fondness for the United States and their loyalty to Castro. On one hand, there was remarkably little violence, either governmental or individual, against U.S. citizens in Cuba. In fact, Bonsal noted an "increased cordiality from all classes of the Cuban people as [a] result [of] recent developments. Attempts to arouse anti-American feelings have been generally repudiated." "Many Cubans are stopping Americans on the streets to apologize for some of the acts and criticisms of the new government against the United States," said one official. "I hope this is true because, in my own experience, there was no place in the hemisphere where Americans were better liked than in Cuba." Church leaders and progressives from the United States, especially, emphasized the ambivalence of Cubans. "The Cubans still feel very friendly toward Americans," said a City College instructor recently returned from Cuba. "After each anti-

American tirade, uniformed militia girls ran over to American visitors and assured them that 'we don't mean you.'"[102]

But the popular mood was changing regardless. The embassy reported more incidents of "molestation and taunts" against U.S. citizens. Public discourse no longer defined "bad Cubans" internally as defenders of Batista, but externally, as "lackeys of imperialism" or "enemies of communism." And in the increasingly divided Cuban press, words with negative connotations such as *yanqui* and *gringo* became more common than the more neutral *americano* or *norteamericano*. Ordinary Cubans, of course, did not eliminate all U.S. influences from their lives. They still played *béisbol*, read U.S. magazines, and used English words on a daily basis. The qualitative change in late 1959 was that they began to suspect all U.S. citizens as being agents of the U.S. government. Or they felt pressure to *pretend* to suspect them. "The anti-American program," reported Santiago's consul Park Wollam, "is gradually wearing away at the friendliness toward the United States that has prevailed in Oriente among the great majority."[103] One officer of the United States Information Service added that hatred was now socially acceptable while friendliness was not. "In one town nicknamed 'Little Moscow' and in other areas, shipments of corn meal sent by the Catholic Church in the United States have been thrown away by the recipients, who said they would not touch anything from the United States. Some had been told that the food was poisoned. In summary, anti-Americanism seems definitely on the rise, with those who would be openly friendly somewhat dispirited and in the minority." After the October 26 rally, the *Times of Havana*, no doubt fearing the dissolution of its own English-language readership, lamented that "the spectre of anti-Americanism in Cuba began to take on definite material form. . . . For Yanks who have called Cuba home for many decades and have always considered Cubans as virtual half-brothers, the week's events were deeply puzzling and touched with disbelief."[104]

Many in the U.S. government, sharing this disbelief, placed Cuba's anti-U.S. sentiment squarely in the realm of pathology. Rather than ambivalence, they spoke of schizophrenia, and not necessarily as metaphor or hyperbole. Congressman Adam Clayton Powell as early as March 1959 judged Castro to have "gone haywire," as evidenced in his rambling, incoherent speeches. More careful observers such as Braddock nevertheless thought of top-level anti-Americanism as "an unreasoning and persistent hostility, moderated at times for reasons of convenience, toward the United States."[105] Bonsal also wondered through most of the year whether Castro was lying or insane. After the October rally, he made up his mind. "[Castro's] performance of October 26 was not that of [a] sane man." Bonsal wrote in his memoirs that the "real Castro" emerged in late 1959.[106] A serious discussion of whether Castro "has good mental equipment" even crept into an NSC meeting in December. Bonsal and Nixon agreed that Castro had "a broad streak of irrationality on the Hitler pattern," and even the normally placid Eisenhower called him a "madman." One aide defended the president's use of the term by saying, "Well, he reserved it for people that had earned it."[107]

Perhaps even more startling to U.S. policymakers was how Castro could maintain the support of a majority of Cubans. Through most of 1959, Castro garnered about a 90 percent rate of support among Cubans. If Cubans were so fond of the United States, and if Castro was so anti-American, then how could he gain their apparently unforced approval so consistently? To U.S. observers, this contradicted the universality of U.S. values. U.S. polling, as in many other U.S. responses, was too slow to provide an explanation. As early as March, USIS officers complained of "insufficient staff and guidance" in their Havana informational program. By April they proposed "to examine Cuban public opinion in some depth. Since January 1, for example, there have been noteworthy expressions of anti-American sentiment. How deep is this feeling? What, or who, feeds it? What elements of society harbor this sentiment?" In July, Bonsal scrapped the project because "the situation was at that point too sensitive to risk a survey of this type." In other words, there was *too much* anti-Americanism to poll it. Instead, the embassy awaited a "more settled situation."[108] With no such situation in sight by December, officials moved to a state of "psychological war" and suggested that a full-time information officer be appointed to write editorials, plant stories, and coordinate with the CIA.[109] In spring 1960, Lloyd Free of Princeton's Institute for International Research finally polled one thousand urban Cubans. He found that, as Castro followers had claimed, only a hard core of 10 percent opposed the revolution, but also that about the same percentage considered economic self-sufficiency or an independent foreign policy a priority. Cubans, the poll suggested, were neither strongly anti-U.S. nor anti-revolution, but rather overwhelmingly pro-Castro. At this point, the Castro government was actively closing down all remaining independent sources of information in Cuba and thus leaving the U.S. government without means to influence Cuban opinion.[110]

Running out of options, the Eisenhower administration decided to subvert the Castro government on the basis of its anti-Americanism. In October 1959, the State Department produced a statement of "Current Basic United States Policy towards Cuba." Early versions—drafted before the "bombing" and the rally—expressed no need for Castro's downfall.[111] In its final version, however, signed by the secretary of state on November 5 and addressed to Eisenhower, the policy statement was as close as the U.S. government would get to stating that anti-Americanism was reason enough to overthrow Castro. The polite wait-and-see attitude was a double failure, the statement implied: it never provided clear evidence of communist control over Castro, but neither did it appease him. Herter noted that "the Department [of State] has in effect applied a series of tests to the Castro regime in the past ten months, meanwhile exercising just restraint in the face of provocations." Castro had failed each test: he had charted "a 'neutralist' anti-American foreign policy for Cuba"; he was supporting other insurrectionist movements in Latin America; he was letting communists work for his government; and he had instituted state control of the economy. Herter concluded that Castro's "deliberate fomenting of anti-American sentiment in Cuba . . . now represents, beyond doubt, the basic policy and orientation of his government." Herter approved the CIA's ongoing efforts to find Cuban partners in working for Castro's downfall.[112]

Evidence of the Cuban government's alignment with outside communist powers soon followed, prompting a sigh of relief of sorts from Washington. In February 1960, the Soviet foreign minister visited Cuba and signed trade agreements, which to CIA director Dulles signaled the Cuban government's "definite espousal" of communism. This, finally, was something Dulles and his colleagues could understand—a government formally hostile to capitalism and clearly conspiring against the United States. For Rubottom, the events of early 1960 swept away any remaining doubt. "I do not know whether the Cuban government is communist," he explained to the House Foreign Affairs Committee. "I would say that it does not make a lot of difference insofar as the treatment given the U.S. because the expressions of anti-Americanism by Premier Castro and others have been so severe that they play directly into the hands of the communists."[113] On January 13, 1960, Special Group 5412, set up to oversee covert operations, resolved to overthrow Castro, and on March 17 President Eisenhower approved a program to transform Herter's "Basic Policy" into a multifaceted program to destroy the Cuban government.[114]

Anti-Americanism by early 1960 was shorn of most of its ambivalence and had proved its value as a political strategy. For Castro, fomenting fear and animosity against an outside enemy, real or imagined, was a master stroke against domestic opponents and international allies. The Eisenhower administration, meanwhile, failed to appreciate the depth and scope of anti-U.S. hostility with or without communism. To them, the worst had happened: anti-U.S. sentiment, earnest and compelling, had provided a gateway into the dark mansion of socialism. Fidel Castro had made defiance of the United States a winning political stance. He had been faster, smarter, and more thorough than officials in Washington. It was a mistake these officials did not wish to repeat.

Cuba's Ripples in Washington

Cuba's successful definition of social revolution as contrary to U.S. interests stirred U.S. policymakers to refine their approaches to anti-Americanism everywhere, and especially in Latin America.[115] In the early 1960s, leaders publicly antagonistic to U.S. policies sprang up throughout the hemisphere and beyond. Attacks against U.S. embassies multiplied. To U.S. officials, there seemed to be a clear and present danger that opposing the U.S. government was spreading as a political strategy. Allies, especially, affected the irascibility and implacability of revolutionary anti-Americanism without embarking on its radical path. This "copycat" anti-Americanism was a great annoyance to Washington. Using the always popular lexicon of pathology, Allen Dulles called this moderate strain of resentment "Castro-itis." The Kennedy administration, however, channeled U.S. feelings of panic into an increased and expanded use of specialists in foreign public opinion. With attentiveness, expertise, and nationalist gusto, U.S. policymakers after 1959 devised systematic ways to understand the sources of anti-Americanism and counteract its effects. It was around this time that the term "crisis management" came into popular use in the United States.[116]

There were certainly crises to manage. In 1959 alone, multinational

3. "Two more about to blow" was the caption on this Bill Mauldin cartoon of late
   1959, which fused much of the imagery employed by U.S. observers to
   characterize anti-Americanism in Latin America. A sombrero (a distinctly
   Mexican hat) equally represented different crises, all of which appeared as
   volatile and destructive. And volcano-like unpredictability was apparently part
   of a carefully waged anti-U.S. "campaign." This failure to see beyond the binary
   categories of the mercurial and the conspiratorial tended to make U.S.
   policymakers either dismissive or reactionary toward anti-Americanism.
   Reprinted by permission of Bill Mauldin and the Watkins/Loomis Agency.

groups of rebels left Cuba in unsuccessful but inspirational attempts to overthrow regimes in Panama, the Dominican Republic, Haiti, and Nicaragua. And in the early 1960s guerrilla movements rose up in Paraguay, Ecuador, Argentina, Guatemala, Venezuela, Colombia, Peru, and Bolivia. Brazil's president, Juscelino Kubitschek, chided Washington for supposedly neglecting the lessons of Caracas, an event which had "presented us to the world as a continent divided by hate and resentment."[117] Now, outside Latin America too, anti-U.S. events became more violent and frequent. In the spring and summer of 1960, riots rocked Turkey, South Korea, Taiwan, and Japan. They were over local issues much of the time, but Castro had directly inspired defiance in underdeveloped countries by declaring his solidarity with "hungry nations." For that, admirers the world over sent him letters of praise, some pledging, "Your cause is ours. . . . Your enemies are our enemies."[118]

It seemed that anything could spark an anti-U.S. protest. In Bolivia, in March 1959, a U.S. embassy official made an off-color remark in the Latin American edition of *Time*, saying that the poor, landlocked country would not be much worse off if it were split in two and handed to its neighbors. Among Bolivians the remark was a common witticism, but U.S. representatives were not to utter it. When a plane carrying the 670 copies of *Time* landed in La Paz, President Hernán Siles Zuazo ordered them seized, denounced the magazine and the U.S. government, and held a six-hour cabinet meeting on the topic. The government paper *La Nación* called *Time* "the fingernail of imperialism's vile claw." After the meeting, Siles stepped out into a crowd of protesting students and entreated them not to give vent to their passions. His words were in vain, and perhaps even intended to stoke those very passions. Whatever the case, the students burned homemade U.S. flags, smashed windows at the USIS library, and stoned U.S. aid offices. Violence spread to other cities, and ended two days later. Herter was furious about his official's "wisecrack" and had to evacuate the embassy staff. *Time* gave the event unapologetic coverage, making sure to point out that the protesters wore U.S.-made blue jeans and included several communists, as if either fact invalidated their cause.[119]

Back in the United States, the years 1959 to 1962 were one of those rare periods in U.S. history when popular authors paid great attention to foreign critics. This was quite a change from 1958, when few studied Cuba and when the U.S. public seemed not to know what a guerrilla was. It was the Cuban Revolution that prompted C. Wright Mills, long a critic of domestic U.S. society, to turn his gaze to foreign relations. In the summer of 1960 he took a quick tour of Cuba and immediately published a book-length paraphrase of rebel philosophy titled *Listen, Yankee*. Mills sympathized with the rebels and prodded his U.S. audience, "It's a big world, Yankee. Why don't you come out into it a bit?"[120] Other popular commentators were more light-hearted. The biographer of the founder of the Christian Children's Fund called his subject "the un-ugly American" and titled his uplifting counter-example to anti-Americanism *Yankee Si!*[121] By 1960, anti-Americanism had become a household word, and Cuba had played the leading role in making it so.

Latin America now even had its own *Ugly American,* 1962's *El Gringo: The Yankee Image in Latin America.* Its author was D. H. Radler, a U.S. citizen living in Honduras, who had quit his job at the United Fruit Company to become a freelance writer. Radler now spent days on horseback meeting ordinary Latin Americans. In *El Gringo* and in articles, he aimed to awaken U.S. readers to the "daily reality" of Latin America as seen from the ground and offer helpful solutions. "One strong reason we aren't liked in Latin America," he asserted, "is simply that we aren't very likable." Culturally based attitudes did matter, he argued, because U.S. citizens abroad seemed to turn inward. Diplomats lived in "modern fortress[es]," tourists looked down on local cultures, and U.S. companies rarely offered stock options to their Latin American workers. Radler's writings were peppered with Latin Americans muttering "Goddam gringo" and threatening further anti-Americanism. As one Honduran told him, "You [in the United States] really believe you're better than anyone else. But the day of the superman is over."[122]

Many U.S. citizens reflected on what exactly was over, and in fact on the changing nature of U.S. national identity. Responding to anti-Americanism was a voyage of self-discovery, a translation of "Why do they hate us?" into "Who are we?" Some grew nostalgic for the early twentieth century, when U.S. power had apparently been too limited for such widespread criticism. According to one wistful author, "In that horse-and-buggy America there was no trace of the apologetic undertone that has of late become the vogue." Now that U.S. citizens had reached "the point of tolerating the insults and expropriations of a Fidel Castro," they should stop "apologiz[ing] for their country." Historian Daniel Boorstin, in his 1962 book *The Image,* likewise worried about a changing national identity due to the "Graphic Revolution" and the fleeting, surface nature of knowledge it created. "I suspect we suffer abroad simply because people know America through images," he wrote. "We hope our nation will have 'prestige.' What does this mean? It means we hope the world will be attracted to, or dazzled by, our image!"[123] Eisenhower officials were not alone in worrying about the inchoate nature of world public opinion.

But they *were* the only ones who could lose the White House over it. U.S. anxiety over anti-Americanism played a significant role in the election of 1960, and in such a close race it may have handed the presidency to John Kennedy. The Massachusetts senator seized on Nixon's embarrassment in South America in a speech in December 1958. "There was a great deal of talk at the time of the demonstrations against Vice President Nixon—a great many promises and assurances—but now . . . the crisis seems to pass from the headlines," Kennedy warned.[124] In the last weeks of the campaign, the headlines were back, as the *New York Times* reported a USIA poll that Democrats said showed the U.S. image abroad to be at an all-time low. Eisenhower demanded a public statement from USIA director George Allen denying those implications. Allen refused. He looked back with distaste on the electoral "furor" of 1960. "I thought it was very undignified for the candidates to put so much emphasis on how we looked to foreign people," said Allen. "It always seems to me to give the impression that we Americans are like an aspen leaf—quivering or holding our breath to find out what foreigners thought about us."[125]

To be sure, Kennedy shared some of the Eisenhower administration's skepticism. Even before he became president, he listed contradictions in Latin America's anti-Americanism:

> Latin American nations have complained about our tariff barriers when embarked upon protectionist policies of their own. They have blamed our government for not making more loans available—and resented us as creditors when they came. They have complained about the selfish nationalism of our agricultural and mineral policies—but have exhibited the same tendencies in their own official programs. They dislike too much foreign capital—yet they ask for more foreign capital. They oppose American intervention in their internal affairs— but think we should have intervened more to help their economies or to oppose certain dictators. They want to be regarded as members of the American family—but they also want to be dealt with as a separate force that cannot be taken for granted.[126]

Kennedy was also a fierce anticommunist in Latin America. He vowed to intervene against any communist revolution, agreed with the diplomatic break with Cuba in early 1961, and when he became president he notoriously gave a green light to the Bay of Pigs invasion in April 1961.

But the principal response of the Kennedy administration to anti-Americanism was to move beyond the mere attitude adjustments that followed the Caracas incident and to devise sophisticated instruments of counter-propaganda. Kennedy was more engaged in establishing a two-way communication between foreign public opinion and the U.S. government. He was more willing to allow that his country had shown shortcomings in Latin America. "The whole place could blow up on us," the president worried to aide Richard Goodwin during his first days in office. "You remember those people who threw rocks at Nixon. I'd like to believe it was just Nixon's personality, but they were sending us a message." Kennedy committed his own disarming charm and energy to Latin American affairs. He displayed a genuine sympathy for the poor and a fierce determination to unseat Castro. In that vein, Florida senator George Smathers recommended to the president-elect that he train a "hard core of dedicated pro-Americans," "dynamic professional propagandists" who would argue "the truth, forcefully presented."[127]

Kennedy took the recommendation to heart. New people and new institutions injected life into the Kennedy pledge to prevent anti-U.S. protests rather than merely respond to them. In February 1960, Costa Rican president José Figueres wrote Arthur Schlesinger, Jr., "It is too bad that you fellows, Yankee scholars, are not better known in the non–English speaking parts of the world. We get enough of coca colas and Mr. Dulles."[128] Kennedy understood the eminence of erudite, sympathetic personalities in Latin American political culture. As a result, he gave his most progressive resident intellectuals, Goodwin and Schlesinger, along with Special Assistant Ralph Dungan, direct access to the Oval Office and great leeway over Department of State old hands.[129] The president also put Puerto Ricans Teodoro Moscoso, Arturo Morales-Carrión, and Jaime Benítez in charge of implementing aid programs and representing the new *simpático* president in Latin America.[130] The change in personnel would signal that anti-Americanism had not prompted only lip service to Latin American "feelings."

These people had a knack for sensitive language. To counter an intangible such as anti-Americanism, Kennedy's aides argued, semantics mattered. As Schlesinger said, "The Latinos resent the idea that money solves everything or that the major problems of life can be comprehended in material terms. . . . It will be necessary to go in for a certain amount of high-flown corn."[131] Within the White House and State Department, officials as high up as National Security Adviser McGeorge Bundy ordered that words be more finely attuned to foreign sensibilities. All correspondents were to change references to "backward" countries so that they now read "developing"; "natives" changed to "citizens"; "terrorists," to "rebels." The terms "pro-West" and "pro-American" were simply discontinued.[132] This rhetorical overhaul seemed also to purge "anti-American" from public speeches. And in private, communist parties were now to be distinguished from those that were merely "anti-American."[133]

Kennedy aides also increased military and economic aid partly to erase once and for all the image of the United States as a gunboat or dollar diplomat. Throughout the 1940s and 1950s, economist Raúl Prebisch and others at the United Nations' Economic Commission on Latin America gathered statistics showing a declining rate in the terms of trade for Latin America. From this basis, "dependency" scholars argued that U.S. encroachments upon agricultural nations impeded or even reversed development, and that import substitution was the answer. In response to such arguments, the Eisenhower administration had already agreed to commodity price agreements, an Inter-American Development Bank for providing public funds, and a Social Progress Trust Fund for public housing, agricultural credits, and education funds. Kennedy's Alliance for Progress, announced in 1961, multiplied the funds promised for such programs and followed with a tremendous publicity campaign rich in idealism. Even Civic Action programs encouraged the Latin American military to undertake public works and thus put a friendly face on U.S. military training.[134]

U.S. confidence in changing foreign public opinion reached a zenith with the creation of the Peace Corps. The relatively independent program entrusted the most altruistic of young U.S. citizens with the task of symbolizing (in the words of historian Elizabeth Cobbs Hoffman) "what America wanted to be, and what much of the world wanted America to be: superhero, protector of the disenfranchised, defender of the democratic faith."[135] Some officials were wary of sending these informal and perhaps disloyal diplomats to places that had witnessed significant anti-Americanism. But they soon realized that the program was a public relations success. To many, it confirmed that anti-Americanism, when it did exist, brought out a healthy U.S. openness to criticism. "The Russians are really squealing about the Peace Corps," the director of the USIA wrote to Kennedy. "They cannot risk sending their youth abroad except under conditions of strict control."[136]

Even as the Kennedy government showed greater sensitivity to anti-U.S. sentiment, hemispheric exasperation with Castro was spreading. Latin American moderates were widely disillusioned that anti-U.S. sentiment in Cuba had lost its spontaneity and become institutionalized into a repressive state. Polls in 1961 showed that Castro's "very good" and "good" ratings had declined all over Latin America to a single-digit total. U.S. officials also noticed that the less they said about Castro, the more he lost favor with ordinary Latin Americans. "The current U.S. policy of ignoring Castro is robbing him of 'Yankee Imperialism' ammunition," wrote the acting director of the USIA to Kennedy.[137] More than any other event, Castro's harboring of Soviet missiles in October 1962 discredited him. The Cuban leader was now endangering the security of the whole Western Hemisphere, not to mention the world, and as a result the Organization of American States in 1962 denied the Castro government participation in its activities.[138] The Cuban Missile Crisis also hardened attitudes among Kennedy's advisers—who would also in large part be Lyndon Johnson's—and emboldened them in times of crisis.

While in ambassadorial meeting rooms hemispheric leaders may have grown skeptical of anti-Americanism as a political strategy, ground-level events persisted and intensified during the Kennedy and early Johnson years. From July 1962 to February 1964 there were thirty protests against USIS libraries, more than half of them in Latin America. Then, in a five-month period starting in October 1964, there were twenty-five more attacks on embassies, consulates, and cultural centers. Social critic John Gerassi, among others, insisted that this hostility was genuine, popular, and ominous. In the early 1960s he visited a slum father in, of all places, Caracas. He related the words of the man, who stared up "at a fifty-foot-wide Coca-Cola advertisement that stood out at the foot of the slum hill. 'None of us in this house has ever drunk a Coca-Cola,' he said softly. 'One day we will kill those who make them.'"[139]

As U.S. responses to revolutionary anti-Americanism grew more anxious because of Cuba, they also acquired a new sophistication. While revolutionary hostility gave the Castro government essentially what it wanted by the end of 1959—freedom from U.S. power through means other than armed collision—it also hinted at three lessons. The first lesson was that anti-Americanism in every country depended on unique social structures and historical relationships with the United States. Castro had been able to count on the support of liberals, for instance, partly because they resented the way U.S. administrators took their jobs in businesses and government offices. Castro also kept opponents at bay largely because Cuba was an island and dissidents could easily escape to the United States. But there was no telling which variant of anti-Americanism might emerge in other places if even slightly different conditions prevailed there. A second lesson was that anti-Americanism's ambivalence was a strength but also a weakness. Castro had had to argue that his reforms pursued fundamental U.S. ideals and had had to proceed with extreme caution because U.S. interests and identities were in many ways Cuban interests and identities. As a consequence, Castro achieved his goals of national independence, social justice, and personal power by sacrificing much of Cuba's identity. The third lesson was that the U.S. government could learn to adjust to anti-Americanism. The Eisenhower administration had jumped recklessly from waiting and seeing to blindly backing Castro's enemies. Kennedy better understood the gray areas between revolution and obsequiousness where anti-Americanism existed. Despite U.S. anxiety about "being liked" in the rest of the world, ideological confidence prompted U.S. officials to respond to anti-Americanism with increasing effectiveness. Variability, ambivalence, and resilience: here were the three themes of U.S. diplomacy in the face of anti-Americanism. They may not have been obvious in 1959, but they would gain definition as other crises erupted in the years to come.

3

Panama, 1964

Conservative Anti-Americanism and
U.S. Pragmatism

As if offering a reprieve to an embattled Washington, the anti-U.S. Panama Riots of 1964 conserved a social order; they did not overturn it. To be sure, by the 1960s, a Panamanian elite came to resent its dependence on supplying goods and services to the Canal Zone, the strip of land surrounding the Panama Canal where U.S. interests were concentrated. That same elite, however, had also grown rich from the U.S. presence. Non-elite Panamanians likewise benefited somewhat from the canal, yet they resented far more the humiliations to which U.S. inhabitants of the Canal Zone—the "Zonians"—subjected them. The growing interplay of these elite and popular ambivalences led to the Riots of 1964—and to the deaths of twenty-one Panamanians and four U.S. citizens—but nevertheless made for a relatively cautious anti-U.S. hostility.

The Panama crisis also highlighted evolving U.S. responses to anti-Americanism since Caracas and Cuba. By 1964, U.S. governments had had decades of practice keeping wealthy Panamanians in power with the seductive bonds of patronage. The intensification of street protests there and elsewhere only made observers grow cynical and impatient at what they saw as the opportunism of elites. Lyndon Johnson, moreover, ascended to the presidency with much less sympathy for anti-U.S. protesters than his predecessor had shown. The newly acquired resolve of Washington toward anti-Americanism paid off nicely in Panama. So did its new sophistication: although Johnson embodied an overall hardening of the establishment that shaped foreign policy, the Riots of 1964 prompted a U.S. response far more calculated than the hawkish retribution for which the U.S. public clamored and which U.S. hegemony allowed. Here was the application of a lesson learned from anti-American-ism: mitigate your own panic by focusing on local variants of hostility. The Johnson White House took into consideration Panama's funda-mental conservatism. As a result, the president and his advisers played a pragmatic diplomatic game with Panamanian anti-Americanism throughout 1964. At times Washington proved more than a match for Panama's brinkmanship, but mostly the game involved propping up the very elites who claimed the leadership of anti-U.S. protests.

Elites and Popular Anti-Americanism

In Panama, firm rule by the elite class and U.S. patronage in favor of that rule fundamentally restrained anti-Americanism in the streets. Through-out more than a century of close relations with the United States, con-servative anti-Americanism—expressed in protests that did not endan-ger local political and economic fortunes—became the dominant variant of anti-U.S. hostility in Panama. To be sure, complex political and psy-chological dynamics emerged from the fact that Panama's economic de-pendence on the United States grew more acute than that of any other country.[1] Dependence created a mass-based anti-Americanism that was often impatient and violent and that occasionally turned against elite rule. Competition between popular and conservative anti-Americanisms up to the very eve of anti-U.S. riots in 1964, therefore, reflected social tensions as much as they did genuine struggles against U.S. hegemony. What set Panama apart was that elites there consistently prevailed in this competition, propelled by an instinct for class preservation and a sense that co-opting popular tactics could win small concessions from Wash-ington. This was anti-Americanism's "go slow" strategy.

In response, U.S. officials expected collaboration rather than intransi-gence from elites despite the occasional flare-up. The U.S. response to anti-Americanism in Panama was also exceptional in that U.S. citizens who lived around the canal, supported by jingoists back home, pres-sured U.S. officials to stand firm even against minor changes in favor of Panama. Thus, to avoid the ire of these domestic opponents and the rad-icalism of poorer Panamanians, U.S. officials long bowed to the political wisdom of the middle of the road.

Even before Panama won independence from Colombia in 1903, anti-U.S. sentiment had emerged among ordinary Panamanians in response to daily contacts with the entrepreneurs, workers, and travelers who were the flesh and blood of U.S. hegemony. The Isthmus of Panama, in some places narrowing to only thirty-five miles separating the Atlantic and Pacific oceans, had long been a hub of world commerce, and U.S. promoters of a railroad from sea to sea understood the land's blessed geography. When prospectors found gold in Sutter's Mill, California, the ink was not yet dry on the 1846 Mallarino-Bidlack treaty between the United States and Colombia. The treaty gave the U.S. government full transit rights on the Isthmus in exchange for protecting it against other powers and conceding official sovereignty to Colombia.[2] With this assurance in hand, the Panama Railroad Company built a track to shuttle gold, as well as everyone and everything involved with gold digging, from one ocean to the other. While passengers waited for the railroad to open in 1855, U.S.-sponsored towns sprang up to serve passengers crossing by canoe, mule, or foot.

The building of the railroad quickly "Americanized" the physical and cultural landscape of the Isthmus and established the United States as the salient foreign power there. In two decades, $710 million in bullion passed through the Isthmus and the dollar replaced the peso as the main currency. English competed with Spanish. Americanization meant jobs for some Panamanians and for thousands of immigrants: West Indians, Africans, Chinese, Europeans, and North and South Americans flooded in to be railroad workers, hotel and restaurant employees, prostitutes, guides, and mule drovers and tenders. Americanization, however, also meant insecurity. New arrivals mingling in unsanitary conditions led to the spread of cholera and other diseases. Bandits roamed about, and so did guards to fight them. Many passengers carried guns and knives.[3] Like other frontier situations, it was far from being "America"; rather, the Gold Rush exacerbated the arrogance, racism, permissiveness, and violence that the U.S. presence generated. Nevertheless, lasting negative impressions of the United States emerged here, where Wild West lawlessness mingled with big-business ruthlessness.

U.S. hegemony also caused booms and busts, which set the tone for events such as the Watermelon Riot.[4] The riot occurred on April 15, 1856, when one haughty U.S. traveler, waiting outside Panama City to board a steamer for California, refused to pay a vendor for a slice of watermelon. A brawl ensued, then an all-out, hate-filled attack on foreigners by poor bystanders and Panamanian policemen. After the killing subsided, two Panamanians and fifteen U.S. travelers lay dead, and dozens had been injured. *Leslie's Illustrated,* a popular U.S. periodical, expressed shock. It portrayed heathen black "savages" brutally assailing well-to-do white women and children.[5] The U.S. government reacted with what were in those days overwhelming punitive measures. It landed 160 soldiers, its first armed intervention ever on the Isthmus, and obtained reparations of more than $400,000 from Colombia.[6]

This popular anti-Americanism emerged as a response to wealth easily won and lost. Watermelon rioters were most probably West Indians, whose influx in the previous years had doubled the population of Panama City. They were lashing out at the iron horse that trampled their budding hopes for a decent life. The railroad, barely in operation a year, already rendered expendable the mule drovers, guides, and peddlers

4. "Massacre at Panama—Terrible Scene in the Freight Room." *Leslie's Illustrated Newspaper* portrayed the 1856 Watermelon Riot, in which sixteen U.S. travelers and two Panamanians died, as a "premeditated thing" by "natives" and "negroes." Yet *Leslie's* also understood the material cause of the riot: "Independent of the hatred of Americans arising from heretical notions of religion, and from blood, it should not be forgotten that the people of Panama are inimical to the [rail]road, from the fact that it is of no practical benefit to the place." *Frank Leslie's Illustrated Newspaper,* 17 May 1856.

who lived along the old routes. Now locomotives thundered through these towns without letting potential customers disembark. Even *Leslie's* could see that "the [rail]road has broken up [Isthmian] business." What the United States had provided with the Gold Rush it was now taking away with the railroad, leaving the local poor powerless and angry.[7]

The Watermelon Riot also proved a harbinger of the next century of U.S.-Panama dynamics. Between the riot in 1856 and the proclamation of independence in 1903, the United States intervened fourteen times in Panama and occupied the Colombian province for a total of two hundred days. Then, in 1904, Article 136 of the Panamanian constitution gave the U.S. government the legal right to intervene "to reestablish public peace and constitutional order"—in other words, to make Panama a protectorate. U.S. bases opened along with the Canal Zone, and U.S. troops spilled out of the Zone and into the Republic of Panama during the elections of 1908, 1912, and 1918, with the acquiescence of the winning party if not an outright request for intervention. In the most naked display of imperial overbearance having little to do with protecting the canal, in 1918 U.S. troops occupied the province of Chiriquí to supervise elections and stayed until 1921 to protect United Fruit Company lands.[8]

It was clear by now that the U.S. government was taking over the roles of both soldier and policeman from Panama, enforcing the inequalities of race and class in the process. U.S. minister Herbert Squiers believed that the Panamanian police were in fact involved in murders of U.S. citizens. As he explained, "The lower classes of this republic hate us, and the police are drawn from that class." Washington not only dissolved the Panamanian armed forces in 1904, but disarmed the police in 1915, partly to minimize fights that broke out with U.S. soldiers at baseball games or during Carnival. Regardless, Panamanians continued to carry guns, and U.S. soldiers did not temper their passions for prostitutes, liquor, cocaine, and a good fight.[9]

With the opening of the canal in 1914 and the wealth it generated, Panamanians grew more ambivalent, despite the occasional violence that still erupted. Much of this love/hate relationship centered on racial issues. Many Panamanians ended up resenting not only the Zone's racism but also its racial composition. On one hand, national myth portrayed Panama as open to ethnic mixing and tolerant of foreign cultures and ideas. To an extent, this was true. Because it was a hub, Panama thrived on its transnational fluidity, perhaps more so than any other Latin American country. Even the Panamanian oligarchy was somewhat porous, letting wealthy Italian, Spanish, or Jewish merchants into its ranks once in a while. French words (many from the clothing trade, such as *chiffon* and *négligé*) and West Indian English (for example *buchimán,* derived from "bushman," a derogatory term for an unreconstructed country migrant, modified to *buchi gringo* for U.S. workers who lacked refinement) infiltrated Panama. By 1960, in addition to U.S. films, Chinese, German, French, and Mexican movies were also being shown. Thousands of West Indians, Asians, and Europeans who worked on the canal settled in Panama or in the Zone. Travelers passing daily through the canal further shaped Panama City and Colón into ethnically diverse cities (the interior remained much more homogeneously mestizo). The already diverse mix of family names such as Boyd (Irish) and Chiari (Italian) now included Yau (Chinese) and Williams (West Indian). By the 1960s, while Panamanians were about 65 percent mestizo, Zonians, according to one count, were 70 percent West Indian, 20 percent mestizo, 9 percent white, and 1 percent Asian (mostly from India). As historian Michael Conniff demonstrated, this mixed heritage contributed to Panamanians' belief in assimilation rather than segregation.[10] Panamanians also believed that everyone should be treated with gentlemanly courtesy—*el trato hidalgo*—which made the Zone's rigid, explicit racism even harder to stomach.

On the other hand, despite their cosmopolitanism, many Panamanians shared a racial contempt all their own. Anthropologists John and Mavis Biesanz studied Panamanians in the 1950s. They found them, white or black, to be particularly contemptuous of West Indians, who were mostly English-speaking Jamaicans, Barbadians, and Trinidadians. Panamanian workers on the canal could not tolerate these *chombo* overseers who spoke only broken Spanish. To native Panamanians, West Indians seemed too subservient to U.S. authority, too Protestant, and too phenotypically different from dark-skinned Panamanians (relatively few Panamanians described themselves as black).[11] To make matters worse, West Indians embodied the dynamism of empire: they had built the canal, and now they held its jobs as well as many jobs on U.S. banana plantations in the interior. Even prominent leftists such as writer Gil Blas Tejeira expressed the concern that "we are a disconcertingly heterogeneous people." He feared that U.S. influence, by facilitating immigration without assimilation, was eroding an already tenuous nationality. Leading scholar Ricaurte Soler sullenly called Panama a "floating culture," doomed by migration to stay undefined—and unrefined.[12]

Another layer of ambivalence settling on Panama in the early twentieth century stemmed from the country's relationship with the almighty Yankee dollar. Panamanians judged that the United States foisted upon them an ethic of materialistic pursuit while it often denied them the means for that pursuit. To one observer, Hispanic "spiritual" principles, even in commercial Panama, were incompatible with U.S. "dollar hungry strictly business jewish ways." Nevertheless, remembered a journalist, while many of his friends complained about the crass acquisitiveness of the Zone, they took its jobs and then agonized over their deal with the devil.[13]

This dilemma essentially provided the plot for Joaquín Beleño's Luna verde, the first novel ever set in the Canal Zone. The title itself, which translates as "Green Moon," refers to the way the rapid influx of U.S. greenbacks, especially during World War II, awakened a money madness in Panamanians. The novel's protagonist, Ramón de Roquebert, climbs up the ranks of the U.S.-run Panama Canal Company (PCC) in the Zone, but grows to resent the Zonians above him and disdain the West Indians below him. He quits, joins the student movement, and permanently resolves his ambivalence by dying at the hands of U.S.-armed Panamanian police in an anti-U.S. protest.[14]

Luna verde reflected widely held frustrations. The attitudes that the dollar spread—utilitarianism, ambition, racial and class antagonism— embarrassed and offended Panamanians rich and poor. Future president Omar Torrijos grew up intensely aware of the wide gap in material comfort between Panama City and the Zone and vowed one day to close it. One "leading Panamanian woman" who had frequent contact with Zonians told the Biesanzes that it was not empire she minded so much, but imperiousness. "I don't want to feel obliged to show my gratitude. . . . I don't want friendship translated into money. . . . I think Americans have no monopoly on setting desirable goals for the world."[15]

After the canal opened, therefore, even popular anti-U.S. political groups displayed a fundamentally conservative ambivalence and chose to criticize the style of the U.S. presence rather than the presence itself. Marrying Panama's cultural conservatism and its populist ambition, the first sustained movement against U.S. influence emerged in the 1920s, not surprisingly a few years after the canal opened. Acción Comunal was at first a nonpartisan nationalist group of professionals—doctors, lawyers, engineers, and bureaucrats—along with some workers and small businesspeople. Its leaders mostly wanted their share of access to the canal's lucrative jobs and contracts.[16] Soon, however, Acción Comunal moved to the far right and dedicated itself to safeguarding Panama from all outside threats. Its members adopted fascist and racist symbols, met semi-clandestinely, wore sheets, and railed against West Indian and U.S. influences. *Acción* magazine's logo, designed in 1923, featured a swastika and urged Panamanians to "speak Castilean, count in Balboas [the national currency—rarely printed, since Panamanians used U.S. dollars] and read *Acción Comunal*." The group's greatest early victory was leading the legislature in rejecting the Kellogg-Alfaro Pact of 1926, which would have prolonged Panama's status as a protectorate.[17] By 1931, Acción Comunal was a full-fledged political party and led a coup against the traditional elite.

Acción Comunal's leader, Arnulfo Arias, embodied both the promise and limits of popular anti-Americanism. On one hand, with the looks of Errol Flynn and the charisma of Benito Mussolini, "Fufo" could give anti-U.S. sentiment a wide cultural resonance because he uniquely captured the imagination of ordinary Panamanians. As a doctor and demagogue, he tended to their physical and emotional needs. The poor of Panama consistently pledged allegiance to Arias, who then created social programs for them when he became president. "I am nothing," said a humble man from the interior in 1960, "but ever since they threw Arnulfo out I have not cared who was president." Arias *was* thrown out several times, and several times he returned.[18]

On the other hand, for a "man of the people," Arnulfo had a rather typical oligarch's relationship with the United States. He had attended a U.S. high school and had returned to his country in 1918 to see U.S. soldiers occupying Panama City and Colón. The scene made him "gloomy and despondent," according to his biographer.[19] Still, he returned to the United States to earn degrees from the University of Chicago and Harvard. Like his brother Harmodio, an international lawyer with a sharp mind, Arnulfo married up, and into the oligarchy. Once there, he profited from rackets, built his own coffee empire, and bought newspapers to give him a voice in politics. Arias' greatest limitation, however, was that he promoted a cultural nationalism that smacked of fascism

more than it delivered economic or political independence. His Pana-
meñista Party, for instance, limited English in outdoor signs, menus,
newspapers, government buildings, and musical performances. It made
schoolchildren and teachers wear uniforms, and it organized paramilitary troops called the Black Berets. Most ominously, the *panameñistas*
passed a constitutional amendment to deport West Indians; drove Chinese, Jewish, and East Indian retailers out of business; and denied U.S.
citizens membership in the Union Club, a country club that defined the
crème of Panamanian society.[20]

While Arias peaked politically in the 1940s and 1950s with an anti-
Americanism that depended heavily on his personality, students slowly
came to embody a more self-sustained blurring of popular and elite anti-
Americanism. On one hand, students displayed the most unequivocal
resolve against U.S. power. Many had bitter personal experiences with
the Zone, whose forbidden fruits could be literal: those who sparked the
1964 riots, for instance, recalled how as children they had tried to pluck
mangoes from trees or pick them off the ground in the Zone, only to
have "tall, blond, blue-eyed" policemen chase them away.[21] And, as in
many Latin American countries, Panamanian students were highly politicized. Those under twenty-one could not vote, but they spilled out
into the streets at a moment's notice (even if, as one confessed, they
might occasionally go on an anti-U.S. strike just so they could skip
classes and study for exams). In 1947, they achieved unprecedented legitimacy with street rallies that forced the National Assembly to reject an
agreement to extend the lease of World War II U.S. bases in Panama.
From 1948 to 1965, University of Panama (UP) students multiplied six-
fold, and their political might soared.[22]

On the other hand, students served conservative anti-Americanism as
much as they challenged it. In general there was no collusion per se between elites and students, and their sometimes violent animosity was
real. But students also practiced anti-U.S. activism partly as training for
later public leadership alongside those same elites. It was widely expected that student leaders, especially privileged children with U.S. degrees, would integrate one day into traditional political parties and per-
petuate the status quo. In exchange, students enjoyed protection against
repression on campus and leniency with schoolwork and attendance.
Studies have concurred that students in Panama, while politicized, had
little sense of public service compared to those of neighboring countries.

Rather, they were more personally ambitious because they emulated the "strong drive for success" characteristic of ruling Panamanians.[23]

Finally, Panama's oligarchy itself developed its own brand of restrained anti-Americanism as a way to preserve its power. Ruling families in Panama had long suffered a crisis of identity, to the point where historians have debated whether there existed an oligarchy at all in the country.[24] Early on, the Isthmus' colonial experience as a commercial hub presented its merchant leaders with a Faustian dilemma: rule unfettered over an impoverished backwater or serve foreigners in a prosperous cornucopia. The latter proved to be the stronger temptation, and it shaped their collective self-image. Panamanian historian Alberto Figueroa's groundbreaking reconstruction of the mentality of nineteenth-century elites found that increased contacts with foreigners shaped clear dispositions—pragmatism, anticlericalism, modernism, and xenophilous tendencies.[25] Trade gave them their privileged status, yet they had to protect that status by criticizing the U.S. administrators who made trade possible.

From roughly the 1930s to the 1950s, conservative anti-Americanism consisted mostly in revising selected provisions of the 1903 treaty, which had given the United States control over the canal, surrounding lands, and much of Panamanian sovereignty. The 1936 Arias-Roosevelt Treaty was a high point of this strategy. The revising process seemed endless—110 conferences took place, and the U.S. Senate ratified the treaty only in 1939—but in the end, Panamanians received an increased annuity, limited U.S. land acquisitions and commissary sales to Panamanians, and ended the protectorate.[26] The Remón-Eisenhower Treaty of 1955, after more protracted diplomacy, provided for a still higher annuity; abolished unfair wage scales for Panamanians and U.S. workers; increased Panamanian suppliers to the Zone (a promise badly kept); and relieved the United States of responsibility for disposing of Panama's garbage.[27]

Revisionism worked well for the elite: new agreements brought higher profits to the already wealthy families providing the Zone with goods and services, and they ensured that favorite sons running for election would have reputations as nationalists. Besides, public opinion was still largely quiescent. In 1949, only 23 percent of Panamanians polled thought that problems with the United States were "most urgently in need of solution."[28]

By the late 1950s, however, elites felt increasing pressure to integrate the radical fervor of students with conservative anti-Americanism. The rising expectations of middle groups all over Latin America, the demographic push of youth, the Castro struggle in the Sierra Maestra, and the apparent sensitivity of Washington to anticolonial protests were all making student strategies difficult to ignore. Panamanian officials often stated that they felt pressured to outdo the students. For instance in 1958 Miguel Moreno, the minister of foreign relations, asked his president to take a strong stand when President Eisenhower's brother, Milton, came to visit. "The country must not get the impression that student groups are the only ones to protest," said Moreno.[29]

To counter that impression, elites embraced the symbolic—and, as it turned out in 1964, pivotal—issue of the Panamanian flag's absence in the Canal Zone. Starting in the 1950s, elites occasionally joined students in symbolic flag-planting pilgrimages to the Zone, and diplomats included display of the flag in their list of revision demands presented to U.S. negotiators. The move implicated conservatives in ever more radical anti-U.S. tactics.

U.S. diplomats in 1955 had strongly resisted any display of the Panamanian flag, mostly for its legal complications. Any concession toward flying the flag implied some sort of Panamanian sovereignty over the Zone, which was the hottest issue between the two countries because no one agreed on precisely what sort that might be. Secretary of State Dean Rusk once said, "Sovereignty, I suppose, is at least a bundle of a hundred sticks. We probably hold 98 or 99 of those sticks but Panama holds one or two of them anyhow." The flag was one stick, as its history demonstrated. The 1903 treaty had said nothing about the flag. Then, in 1906, a visiting U.S. senator had complained that not even the U.S. flag flew in the Zone. No one had given the matter much thought, but once it had been raised Panamanian flags quickly disappeared.[30] If they now flew on U.S. bases, the Pentagon argued in the 1950s, Panamanian flags would endanger the canal because Panamanians would claim a say in defense decisions. To Panamanian nationalists, a flag in the Zone would indeed be proof that sovereignty resided with Panama. Panamanian presidents, however, merely reiterated that the logical, harmless, and "moral" thing to do was to allow Panama to fly its flag where it had "titular sovereignty."[31]

What Washington understood less clearly was that a folded up flag aggravated the cultural malaise in Panama's national identity. By the late

1950s Panamanians were speaking of their "dependent society complex" or "national inferiority complex" toward the United States.[32] They claimed none of what Latin American culture held highest: no national ideology such as bourgeois liberalism or socialism; no wars, hence no martyrs; no great art or literature to elevate as "spiritual" masterpieces; and no racial, ethnic, or linguistic homogeneity.[33] Anti-Americanism was so well founded precisely because nationalism was so hollow. The Biesanzes cited a 1947 poll of students' sources of pride, the most common of which was "national pride." "They are proud of being proud!" exclaimed the Biesanzes. "We do not know who we are," agreed a UP dean in 1966.[34]

The quartered Panamanian flag—colored red, white, and blue, as if a reminder of U.S. midwifery of the nation—thus became a fetish with immediate aesthetic and emotional resonance, an object of almost religious devotion that provided a modicum of gravitas to the unbearable lightness of being Panamanian. High school students, for instance, practiced the flag's dainty handling and pledged to defend its integrity. In 1964, they carried into the Canal Zone a banner literally stained with the blood of martyrs from the 1947 anti-U.S. protests.[35] In the postwar era, planting the flag in the Zone became a standard motif in the repertoire of Panama's macho politics, a gendered imperative to "penetrate" into the forbidden area and drive the staff of national affirmation into the pristine lawns of Zonians. The move was aggressive, perilous, and irreversible. As El Día proclaimed in 1960, "sovereignty, like virginity, is or is not—there is no halfway measure."[36] In all these ways, the flag became a unifying symbol for popular and conservative anti-Americanisms.

The Zone and the Riots

Anti-U.S. sentiment in Panama turned violent in 1959 and far more seriously so in 1964. U.S.-Panama relations tensed up at this point not only because the elite co-opted the strategy of flag planting, but also because Zonians voiced a U.S. response outside the Washington, D.C., Beltway—a people's response to anti-Americanism—that proved as emotional as any Panamanian hostility toward the Zone. The hard attitude of Zonians, in fact, reflected how most U.S. citizens would react to the Riots of 1964.

Zonians were not so atypical of U.S. public opinion as critics of U.S.

foreign policy made them out to be. To be sure, they were disproportion-
ately Southerners in the early decades of the canal's construction and operation. But by 1954, the PCC found that only 11 percent of its employees came from South or Gulf states. Furthermore, by the 1960s, only 15
percent were second-generation Zonians, who tended to be more jingoistic. Demographically, the Zone was becoming a small-scale replica of
the mainland. Polls and local press from the United States consistently
showed that attitudes in the Zone were fairly representative of those
back home.[37]

To Panamanians, Zonians represented U.S. civilization in all its contradictions: peaceful, wealthy, and orderly, but also socially exclusive
and obsessed with security. The PCC's need to protect the canal regi-
mented Zonian life, a life burdened by purpose and precision. Though it
looked like a suburb, the Zone was run like a military base. The authorities viewed free speech as a privilege, not a right. "It is clearly indicated
to us that our personal lives are expected to be above suspicion," one
Zonian complained anonymously to a local paper. "One of the responsi-
bilities of our jobs is to live up to the ideal of what an exemplary American should be." Grounds for dismissal, the writer explained, included
communist leanings, adultery, illegitimacy, and homosexuality. Official
racial segregation, moreover, survived well into the 1950s in hospitals,
schools, trains, drinking fountains, and pay scales.[38] More generally, social conformity also ruled. Houses, for instance, looked the same—big,
clean, single-family homes with screened-in porches and, after the in-
vention of air conditioning, tightly shut windows. The result was what
one author called "a kind of tropical Levittown," where the midcentury
tensions of Organization Man—the stifling of individual expression in
a free society, increasing sameness amid consumer choice—were only
heightened by Cold War paranoia and U.S. racism.[39]

Given these insecurities, Zonians kept their distance from Panamanians. "Enclave" rather than "colony" was the *mot juste* to describe Zone
society. A woman signing herself "American Mary" wrote to a local paper about the dispirited state of Zonian women, who felt responsible for
promoting domestic bliss but who often faced daily hostility from Panamanians, mostly maids and grocers. "How can we have any kind of good
relations with them when they go out of their way in every instance to
let us know they don't want us here and don't like us? . . . We're happier,
too, when we stay away from town because then we can forget how we're

hated by the country we're here to defend."[40] In this context, U.S. citizens who lived in the Zone naturally resented efforts to fly the Panamanian flag on "their" lands. In their eyes, admitting any Panamanian sovereignty over the place where they lived not only imperiled their mission to run and protect the canal but also endangered their social peace as a privileged middle class, their national identity as U.S. citizens, and their supremacy as whites.

Washington would have preferred to avoid Panamanian issues altogether. When responding to Panama's demands, the Eisenhower administration, it seemed, could not help expressing arrogance, insouciance, and beleaguered feelings all at the same time. Secretary of State John Foster Dulles, for instance, considered Panama to be as close to a colony as the United States had, and he liked it that way. He dismissed the republic's concerns, and kept Panama away from all talks on the sovereignty of Egypt's Suez Canal so as to avoid any association between the two waterways in the minds of Panamanians.[41] President Eisenhower was more commonsensical, perhaps too much so. He would spontaneously ask why Panama was not getting much in annuities or did not have the right to fly its flag on U.S. bases as other countries did. "Legalisms" bored him and he paid them little attention. He did present to Panama a detailed study of outstanding problems, mostly answering charges of his administration's bad faith and poor enforcement of the 1955 treaty.[42] But otherwise, the president let his brother handle the diplomacy. Milton visited Panama in 1958 as part of his Central American tour following the Nixon trip, and came away with a sad foreboding. The flag, he said, was "far and away the hottest issue" in Panama. He regretted that Panamanians were being militant and ungrateful, and saw little that Washington could do to improve relations. "I left Panama with a feeling of impending disaster weighing heavily upon me."[43]

Disaster struck a little over a year later. In November 1959, anti-U.S. rioting catapulted the flag campaign to number-one priority among Panamanians. Trouble loomed on the horizon when, in mid-July, just as revolutionaries were boldly seizing U.S. farms in Cuba, the respected Panamanian historian Ernesto Castillero Pimentel announced he would head a march into the Zone on November 3, Panamanian Independence Day. "It is necessary to open a new front—the front on the street, on the public park," said Castillero. The U.S. embassy staff, reading the papers, feared that these elite organizers were "unfolding a new radical anti-U.S.

and Canal Zone strategy."[44] The flag march gathered steam. Media barons advertised it, President Ernesto de la Guardia gave it his silent acquiescence, and fiery National Assembly deputy Aquilino Boyd promised to lead it.[45]

The morning of November 3 started out peacefully as Boyd and Castillero made good on their pledges and led a group in a peaceful planting of flags in the Zone. In the afternoon, however, crowds spilled out from patriotic marches and gathered near the Canal Zone–Panama City border, some with signs reading DEATH TO THE GRINGOS and YANKEE GO HOME.[46] Fighting broke out when a sixteen-year-old boy wrapped his flag around a Zone policeman's head and shouted, "It's dirty, now!" Such theatrics sickened police, who considered their "forbearance" exploited. Crowds then attacked several U.S. properties, burned cars, threw rocks, and shattered the windows of the United States Information Service (USIS). They marched over to the embassy, where they pulled down the U.S. flag and tore it up. Most egregious to Zonians, the Panamanian government soon protested that it was Zone authorities who had "desecrated" a Panamanian flag by plucking it out of the ground (and perhaps dropping it or trampling it). Nationalist writer Gil Blas Tejeira, then serving as private secretary to the president, promised he would try to reach de la Guardia to quell the violence. The National Guard (GN), as close to an army as Panama had at that point, never showed; in fact it instructed its units to stay away from rioters. U.S. troops, for their part, used tear gas, fire hoses, bayonets, and bird shot against the rioters. Between 80 and 120 U.S. police and Panamanians were hurt. No one died.[47]

Privately, Panamanian officials knew that their co-opting of popular anti-Americanism ran counter to their duty as keepers of law and order. They also knew that this was the very essence of their diplomacy of defiance. Two days after the riots started, the National Council of Foreign Relations—a gathering of Panama's "wise men"—met in an extraordinary, closed-door session. All agreed that Panama had failed to police the riots. But they also decided to conceal their negligence. "It seems to me that this is a really delicate issue," said Harmodio Arias, Arnulfo's less boisterous brother, at the meeting. While Panama's rulers could keep the facts from Panamanians, the sharp "Anglo-Saxon" mind would see through any excuses, he feared. Arias concluded that they must "demonstrate emotion" without offending the U.S. government. Others agreed. Subsequent meetings of the council in November reiterated this same conservative, evasive strategy. When new riots threatened on November 28, the GN came out in force and effectively put down the rioters.[48]

The oligarchy's efforts to appropriate the flag issue had almost backfired. Almost, but not quite. The gamble paid off nicely. Weeks after the November riots, Eisenhower recognized Panama's "titular sovereignty" over the canal and declared that Panama should have "visual evidence" of it in the Zone—that is, it could display its flag.[49] With this announcement, elites scored a victory for anti-U.S. violence without explicitly endorsing it or endangering their rule. Boyd and Castillero, the only two leaders to place themselves in harm's way, frankly sanctioned the rioters in a post facto press conference. "We believe," they declared, "that demonstrations of this kind are necessary and useful for the Panamanian cause." Other endorsements were indirect. The National Assembly, for instance, voted Daniel Flood, a member of the U.S. Congress who vehemently defended Zonians and excoriated Panamanian nationalists, as Panama's Enemy Number One. Cartoons in Panama papers portrayed U.S. policemen as dogs, devils, or gorillas attacking defenseless Panamanians. And in the presidential elections of 1960, candidate Roberto Chiari accused his opponent, "Dicky" Arias, of being a *gringo*. Dicky lost.[50]

Yet elite manipulation of popular sentiment, real or apparent, also cemented U.S. cynicism. Panamanians were often the worst advocates for their cause, notorious for their undisciplined (sometimes drunken) meetings with U.S. diplomats, non sequiturs, and self-serving professions of meekness or patriotic sacrifice. In his Foreign Ministry's report for 1960, Miguel Moreno made the oft-repeated argument that tiny Panama could not possibly pressure the all-powerful United States. He knew perfectly well that that was the strategy.[51] U.S. officials repeatedly fumed that "the Panamanians are at it again"—meaning they were using anti-Americanism to extort concessions from Washington.[52]

More than other Latin Americans, in fact, Panamanians seemed to elicit the disdain of U.S. citizens, who refused to be intimidated by a tiny nation whose very founding was due, they said, to U.S. protection. Representative Frank Chelf of Kentucky, for instance, denounced "using Uncle Sam as 'the big bad wolf' who is responsible for everybody's troubles all over Panama and the world." Zonian Arthur Wynne wrote to

the president that "Uncle Sam has let a bunch of money-mad dema-
gogues and business barons kick him in the teeth—he turns his back
and they kick him in the pants."[53] In memo after memo, U.S. officials described themselves as a "whipping boy" and a "convenient scapegoat"
for "Panama's alleged grievances." Many were shocked that "at no time
was there any gratitude expressed for anything done for Panama by the
United States. The feeling is that anything from the United States was
theirs by birthright and their just due." "No country in history ever
treated another country better than the United States has treated the Republic of Panama," wrote former PCC director Charles Reed to the
president.[54]

Following the riots, U.S. reactions to Eisenhower's "titular sovereignty" concession were wholly negative: Zonians boycotted Panamanian goods, and House representatives voted 371 to 12 against it. Daniel
Flood—"the all-time nut on the subject of Panama," according to a
presidential aide—even hinted that Eisenhower should be impeached.[55]
Public opinion, too, was firmly against Eisenhower—20 to 1 among editors, and 180 to 3 among letter writers to the White House.[56]

This buildup of resentment against the Panamanian elite in Washington helps to explain President John Kennedy's strategy of delay. When
the new Panamanian leader, Roberto Chiari, visited Washington in June
1962, Kennedy told him that he understood Panama's nationalists, and
he seemed to be sincere. But Kennedy also knew that he faced not only
a jingoistic U.S. public but a Department of Defense that feared sharing sovereignty with Panama in such a strategic area. Kennedy advised
Chiari to wait two to four years for a "basic document" revising the 1903
treaty and the flag issue, and kept giveaways small and economic.[57]

Chiari, however, was expressing an anti-Americanism that could no
longer be bought—at least no longer at such bargain basement prices.
Kennedy's inability to recognize the patron-client assumptions in the
elite's anti-Americanism astounded the Panamanian. Chiari was surprised that U.S. officials thought Panamanians wanted to run the canal
themselves, insisting "that not for a single moment does Panama wish to
participate in the maintenance, operation, and protection of the Canal."
Kennedy eventually did send representatives to bilateral talks, which
eventually produced a resolution to fly both banners side by side.[58]

But by early 1964, as the film version of *The Ugly American* ran in Panama's movie houses, Zonians vehemently resisted implementation of the

flag resolution and succeeded in slowing it down. Among the many who disobeyed that resolution on January 7 and 8, 1964, were the U.S. teenagers of Balboa High School (BHS), where the Zone's governor had unwisely decided to fly no flag at all. The BHS students could not stand to see Old Glory lowered just to achieve a symbolic equity with the Panamanian flag, and so they raised their own flag. As they did so, a plan to counter-protest the BHS gesture took shape among the teens of a nearby Panamanian high school, the National Institute (IN).

The violence that began on January 9 and continued for four days was a conflict not just between two schools but between two societies.

5. National Institute student Napoleón de Bernard arguing with Canal Zone Police Captain Gaddis Wall at the base of Balboa High School's flagpole on January 9, 1964. De Bernard claimed that, moments later, he threw the first punch and broke a policeman's jaw. To the left of him, holding a corner of the Panamanian flag, is another National Institute student, César Villareal. Villareal remembered feeling, at seventeen, that "the bullets of imperialism could not kill me. . . . Self-immolation for the fatherland did not seem like much." Both were interviewed for this book. National Archives and Records Administration.

Parents and friends brought blankets and sandwiches to the BHS teenage protesters, who hoisted a makeshift flag up their flagpole and camped at its base overnight.[59] The Panamanian IN students also had support: according to the one who threw the first punch in Balboa High's front yard, the dean of the IN gave them permission to use the revered 1947 Panamanian flag to lead their march to BHS. The Ministry of Foreign Relations also knew of their intentions.[60]

When the IN students got to Balboa High, they insisted that their flag fly next to the Stars and Stripes. The BHS students vehemently refused, and in the ensuing scuffle the Panamanian flag was torn. The Panamanian students soon ran away in anger and humiliation, and the violence might have ended there. But an hour or so later, riots flared up in Panama City and Colón. By then, radio broadcasts were urging listeners to join the protest against "the outrage"—a reference to the tearing of the Panamanian flag. The thousands who responded to the broadcasts charged several of the Zone's buildings, especially the enduring symbol of U.S. colonialism, the Tivoli Hotel, which was hosting several parties at the time.[61]

At around 8 p.m. that evening, the few dozen Zone police realized they were outmatched. They handed over control of the Zone to U.S. armed forces. It was around then that Panamanian teenager Ascanio Arosemena was shot as he dragged a wounded friend to safety. The news of his martyrdom spread like wildfire, and guns came out on the Panamanian side. The crisis had begun when Zone police overreacted to a protest by probably shooting into rushing but unarmed mobs; it escalated into riots and a bizarre four-day standoff in which each side was technically shooting into a foreign country.

The violence directed against U.S. citizens in those four days was unprecedented, widespread, and indiscriminate. "We should lynch the Zonian savages!" shouted Harmodio Arias to the National Assembly. Spurred by such battle cries, many Panamanians jumped up on Zonian cars, bashed in windows, pulled out drivers, and beat them. Foreigners, notably Canadians, made sure to set themselves off from U.S. citizens. Cornered by a crowd, one U.S. citizen escaped by yelling, "Je suis français!" Rioters also focused on U.S. symbols. They destroyed diplomatic property, including the twelve thousand books in the USIS building. They also trashed businesses that just looked Yankee, such as the Panamanian-owned Good Neighbor bar. Maybe partly to protect his establishment, the owner of Club 27 posted a sign after the riots that wryly mocked U.S. racial discrimination: NO DOGS OR ZONIANS.[62]

U.S. citizens did not show much more discrimination or restraint. While Zonian civilians did not come out in great numbers to counter-riot, some, possibly off-duty policemen, shot at Panamanians.[63] A few Zone policemen, when initially faced with angry mobs, also probably fired directly into groups of Panamanians. U.S. soldiers, too, released pent-up hatred. "Kill the Panamanian dogs!" they shouted as they kicked Panamanians and beat them with rifle butts.[64]

The suddenly unleashed violence terrified U.S. citizens. Thousands of them lived not in the Zone but in the Republic of Panama. They were far more integrated into Panamanian life than were Zonians and had Panamanian neighbors, family members, household help, and co-workers. Yet rioters targeted them anyway—even more so because, unlike Zonians, U.S. citizens in Panama were unprotected by the U.S. Army. As striking evidence of ambivalence, it was often Panamanians who protected these helpless U.S. citizens. "For every Panamanian fighting there were ten helping you," said Judy Kriz of Iowa, a survivor of the riots. Living in Panama City, another woman, originally from New Jersey, received anonymous phone calls asking her nationality. "We wouldn't say anything," she recalled. Her maid would answer the door while "seven of us hid in the shower."[65] Others replaced Canal Zone license plates with Panamanian ones to protect cars from arson or stoning.

The violence and fear spread far beyond Panama City and Colón. At a Santa Clara beach resort, Panamanian airline workers pulled away twelve U.S. citizens who were being threatened by a drunken mob and flew them out in small planes. Even farther away, in Santiago, Peace Corps doctor Robert Waldron, the only U.S. citizen in town, heard of the violence in the capital. "I immediately sensed the feeling against me. . . . The people looked daggers at me for being a gringo. . . . The mob . . . marched to the hotel and more or less stormed it with clubs, looking for me." Friends spirited Waldron out of town in a disguise.[66]

In such an atmosphere of lawlessness, accountability was not at a high premium. For instance, nobody knew for certain how many died on each side, or how they died.[67] Three U.S. soldiers were killed and a fourth probably took a fatal step off a cliff in the Zone, but Panama's media rarely acknowledged that fact. As for Panamanian casualties, few knew that seven to eight of the (probably) twenty-one dead were victims of asphyxiation or burns while looting or setting fires; that another may have been a victim of a hit-and-run; that many were felled by ammunition not used by U.S. forces; and that three were innocents—a baby, a little girl, and an old fruit peddler caught by a stray bullet. Even the most liberal computation, therefore, placed the total of Panamanians killed by U.S. forces or Zonians, purposefully or otherwise, at thirteen out of twenty-one.[68] The grim possibility that some of those were victims of other Panamanians cannot be dismissed.[69] Miguel Moreno, ambassador to the Organization of American States (OAS) during the riots, was aware of the political dangers of this possible fratricide. He wrote to Foreign Minister Galileo Solís a month after the violence that they should aim to prove that U.S. forces had killed at least a "majority" of the dead Panamanians.[70]

In public, however, Panama's leaders blamed all casualties on U.S. soldiers and charged unmitigated "aggression" against the U.S. government. Panamanians, who in sixty-one years of independence had never had one of their own die at the hands of foreigners, treated their dead and wounded, whoever they were and however they had died, as pure-hearted fallen soldiers in an all-out patriotic war. They *needed* this martyrdom. Radio commentators and cartoonists told tales of U.S. forces rolling tanks into Panamanian territory and machine-gunning innocents. "Our fellow Panamanians are being tortured and are undergoing great sufferings for the insults inflicted on our national flag," declared one radio personality during the riots, interpreting liberally the word "torture."[71] Some Panamanians eventually admitted that when they said "tanks" they meant armored personnel carriers and that automatic weapons were not actually fired, only mounted.[72] Most Panamanians also ignored the fact that the Canal Zone's borders extended further than generally thought, which meant that U.S. soldiers stayed within their jurisdiction even when in Panama City. Many also assumed that more Panamanians died after the U.S. soldiers took over, while in reality the armed forces limited casualties by aiming only at snipers.[73]

As in the riots of 1959, the Panamanian government in 1964 was aware that it bore its share of responsibility. Panama's security forces, following direct orders from President Chiari, had stopped the riots only after several days. Several Panamanian officials admitted dragging out the riots because they dreaded reprisals from nationalists. "They would have accused us of being traitors and anti-patriots," explained GN com-

6. A young man throwing a rock or a tear gas canister at U.S. soldiers in the Canal Zone. The Panamanian government presented this photo to the Organization of American States as evidence of U.S. "aggression," though the soldiers were within their jurisdiction. National Archives and Records Administration.

mander Colonel Bolívar Vallarino. "The situation of the National Guard was very difficult. [Restoring order] would have had internal repercussions."[74] As Vallarino pointed out, the GN after all did do *some* policing—it performed ambulance duty, beat on some of the worst rioters, evacuated U.S. citizens in Panama, protected U.S. businesses, and guarded the U.S. embassy. Regardless, negligence was clear. Zone officials made eight calls to Panamanian officials, including Vallarino and the president's aides, all of whom either promised action or remained noncommittal and then did nothing.[75] Zonians provided the GN with tear gas. It never used it. The GN promised to pinpoint snipers—who were shooting from the Legislative Palace, no less! It did not. For the first few days, some Panamanians even wanted Chiari to send out the

SOLIDARIDAD

7. In the summer of 1964 the Panama Ministry of Education published a new edition of the civics textbook *Educación cívica*, which contained this interpretation of the January riots. The cartoon conveyed a widely shared collective memory of unrestrained, unprovoked U.S. violence against defenseless youths. Contrary to this perception, Panamanians and U.S. forces had each shot at the other, and there was no evidence that the U.S. side had fired automatic weapons. Cartoon by Alfonso Pinzón, in Diamantina de Calzadilla and Etna de Martínez, *Educación cívica*, 4th ed. (Panama City, 1964–1965).

GN against the United States.[76] Whatever the causes of the riots, one thing was certain: the Panamanian elite would be at the center of the aftermath, either as the main beneficiary or the main casualty.

Tough and Tender: Post-Riot Diplomacy

The Riots of 1964 stood as a test of U.S. resolve against the spread of anti-Americanism as a political strategy. A new administration had just taken over in Washington, secure in the conviction that the U.S. government would no longer be caught napping as it was in Cuba. At the same time, U.S. citizens in and out of Washington were moving close to a consensus: elite-manipulated anti-Americanism should meet with a firm yet practical U.S. attitude. U.S. officials did feel that their supposed allies in Panama City were playing them for fools, yet their long-developing cynicism about Panama told them to respond to riot strategies not by weakening elites but by strengthening their rule so that conservative anti-Americanism would never again have to co-opt the street-level tactics of popular anti-Americanism.

The idea that Latin America's conservative anti-Americanism was insincere and opportunistic found increasing favor among U.S. officials in the early 1960s. In U.S. eyes, the wealthy in Latin America were trying to have it both ways: they were unwilling to take a public stand against Castro, yet they refused to abide by any tax or land reform that would help to prevent Castro-type revolutions.[77] John Moors Cabot, ambassador to Brazil under Kennedy and himself quite the blueblood, complained to Arthur Schlesinger, Jr.: "I get very irritated when people blame the problems of Latin America on the United States policy. . . . The source of the difficulty is that the haves in Latin America do not realize that their day is over. The selfishness and blindness of the oligarchies in these countries is the reason why a storm is brewing."[78]

Besides, many added, polls were suggesting that the poor simply were not prone to anti-U.S. violence. One USIA survey of Central American cities showed that only 2 percent of respondents gave priority to "resisting foreign influence." These results echoed dozens of other Latin American urban surveys. As for the people in the countryside, one USIA poll in 1961 claimed to be "the first time anyone had systematically sought the views of the semi-literate, poor campesinos." Interviewers completed the study "despite great difficulties," as local elites denied them permits and jailed them. Elites, it turned out, were right to worry. According to the polls, peasants rejected both capitalism and communism as a way of life. They preferred "socialism," by which they meant land reform. They also felt, oddly enough, that the U.S. government was sympathetic to these hopes.[79]

The irony of finding pro-Americanism among the poor was that U.S. officials quickly stopped paying attention to their views. And so the gap between U.S. policymakers and poor Latin Americans gradually came to resemble that between elites and the poor. In mid-1963, a research paper that had digested recent insights from social psychology and national character studies concluded that "the U.S. is a wealthy country, therefore it is expected to act as do wealthy persons in Latin America. Without going into detail, one can say that this involves bribery, tax evasion, removal of profits from the country, high interest and profit expectation and the like in the Latin American socioeconomic system. These practices are not denied, even by the wealthy themselves—in fact, they seem so 'normal' as to be expected." The contempt of Latin American elites toward social egalitarianism appeared to be rubbing off on even the most idealistic of U.S. policymakers. When in Bogotá thousands of workers cheered the visiting President Kennedy, the president of Colombia leaned over and explained, "They think you're on their side."[80]

The violence in Panama also coincided with a key personnel change in the Johnson administration, a change that reflected this wider exasperation. The appointment of Thomas Mann as assistant secretary of state for inter-American affairs in December 1963 crystallized impatience, especially toward elite anti-Americanism. It is true that Mann sent out the message that military regimes would now meet with a more "open" attitude in Washington. But the "Mann Doctrine" was not simply a return to Eisenhower complacency. As historian Walter LaFeber has argued, Mann's professional trajectory mirrored Washington's evolving mood toward Latin American policy. He had gone from aggressive anticommunist in the Eisenhower years to liberal reformist in the early Kennedy government to grumpy cynic by 1963.[81]

In 1964, Mann articulated an active, calculated approach to anti-Americanism that was gaining favor in Washington. He drew up his own list of anti-U.S. "clichés." Out of twenty-seven, twenty-five were economic; Mann paid little attention to the political or cultural aspects of anti-Americanism. "I think the American people, naively, expected love and affection to be the product of aid programs," he later said. "Now no sophisticated person in the State Department ever thought that, nor did we ever say that." Since the Cuban Revolution showed the economic and political destructiveness of both inaction and panic in the face of anti-Americanism, he argued, "our policy should be one of quiet confidence which avoids even the appearance of appeasement."[82] Soon, Mann's language of resilience spread. "I am for being hard-nosed" against the "fad" of throwing rocks at U.S. embassies, wrote Carl Rowan, the new director of the USIA, to President Johnson. He added that the U.S. government should demand public apologies and full reparations from leaders of countries where these events took place.[83]

The new president, finally, was the right boss for Mann. Lyndon Johnson claimed that his uncompromising stance toward anti-Americanism was the result of personal experience with Latin Americans. Johnson had been raised in Texas with Mexican American ranch hands and had taught their children as a schoolteacher during the Depression. Perhaps as a result of that experience, he seemed to reason that Latin Americans young and old were like children. Some were spoiled: when he heard that a Latin American leader was unhappy with the attention he received from the White House, Johnson ridiculed him. "I don't know how much more we can give him. We had him in here and we had a picture made. . . . I could put him on my knee and bounce him."[84] Others needed a firm hand: "I know these Latin Americans," he once privately told reporters. "I grew up with Mexicans. They'll come right into your yard and take it over if you let them. And the next day they'll be right up on your porch, barefoot and weighing one hundred and thirty pounds and they'll take that too. But if you say to 'em right at the start, 'hold on, just wait a minute,' they'll know they're dealing with somebody who'll stand up. And after you can get along fine." Anti-Americanism gave Johnson the opportunity to teach Latin Americans to "get along." He told a close adviser by phone that he was "damn tired of packing our flag and our embassy and our USIS every time somebody got a little emotional outburst. . . . They better *watch* it."[85]

Yet the Riots of 1964 confronted Johnson with a more subtle choice than packing or staying: the United States had to either negotiate with a largely rhetorical anti-U.S. hostility that had temporarily turned violent or else open the door to more radical alternatives. Mann and others advised the president to opt for the former. To assist Panama's conservatives in policing both radicals and themselves, therefore, U.S. diplomats in 1964 avoided overreaction. By keeping quiet about the collaborationist impulse of conservative anti-Americanism, U.S. officials not only avoided revolution but kept their losses to a minimum. Johnson's promise to scrap the 1903 treaty, made at the end of 1964, was more advantageous to Washington than Panama let on.

It helped that, soon after the shooting ended, divisions in Panamanian society resurfaced. The militant Panamanian media offered an illustration of that dynamic. It was often the conduit for what one commentator called a "symbiosis" between oligarchs and students, but oligarchs clearly dominated that partnership.[86] Panamanians were highly literate—72 percent—and exposed to several newspapers and more than sixty radio stations. But a media oligopoly—comprising about seven families—owned all the newspapers and many of the radio stations, and through the press it openly conducted political campaigns. In a clear illustration of the workings of conservative anti-Americanism, rightist owners hired leftist journalists to provide nationalistic credibility. These were strange bedfellows indeed, yet journalists were convinced that they were free opinion leaders in Panamanian society. All claimed to speak for "the people" but none bothered to conduct polls. "Polls were sentimental," explained Ramón Pereira, the popular host of Radio Mía.[87]

Following the riots, media barons walked a finer line than usual between reassuring U.S. officials that they were in control of anti-U.S. discourse and admitting that they exploited it. For the first few days, Chiari aimed to moderate news by funneling it through his office. Then, for a few weeks, editors loosened the reins of reporters a little because strong anti-U.S. language was to the advantage of Chiari, who was eager to showcase for Washington an outraged public opinion.[88] Then, on February 24, apparently in reaction to growing solidarity on the left, Harmodio Arias and other publishers told embassy staffers that they "agreed to a complete shutdown on anti-American news" to allow smoother negotiations.[89]

The back-and-forth in Panama's media message reflected the ambivalence of the Panamanian president himself. Chiari, it turns out, hesitated before suspending diplomatic relations with the United States in the early hours of January 10, the key diplomatic move of the crisis (he broke off relations soon after). It took pleas from the minister of education, Manuel Solís Palma, to awaken Chiari's sense of honor and his political instincts for survival. A founder of the student federation and a man whom the U.S. embassy considered a communist (he denied he was), Solís Palma met with Chiari at the palace at around 9 p.m. on January 9, just as the riots were escalating. At this point the president was "outraged" but was without a plan, and so he considered consulting his cabinet. Solís Palma was wary of the radicalism of students and of the conservatism of cabinet members. He offered Chiari the following logic: "*Presidente,* if you have decided to sever relations, just do it and then inform us. But if we go to a cabinet meeting to argue, we'll still be at it tomorrow." Chiari took the advice. The move was brilliant. It both bypassed the ministers and outpaced the students by calling for a renegotiation of the 1903 treaty that would give Panama sovereignty over the Canal Zone and so scrap the clause that gave the United States control "in perpetuity" over the canal. Chiari, upon making this announcement, also posed with the torn 1947 flag for photographers, again wisely associating his elite-staffed government with student martyrdom. Solís Palma's day in the sun cast a temporary shadow over Vice President José Bazán, the pro-business manager of the Colón Free Zone and the usually more influential adviser, who worried that a break in relations would lower U.S. consumption in Panama and damage the import-export sector.[90]

As time went on, however, the stoic pledge to "live off sovereignty" as opposed to living off canal revenues lost its appeal. Investment flowed out of the country and Chiari felt mounting pressure from Bazán and other pro-business elites to renew talks without a guarantee of renegotiations.[91] Students themselves began to show signs of breaking with the elite-led face-off with the U.S. government. Some student leaders distrusted the suddenly ultra-patriotic elites. One of them, Federico Britton, suspected that Chiari's stance "was a result of the pressure from the crowds in the street—that it wasn't voluntary." Others threatened to turn against Chiari if he backed down.[92] Then the students themselves grew divided. Radical groups broke with the pro-Chiari mainstream, and the schism made student rallies less effective. In March a Youth Congress against imperialism, which had been funded by Solís Palma, collapsed after a pro-democracy faction booed and hissed and walked out on radical organizers.[93]

Among the U.S. public, meanwhile, the situation in Panama exacerbated concern over worldwide anti-Americanism. Part of the reason was that, as with Caracas in 1958, an anti-U.S. event there coincided with protests in other countries—in this case, Cyprus, Cuba, Cambodia, Ghana, Congo, and France. This new wave of anti-Americanism met with a hawkish public reaction. Poll numbers confirmed that U.S. citizens, when it came to Panama, had mellowed little since the days of Theodore Roosevelt. Following the riots, 56 percent of respondents supported a "firm" stance against Panama, and the large majority of those rejected any concessions. Moreover, the 1,484 who wrote to the White House or State Department in the first two weeks following the riots were almost unanimously incensed at Panama's behavior. The State Department classified seven out of ten as "'Hard Line' (Send the Marines, Remember the Alamo, etc.)" and another two out of ten as "Pro-Administration." A tiny fraction even suggested making Panama the fifty-first State or a commonwealth such as Puerto Rico. Most of the other 10 percent favored either a multilateral solution (letting international organizations decide) or a more pragmatic one (building a new canal). In negotiations, Mann was able to remark quite correctly to Panamanians that "we have 190 million Americans who feel very strongly about this thing."[94]

Events in Panama also gave U.S. media commentators the opportunity to articulate a common paradox in U.S. responses to anti-Americanism: fear of declining U.S. prestige just as U.S. world power peaked. *Miami Herald* columnist Robert Ruark, for instance, could not understand how "the greatest, richest nation of them all, big brother to all the world, conqueror of mighty Germany and mighty Japan, inventor of the atom bomb, wheat-seller, hog-butcher, proprietor of Frank Sinatra and Mickey Mantle, continued to be knocked off constantly by a global approximation of the Mets." Many were concerned, again, that impressions were prevailing over facts. A widely disseminated editorial, "Panama Emotionalism," argued that the U.S. government could not win a public relations contest against "tiny Panama." "In the modern drift of world opinion, [Panamanians] have a sentimental case." Only a few argued that the Johnson government should concede that the Canal Zone was a misguided colonial venture, yet these more liberal commentators also recognized the inevitability of anti-Americanism. The *New York Times* unveiled colonialism as the "disguised inner issue." "We cannot masquerade as anti-colonial unless we are wholly so; there is no such thing as a partial virgin." Theologian Reinhold Niebuhr agreed. Welcoming the crisis as "a flash of light to a sleeping American giant too drugged by his sense of a messianic mission to sense the perils of great power," he counseled the U.S. government to fully recognize Panama's sovereignty over the Zone.[95]

In tune with this battle pitting realism versus idealism, the U.S. media translated complex U.S.-Panamanian relations into simple emotions: "A Nation That Hates Gringos," "Why Do They *Hate* Us?" and "Panama: Why They Hate Us" were notable headlines.[96] Zonians expressed a more personal dismay. "It seemed incredible to suddenly see this hatred around me," wrote Amy McCormack in *U.S. Lady.* Another Zonian woman wrote to her parents in Nebraska: "You don't know how awful it is to be called such horrible names on television, radio and press. Day after day, of how murderous the bloodthirsty Americans are. . . . I don't mind being out of eggs, bread, Panamanian coffee, etc. . . . but I can't stand the hatred."[97] As in many anti-U.S. crises, U.S. citizens expressed genuine disbelief at the hostility of foreigners and chose to brand them as ungrateful or hateful—in other words, as somehow irrational.

Given that many U.S. citizens believed the United States could be an anticolonial superpower, the Johnson administration's attitude placed it to the left of most of the public. The priorities of Johnson's advisers were to maintain the security of the canal and to safeguard the image of the United States. Their genius was in realizing that the latter strategy, the ideological touch-up, was necessary to sustain the former. Two issues framed Johnson's relatively moderate carrot-and-stick policy.

First, Panama was important for its linkages with world diplomacy, and so the similarity of events in faraway Ghana or Cyprus did matter. While Johnson disparaged the Republic of Panama as "no larger than the city of St. Louis," he realized that the tiny nation could make "the Colossus" look recalcitrant on the world stage—and more precisely in the Western Hemisphere. "On Panama we are taking a shellacking from the Communists," reported intelligence services to Johnson.[98] The president could do little about bad press in Havana, Beijing, Moscow, or Cairo. But he did heed Secretary of State Dean Rusk's warnings not to ignore the neocolonial aspects of the situation.[99] The press in the hemisphere, while not indulging in a "shellacking," generally did dismiss the importance of communism in the riots and support Panama's claims for a new treaty. Johnson could not ignore such opinions. He worried that if he did not handle Panama with at least some of what he called "social consciousness," Georgia senator Richard Russell's prediction would be right: "You're gonna have trouble there all through your tenure as president in that area down there. . . . That's gonna be a trouble spot."[100] On the other hand, if Johnson capitulated, Panama would set an example for other countries to blackmail the U.S. government with riots. Panama, therefore, presented an opportunity to halt what could be called the "domino effect" of anti-Americanism.

The second issue balancing Johnson's approach was that the Panamanian elites' preponderance of power still held after the riots. There was evidence of Cuban and communist participation in the violence, but most reports warned not to overestimate a few hundred communists who had few weapons and little support among the public and in government.[101] Wealthy Panamanian diplomats would spout anti-U.S. rhetoric, most felt, while they winked toward Washington and kept the other eye firmly on social revolution. U.S. officials, therefore, talked only to those with real power—not the students, not the communists, and not left-leaning ministers such as Solís Palma—but the leading elite parties and the military. The most sympathetic assessments of Panamanian nationalism noted its "schizophrenia." Panama was "curious," one Panamanian representative told U.N. Ambassador Adlai Stevenson, "in that many of [the] most conservative persons are anti-American either on [the] emotional issue of Canal and national pride or as opposed to U.S. efforts at economic and social reform."[102]

In the carrot-and-stick policy that followed the riots, the stick came out first. Mann, especially, resented the fact that during his rushed trip to Panama on January 10 to assess hostility, his Panamanian hosts took secondary roads, used back doors, and subjected him to mobs shouting "*Gringos* go home!" and throwing rocks at the windows of a meeting room. Mann found the experience to be "pure theater" and was disgusted with the "perfidy of the Panamanian people."[103] He responded with a laconic stance. While in Panama, he remained noncommittal on the issue of renegotiating the 1903 treaty and suggested that no one back home would give in to such a demand.[104]

Mann returned to Washington on January 13 for a fascinating White House meeting that outlined the U.S. response. Behind closed doors, the first order of business was to deal with a little-known threat of a coup d'état against Chiari. The riots had quieted down, but there still existed an outside chance of a communist overthrow. The CIA reported that the local Communist Party, along with none other than Arnulfo Arias, now Chiari's opponent in the coming elections, was plotting to strike at the presidential palace that very evening. Upon hearing those CIA rumors, Johnson's advisers played out a scene of Cold War paranoia worthy of *Dr. Strangelove*. Since it was already 10 p.m., all immediately agreed that the U.S. government would send troops if any coup involving communism appeared to succeed. Secretary of Defense Robert McNamara then went into the adjoining room. He called the commander of the Southern Forces to request that he inform Chiari. With Johnson standing next to him, McNamara, through the commander, gave the Panamanian the pledge of assistance and made sure that "communist sympathizers" were in the room with Chiari to hear the thinly veiled threat. (Solís Palma, most likely the sympathizer to whom they referred, was at Chiari's cabinet meeting but later did not recall any U.S. warning.)[105]

Thus reassured that Chiari was unlikely to tolerate a Castro-type assault, Johnson's men returned to their meeting and resolved to elaborate a "tough" stance against Panama precisely because of Panama's conservatism. Johnson's advisers agreed that, although several Latin Americans were already losing patience with Chiari, Chiari was still behaving like a typical Panamanian oligarch. The Panamanian president, himself a businessman dependent on the Canal Zone for his family's milk business, would eventually buckle under pressure from the military and business sectors. The best approach was to be "low key," as Mann said.[106] As he had already indicated to Chiari earlier that day in Panama City, the White House would refuse to negotiate anything as long as the threat of violence loomed, and furthermore, President Johnson was prepared to wait the Panamanians out. The U.S. government would speak softly and carry a big stick.

At the same January 13 meeting, Mann and Johnson also decided to present Panamanians with an impressive carrot—eventually. Officials largely agreed that the U.S. government had been, as Rusk said, "heavy-handed" with Panama in the past. In order to correct that imbalance and prevent future riots, the White House would immediately draw up a "long-range plan" of "major changes," including a sea-level canal to replace the existing lock-operated Panama Canal, which all observers agreed was too narrow for the new aircraft carriers and too slow for the increasing traffic. The White House and its closest advisers, in short, were ready to give in to Panama's key demand and abrogate the 1903 treaty. They refrained from saying so in public. They knew the U.S. public would cry out against this alleged modern-day surrender of the Alamo. They also concluded that Panama would read the abrogation as too easy a victory and demand more. Panama's surface anti-Americanism would reap some rewards, but only when it reverted to its conservative guise. Secretary Rusk explained the Johnson-Mann approach to U.S. senators by calling it "a kind of minuet" between the U.S. and Panamanian governments. Some steps would address the demands of popular anti-Americanism; others would satisfy the elite. It was all choreographed, almost pro forma, he implied.[107] Here was the "go slow" strategy reinvigorated. The difference this time was that the United States would set the pace.

For now, the public U.S. refusal to renegotiate the 1903 treaty meant that relations remained broken, and so both countries embarked on a gingerly post-riot diplomacy to restore them. The two governments did share fundamental goals: first, to reach a mutually satisfactory agreement on the future of the canal, and second, to have Chiari's pro-U.S. successor win the presidential elections in May. Both sides seemed aware that the second goal would likely be impossible if the first was not met by the time Panamanians headed for the polls. Mann was right that time was on the U.S. side, and so Johnson was free to be the most recalcitrant member in the White House, concerned as he was with his own elections in November 1964 and fearing the power of Congress to block whatever treaty he might rewrite with Panama. Both men wanted any new language to provide what Mann called "protection" against an outright giveaway of the canal.[108] But what was that language?

"We've got to agree that rhetoric is a means of meeting of the minds. It's something we employ to understand each other, isn't it?" asked a frustrated Lyndon Johnson of his national security adviser McGeorge Bundy on January 17 as a semantic disagreement stalled talks for the first of many times. Seemingly taken aback by the president's naïveté, Bundy responded, "Um, sometimes, and sometimes the opposite, Mr. President."[109] Both sides learned in the months following the riots that finding words for the U.S.-Panama relationship was a challenge because they preferred to describe what it should be rather than what it was. Reaching an agreement on paper happened in three stages, a rough process that smoothened out only as elections drew near and U.S. and Panamanian elites recognized the urgency of collaboration.

From January 10 to January 28 came the first stage, the first wave of hope and disillusion, as both sides realized that words mattered more than they had thought. The OAS's Inter-American Peace Commission (IAPC), which mediated when OAS member nations broke relations, was in no position to find those words. From the moment of the commission's arrival in Panama at the end of the riots, its members were ineffective and highly suspicious of what they considered to be Chiari's about-faces. In mid-January, all parties thought they had an agreement, only to have talks break down over which word, the English "discuss" or the Spanish *negociar,* described the pledge they had just made.[110] The semantics, it turned out, were meaningful: Panamanians wanted a new treaty, while the U.S. promised only wide-ranging talks. The "misunderstanding" showed that Johnson had to appreciate the pressure Chiari was under. "Now you are learning about the Latins," Mann told a colleague who expressed exasperation over Panama's casuistry.[111] On January 28 the Latin American delegates realized they would be unable to bring the two parties together. They pulled out of Panama.

Moreno, Panama's ambassador to the OAS, set in motion the second stage as he requested the formation of a more high-level OAS delegation, the Organ of Consultation, on January 30. His speech, the *New York Times* reported, "was regarded as the most violent attack by a Latin-American government on the United States since Fidel Castro seized power in Cuba." Moreno went so far as to ask for OAS protection against any future aggression by the United States. In reaction, OAS members sided with Washington, but not openly. "Privately, most Latin-American diplomats deplored the violence of Mr. Moreno's speech and praised the moderation of [U.S. ambassador at the OAS] Mr. [Ellsworth] Bunker's reply," said the *Times*.[112] Moreno knew perfectly well that Panama was playing a risky game with both the OAS and Johnson. "When [my] speech was over," he recalled, "not one person applauded. And when we left the building, I talked to the Mexican ambassador to the OAS, a career diplomat, Vicente Sánchez Gavito. He said, 'Miguel, I'm sorry to say that with this speech, you've done what Hernán Cortés did when he discovered Mexico: you burned your ships. Your mission to Washington will fail.' I told him, 'Look, Vicente, I appreciate your sincerity, but my speech had to be strong because otherwise my government would collapse.'"[113]

From early February to late March, still during this second stage, another semantic tug-of-war came about as U.S. and Panamanian negotiators disagreed on proposal after proposal.[114] The Panamanians seemed to play dumb, but in reality they articulated two smart arguments: first, that a U.S. promise to negotiate would not make a new treaty a foregone conclusion but would simply shore up the Chiari government; and second, that a new treaty would not exacerbate anti-Americanism but rather eliminate it.[115] In other words, Chiari and his aides were hinting that negotiations would silence public violence. As with media barons, it was close to admitting that they controlled rioters—a fine line for conservative anti-Americanism to walk.

After the OAS gave up again, Johnson on March 21 set in motion the final stage by making a conciliatory speech that plucked the right cultural strings without giving away anything substantial. He explained that "circumstances change, . . . history shapes new attitudes and expectations," and conceded, "We are well aware that the claims of the Government of Panama, and of the majority of the Panamanian people, do not spring from malice or hatred of America."[116] Here, finally, was the public carrot that Panamanians had been waiting for, at least in tone: recognition and appreciation of anti-U.S. ambivalence.

The affirmation of friendship healed much of the animosity and hurt pride in nationalist circles. "All Panama has waited sixty long years to hear words such as those spoken by President Johnson on Saturday afternoon," wrote one columnist.[117] The statement freed the elite from its rhetoric of *ni un paso atrás* ("not yielding one step"). Moreno, despite being an *antiyanqui* hero since his January 30 speech, considered the U.S.-Panama relationship as similar to a Catholic marriage: "there could be no divorce."[118] He and his U.S. counterpart Ellsworth Bunker followed up on the Johnson statement by meeting in a private club in Washington, D.C., away from the media. They put behind them twenty-eight failed proposals, soberly ordered coffee, and within days they agreed, of all things, on the word "agreement." On April 3, 1964, Johnson approved the new statement, which renewed diplomatic relations and promised open-ended talks and an "agreement" between Panama and the United States, but not necessarily a new treaty. Satisfied that he had saved face, Chiari phoned his most recalcitrant minister, Manuel Solís Palma. "Tonight I will not join you in voting against the memorandum [of April 3]," the president told him. "I have the impression that you will be a lone dissenter in the Cabinet."[119] The April statement was a triumph of the long U.S. alliance with conservative anti-Americanism.

Panama's presidential elections of May 1964, close on the heels of the April agreement, further showed the wisdom of the pragmatic U.S. approach. Since the president could not serve two consecutive terms, his Liberal Party's candidate was Marco Robles, Chiari's cousin. Robles, like Chiari, vowed to scrap the 1903 treaty. The problem was Arias, his opponent, who seemed as popular as ever with the masses. Before the riots, the election of 1964 seemed as if it would once again pit a traditional oligarch (Robles) against a populist oligarch (Arias). After Chiari had broken relations with the United States, however, a strange thing happened: the populist Arias, who once fined bars for playing too much foreign music, now urged Panamanians to settle for a "fair" deal from Johnson. He also distanced himself from the student movement, and student leaders considered Arias' "anti-U.S." attitudes old-fashioned compared to their own "anti-imperialist" program.[120] As Chiari and Robles moved toward anti-Americanism, therefore, Arias moved away.

Neither fooled U.S. officials. Aides reported to Mann that "among U.S. personnel here [Arias] continues to be highly controversial. Many doubt [the] sincerity of his pro-U.S. 'conversion.'"[121] Mann himself considered Arias two-faced, unpredictable, anachronistic, and racist. In contrast, U.S. officials were rather accommodating with Chiari and Robles. They pleaded with each other to let the Liberals play their local political game, and noted again and again that they should help Chiari out of the "box" he was in or the "corner" into which he had painted himself.[122]

In a classic instance of intervention through nonintervention, the U.S. government turned a blind eye to an election marked by ugly smear campaigns and almost certain fraud. The Chiari family's paper, *La Prensa*, savaged Arias as a pro-Yankee, racketeering, drug-smuggling, arms-dealing, counterfeiting Nazi "Führer" plotting to sterilize Panamanian blacks.[123] *El Día* accused Arias of being "the candidate of the *gringos*," and *Gráfico* reported that Zonians campaigned for Arias and intimidated West Indian voters. On the eve of the vote, Robles' *Guerra* falsely accused Arias of having married a *gringa* in the Canal Zone.[124] Desperate tactics were the result of what Jack Vaughn, the new U.S. ambassador, called a "widespread mood of uneasiness" among elites who realized the growing difficulties in stealing elections.[125] Throughout the campaign, it was an open secret that in the event that Arias won, Robles would just take the election by using the GN, whose commander was exhorting his troops to vote for Robles. As it turned out, Robles won with a slim margin, and the GN stayed in its barracks. Arias' supporters charged fraud, and Vaughn concluded that this was "likely." But, as the embassy noted with a tinge of relief, Arias had no evidence.[126]

With elections out of the way, elites could go back to being elites. Throughout the Chiari-Robles transition from May to October, most notably, Fernando Eleta was there to remind U.S. officials that Panama's battened-down hostility was indeed the minuet that Rusk had described. Eleta was a walking monument to conservative anti-Americanism and a fine dancing partner for the United States. He had built a classic Panamanian fortune by intertwining his commercial, political, and media power. He had held several cabinet posts, and, following the break in relations, had secured bailouts from Spain. Yet Eleta proudly recalled his youth as an amateur Marxist and a friend of U.S. foreign policy critic Eugene Burdick, co-author of *The Ugly American*. To achieve equilibrium between these contradictory pasts, Eleta employed a romantic anti-U.S. rhetoric in public and offset this with friendly collaboration in private. His special skill was denigrating Latin America's "inferiority complex" while comforting U.S. officials with a beguiling, gendered subaltern personality. "The same way a man treats a woman who bears complexes," he suggested for instance, "is the way politicians should treat Caribbean peoples: 'You're so pretty'—you know—'I love that skin color.' You don't want her to feel inferior because she's a little dark-skinned."[127]

Eleta became Robles' foreign minister, and both men immediately let it be known that the days of popular anti-Americanism were numbered. Protesters, who were gearing up for more street demonstrations as the Fourth of July approached, were the first order of business. With the election over, *La Prensa* now criticized protesters as "confused rebels" and drew a fuzzy distinction between the "patriotism" of January and the present "chaos." "Repression by competent authorities," the paper warned, "needs to be unleashed this time without hesitation." It was. Marco "the Rifle" Robles did not disappoint those who knew him as the law-and-order minister of justice. For at least two years after the election, he sent the GN out to beat and arrest students, journalists, and even Arnulfo Arias himself. Robles also made it clear that he would not pressure his counterpart before the U.S. presidential election in November. He had anti-U.S. graffiti painted over, and went so far as to disagree with Chiari's "thesis" that the U.S. government had been the "aggressor" back in January.[128]

Robles and Eleta also largely purged their government of those who did not appreciate the cooling down of the anti-U.S. strategy. During a poker game in July, the president-elect confided to a prominent U.S. businessman that "no Ambassadors, Consuls or foreign representatives that are in any way anti-American will be appointed after October 1st [his first day in power]."[129] Eleta kept Robles' poker-game promise with all the drama of a Spanish duel. After a public exchange of harsh words with strongly anti-U.S. negotiators, he restaffed the whole team. And in late November, Eleta successfully defended himself in a closed-door meeting of the National Assembly. From then on, said Eleta, "all of [the old] negotiations, we swept all of that away. And a totally different process began."[130]

The process that began in November 1964, however, was no giveaway of the canal. In fact, talks were firmly under U.S. control. To be sure, U.S. officials knew that Robles did need the promise of a new waterway to survive in office, and one chargé reported that Eleta was convincing many with his anti-U.S. gambit that "Panama might . . . simply choose to live on its *dignidad* even if it meant starving."[131] But Mann, since the White House meeting on January 13 almost a year before, had already allowed for a new canal. The problem was how to deliver it at the lowest diplomatic cost.

In late 1964, therefore, Mann confronted conservative anti-Americanism with its humiliating dependence. Ordinarily impatient with Latin American bluffing, Mann now played along with it. Using January 9, 1965, the first anniversary of the riots, as a looming deadline that would surely bring violence if no deal were reached, Mann spearheaded a unilateral U.S. declaration supposedly giving the Robles government what it wanted. He convinced the secretaries of Defense and the Army to forget merely tinkering with the 1903 treaty and instead to commit to negotiating a brand new treaty. Johnson, after all, said he wanted "some coonskins on the wall after eleven months." And so his men fanned out around Washington and obtained support from recalcitrant members of Congress, the Joint Chiefs of Staff, former presidents Harry Truman and Dwight Eisenhower, and even FBI director J. Edgar Hoover.[132]

The resulting statement of December 18 was as close as the U.S. government came to a ringing success during this era of anti-Americanism: it reassured U.S. nationalists and the Army that a new sea-level canal was Johnson's top priority, yet it also acknowledged Panama's dignity by conceding sovereignty over the existing canal.[133] In November Mann had expressed his doubts to Johnson that they could get all these foreign policy hawks to "make sweeping concessions on sovereignty and on perpetuity, . . . the two gut issues that the Panamanians are going to insist on," and so in December he was delighted by their success. Almost every segment of official and press opinion in both countries could find something to rejoice about in the December 18 statement.

"It's a very reasonable thing we're coming out with," Mann told Johnson in the same conversation, "but it's likely to be unsatisfactory to the Panamanians."[134] Indeed, despite the good immediate feedback, Mann sensed that the Panamanian elites would soon grasp how he had outmaneuvered them. In an ideal world, they would have won sovereignty over the canal while the United States continued to run it for them. Panamanians *had* won a symbolic victory by getting Washington to admit that the Panama Canal should one day be Panama's canal. But for now they felt the sting of U.S. resilience. The December statement did not promise that the U.S. government would build the new sea-level canal *in Panama;* rather, it said that "the United States should press forward, with Panama *and other interested governments,* in plans and preparations for a sea-level canal in this *area.*"[135] Very publicly, Mann soon canvassed other possible host nations in Latin America.

Panamanian negotiators were furious. They were trapped in Mann's carrot-and-stick scheme: on one hand, they needed U.S. funds and minor concessions, and genuinely feared student protests if the U.S. Army did not strengthen the GN; on the other, they faced the possibility of running an obsolete waterway abandoned by the great shipping lines, who would use the bigger, faster, still U.S.-run sea-level canal, possibly located in another country.[136] As if reflecting conservative anti-Americanism's embarrassment, in early 1965 talks went underground, conducted away from the eyes of an impatient public. Throughout the process, U.S. negotiators stayed in command, listing talking points, doing feasibility studies, proposing drafts, hurrying Panama into counter-proposals, and, as Johnson said to Mann, "throw[ing] a few bones" such as higher wages for Panamanian employees. "Ridiculous! Shameless!" Panamanian statesmen exclaimed privately to colleagues when faced with U.S. proposals. Some became paranoid, fearing mafia or CIA machinations.[137]

The riots of 1964 presented the U.S. government with a variant of anti-Americanism that proved inherently manageable. A White House reporter looked back on Johnson's 1964 Panama diplomacy as having garnered "probably too little praise," since by the end of that year things had taken "an astonishing turn for the better."[138] The threat of social revolution seemed temporarily effective against a U.S. government wishing to preserve at least some anticolonial credentials in a Cold War world. Yet the Johnson administration limited the damage to its reputation and interests by mitigating the impulse to be cynical toward conservative anti-Americanism with a deeper knowledge of local politics in Panama. Mann and others understood the underlying social conflicts between popular and conservative groups there, and they correctly placed bets on an outcome that would favor the latter. As the long-time patrons of an elite that resorted to brinkmanship, U.S. officials used every diplomatic response at their disposal—direct diplomacy, semantic sleight of hand, carrot-and-stick manipulation, and an underacknowledged dose of restraint—to fool elites into believing that they had won more than they did. By 1965, Panamanians realized that their moral victory was little more than that. Only the revival of negotiations in the 1970s saved the memory of 1964.

On the broader issue of anti-Americanism in Latin America, however, the Panama Canal riots did not completely assuage the U.S. government. To be sure, Panama's variant on anti-Americanism was a welcome counterpoint to Cuba's. It showed that, in each country, specific social and political configurations set the patterns of hostility. It also suggested that ambivalence would most likely moderate diplomats in any nonrevolutionary situation. But there, too, lay the problem. Panama, despite a similar degree of dependence on the United States, was a polar opposite to Cuba. It did not represent the rest of Latin America or even the Caribbean, any more than Cuba did. Cuba and Panama were both unique, and neither could be counted on to help to predict how other governments might express anti-Americanism. The 1965 U.S military intervention in the Dominican Republic would present a third variant of anti-Americanism, with characteristics all its own but with a more satisfying impact for Washington.

Dominican Republic, 1965
Episodic Anti-Americanism and U.S. Containment

The dominant variant of anti-Americanism in the Dominican Republic revealed itself not as an offshoot of a consistent political ideology but in a series of diffuse and ephemeral protests. Two conditions shaped what could be called episodic anti-Americanism. First, potentially anti-U.S. groups—communists and Cold Warriors, urbanites and campesinos, democrats and dictators—displayed little unity throughout Dominican history. Second, rapacious outside powers formed alliances with Dominican collaborators to exploit this internal lack of cohesion. The reaction to U.S. intervention in the 1965 civil conflict added one more episode in a tradition of protest marked by these two characteristics. That year, Dominicans quickly gained but then lost resolve against the U.S. enemy.

What was for Dominicans merely another episode in its anti-Americanism became for Washington a closure of sorts in its learning process. By the mid-1960s, as with Panama, U.S. officials aimed to craft their responses to anti-U.S. crises in keeping with national ideological variants of hostility. In the Dominican Republic, U.S. officials realized that the atomized nature of anti-Americanism made leaders vulnerable to U.S. pressure and likely to turn against one another in the long run. Also as in other anti-U.S. crises, U.S. policymakers sometimes disagreed on the methods of U.S. power but nevertheless responded to critics by reaffirming what they believed to be that power's fundamental benevolence. The unusually volatile nature of anti-Americanism in the Dominican Republic, therefore, made for one of the sharpest contrasts with the ideological resilience of the U.S. response. These conclusions, overlapping with the buildup in Vietnam, may have helped lead Washington toward a hardened, cynical approach to critics everywhere.

Empire, Dictatorship, and Atomization

From the nineteenth century to the eve of the 1965 intervention, anti-Americanism in the Dominican Republic lived many short, discon-nected lives. Hostility to the United States typically lay dormant for years, after which it would wake, thrash about, then go back to sleep. This episodic anti-Americanism was the result of centuries of internal and external pressures bearing down on any effort at forging a national identity. Internally, Dominicans were not simply divided, but atom-ized—mostly by region, class, and race. As a result, political leaders, even elites, developed a culture of fear and violence. Externally, Domini-cans, more than others in Latin America, faced the persistent rapacious-ness of several foreign powers and regularly handed the country over to one or more patrons and protectors. Together, these tendencies—atom-ization and collaboration—made Dominican national identity extremely inchoate and rendered Dominican political leaders wholly unprepared to resist U.S. influence. Finally, because Dominican anti-Americanism remained unformed as a political strategy before 1965, the U.S. govern-ment grew unresponsive to what negative sentiment there was in the country.

At the root of much of the republic's atomization was its long neglect by the Spanish crown. Ironically, for a few decades at the end of the fif-teenth century, *la Española,* or Hispaniola, the island Dominicans now share with Haitians, was "the land that Columbus loved." It served as a launching pad for the conquest of the Caribbean and was the seat of many of the hemisphere's firsts—first settlement, first university, first church. After Columbus died, however, Spaniards warred against the is-land's native Tainos, depleted its gold, and built a short-lived slave-based sugar plantation system. Runaway slaves further disrupted social peace and economic development. Then came the *coup de grâce* to the colony. On August 4, 1603, Philip II of Spain ordered the depopulation of the north coast in order to curtail the bounty of buccaneers who defied his commercial monopoly. The depopulation of 1603 had a lasting legacy, what some historians have called "the miserable century." For nearly three centuries, in fact, the colony became a sleepy economic backwater where peasants eked out a living raising cattle rather than diversifying agriculture or creating manufactures. Until the twentieth century, poor roads or no roads at all largely cut off rural areas from coastal towns, and all civil, military, and religious activity remained in the capital city.[1]

Subjection to foreign powers was constant. European buccaneers raided Dominican shores from the very beginnings of Spanish settlement. Eventually, the colony itself was in dispute. French Haiti, the western third of Hispaniola, known then as Saint Domingue, prospered while the Dominican Republic, with a lesser population density, stagnated. France took over the whole island from 1795 to 1804. From 1804 to 1821, Haitian, French, and English troops as well as the Spanish crown fought over the eastern part of Hispaniola. Finally, Dominicans declared their independence from all foreign powers in 1821. This lasted three months. In 1822 the Dominican Republic succumbed to Haitian rule, which endured for twenty-two years. A second declaration of independence then gave birth to the First Republic, which ended in 1861. That year, Dominican leaders voluntarily rejoined Spain before ultimately achieving a lasting independence in 1865.[2]

The Haitian occupation of 1821 to 1844, especially, scarred Dominican national identity. The "Black Occupation" fueled a fear of Haiti among Dominicans and forged their racial self-image as a people of supposedly non-African descent. Benjamin Green, U.S. commissioner in the Dominican Republic, remarked in 1849 that "the cruelties of the Haitians toward all who spoke the Spanish language have given such force and universality to the feeling in favor of the whites in the Dominican Republic that it is not uncommon to hear a very black negro, when taunted with his color, reply: 'Soy negro, pero negro blanco.'"[3] Already in the nineteenth century Dominicans defined themselves as white rather than black.[4] Ever since, Dominicans have felt threatened with war by Haiti's government, with economic bloodletting by Haiti's workers and settlers, and with racial degeneration through miscegenation with Haitians.[5]

The U.S. government entered the fray of Dominican foreign relations in the late nineteenth century, taking advantage of the republic's weaknesses. From 1865 on, U.S. adventurers and political figures schemed to gain land or annex the country. Not only did Dominican presidents not resist, but they repeatedly lobbied for annexation in one of the most overt displays of *entreguismo,* or "hand-overism," in Caribbean history. The collaboration of elites was so calculated to ward off internal enemies and competing foreign nations that the U.S. government seemed a rather reluctant bully in contrast. Even Ambassador Frederick Douglass, the legendary abolitionist, and the 1871 National Convention of Colored Men, approved of annexation on the grounds that any contact with

U.S. citizens could only improve bleak Dominican lives.[6] By the end of the nineteenth century, an old Dominican poem was sporting an added final line:

> Yesterday I was born Spanish
> In the afternoon I was French
> In the evening I became Haitian
> Today they say I am English
> Maybe tomorrow I'll be American.[7]

Widespread anti-Americanism did take hold in the Dominican Republic during the U.S. occupation of the country from 1916 to 1924. The Marines' rule was brutal, racist, and paternalistic, and rapacious U.S. investors took over Dominican lands during the occupation. In response, urban political and intellectual Dominican leaders organized protests and eventually negotiated a withdrawal in the early 1920s. In the countryside, most notably, a guerrilla war raged for five and a half years, a reaction to the loss of land and to Marines who frequently tortured prisoners and sent innocents to jail. Marines, often in vain pursuit, burned villages and even banned *gabillero* cigars (named after the guerrilla fighters).[8]

Yet the two major characteristics of the Republic's politics—atomization and collaboration—weakened Dominican resolve against the U.S. occupation, just as they would in future episodes. The persistent rural-urban gap, especially, reinforced the divide among Dominicans. Many in the cities showed ambivalence. The landing of the Marines on May 15, 1916, met with some physical and verbal resistance, but also with "a rash of self-criticism" in the Dominican press. Some Dominicans blamed "national character" and the corruption of politics for inviting occupation. The proclamation of U.S. military government the following November met with even less opposition. Words were often urbanites' only weapons. Historian Bruce Calder believes that elites in Santo Domingo, wrapped up in the day's liberal and positivist ideas, generally accepted the U.S. characterization of the peasant rebels as "bandits." They forged links with intellectuals and politicians elsewhere in Latin America and in the United States rather than with poor campesinos in the interior.[9]

In the countryside, meanwhile, the *gabilleros* consisted mostly of east coast peasants whom large U.S. sugar landowners had displaced. They were hardy fighters, but they proved faithful mostly to local caudillos (leaders), and their motivations ranged from national revolution to simple looting. U.S. occupiers adjusted to guerrilla warfare by bringing in more troops, turning a few Dominicans into traitors, and methodically sweeping certain areas. They quickly destroyed the rebels. Here, then, was the tragedy of Dominican anti-Americanism in a nutshell: two resistance movements, each somewhat compelling but both burning out quickly or remaining weak for lack of cooperation.[10]

Faced with the relative ineffectiveness of Dominican resistance, U.S. responses to this first episode of anti-Americanism were dismissive and self-congratulatory. Marine Colonel Joseph Pendleton believed that "95 percent" of Dominicans "have wanted just what they are now getting but have been afraid to say so, fearing the small percentage of politicos and professional disturbers." According to U.S. minister William Russell, most Dominicans thought "that present control by the United States was what the Dominican Republic needed and that petty politicians are the only people dissatisfied."[11]

For a generation following the intervention, more episodes of anti-Americanism took place, this time involving both a dictator and his democratic opposition. Hostility was especially marked in the last few years of the Machiavellian reign of Rafael Leonidas Trujillo Molina. For the vast majority of his three decades in power, in contrast, Trujillo cooperated with Washington. He showed symbolic deference to the United States, for instance by naming streets after George Washington, the U.S. Marine Corps, and U.S. diplomat Sumner Welles.[12] In a private letter to his son Ramfis, he indicated his practical view of the North: "An overwhelming majority of Americans are good people," wrote Trujillo, "and we know how a certain percentage are—perverted, bad, gangsters, etc. —but we need to get along with them." Trujillo said that it was he who controlled U.S. policy, not the other way around. His propaganda apparatus extended overseas to plant hundreds of pro-regime articles in newspapers, and he boasted of how he bribed many a U.S. lawmaker.[13]

Events in the late 1950s, however, suddenly made Trujillo a dangerous U.S. asset. In 1956, Jesús Galíndez, a Basque living in the United States and a vocal opponent of Trujillo, vanished, followed by an aviator from Oregon, Charles Murphy. The democratic Caribbean community widely perceived Trujillo to be responsible for the disappearances. In 1959, Fidel Castro took on Trujillo as an enemy and permitted an expedition to launch from Cuba's shores against the Dominican Republic.

Simultaneously, Venezuelan president Rómulo Betancourt called for the Organization of American States (OAS) to intervene diplomatically against Trujillo. Surveying this growing antidictatorial agitation, Eisenhower officials decided that opposing Trujillo would counterbalance plans to overthrow Castro. By helping to bring down authoritarian regimes from the extreme left *and* extreme right, they thought, they might maintain prestige in the hemisphere and perhaps turn more moderate anti-Americans in their favor. The last straw came in the summer of 1960, when Trujillo ordered the assassination of Betancourt and the attempt nearly succeeded. Eisenhower now judged Trujillo, long a stable if brutal ally, to be a factor of *in*stability, and the Dominican Republic a breeding ground for communism. In August 1960 Eisenhower followed the OAS's lead and broke off relations.[14]

Dominican officials reacted to the new chill in Washington with what one U.S. official called "reactive Xenophobia." As early as 1958, the Dominican Congress had ended all technical and military cooperation with the United States. By early 1960, Trujillo's head of secret police, Johnny Abbes, denounced U.S. efforts to "disrupt" Trujillo's rule. Abbes, one journalist remembered, was "violently anti-American . . . and he incited these hatreds in Trujillo." Abbes also enjoyed free rein over Radio Caribe. In January 1960, the station took a sharp turn away from its anticommunist line and started broadcasting dispatches from the Soviet news agency TASS. Trujillo then sent emissaries to Moscow and signed a nonaggression pact with Castro. Trujillo's son took a similar turn toward anti-Americanism. In 1958 Ramfis had flunked out of a college in Fort Leavenworth, Kansas. Feeling betrayed by his U.S. hosts, he commissioned translations of Egyptian leader Gamal Abdel Nasser's speeches, and, like Nasser, he initiated import substitutions to free his country from U.S. dependence. Finally, he arranged for Dominican diplomats to slight their U.S. counterparts.[15]

In 1960, the Trujillo regime stepped up its anti-American campaign. Crowds of Dominicans "spontaneously" emerged to protest U.S. policies, sometimes holding signs that maladroitly told the U.S. ambassador to COME HOME rather than GO HOME. Trujillo's press also lashed out at racism in the U.S. South—criticism unlikely to stir U.S. officials, since it came from a man who had ordered the massacre of thousands of Haitians in 1937. Trujillo himself even resorted to name calling: on CBS-TV he denounced Franklin Roosevelt and his secretary of state Cordell Hull as *pendejos*. The Dominican press lobbed insults at Eisenhower and *his* secretary of state Christian Herter, and accused Thomas Mann, already a respected leader in inter-American affairs, of bribing the OAS into breaking relations with Trujillo. "It is well known," one source said, "that Señor Mann has diabolical intentions and is effeminate, like Betancourt."[16]

Most explicitly, the anti-U.S. campaign focused on one of the republic's five bishops, a U.S. citizen named Thomas Reilly, who publicly denounced Trujillo's human rights abuses. The tyrant's attacks on Reilly called forth common stereotypes of Yankeedom: Radio Caribe characterized "Reilly the North American" as a blowhard soaked in "low-grade whiskey" who cavorted with whores and communists.[17] Organized groups harassed and stoned other priests, sacked their houses, and burned their churches. All the while the Dominican press accused the "imperialistic Yankee bishop" of hatching bomb plots.[18]

Partly because Trujillo had turned against his long-time ally, but also for deeper reasons, anti-Trujillo forces of all kinds—even after the dictator's death in 1961—were unable to unite or get past their ambivalence toward the United States. The Dominican resistance limited itself to episodic anti-Americanism partly because it lacked ideological foundations. Unlike Cubans, Dominicans had little use for the worldview of revolutionary anti-Americanism and barely any ability to follow through on it. No communist group had more than a few hundred members, plus perhaps a few thousand sympathizers. It took exiles in Mexico to found the Socialist People's Party (PSP), or Soviet-line party, in the 1940s. The other important socialist group, the Dominican People's Movement (MPD), was made up of expelled PSP members who regrouped in 1956.[19] All these groups published small, badly typeset— sometimes typewritten—newspapers, often printed clandestinely and distributed by hand. Because they had little training or money, they also failed to apply their socialist analyses to Dominican situations, rarely benefited from empirical evidence of U.S. exploitation, and never freed themselves from the hackneyed Moscow-Beijing lexicon of anti-imperialism. As one communist leader admitted, the U.S. presence in the Dominican Republic was simply not tangible enough. "Our trouble," he said, "is that we have no issues."[20] Revolutionary anti-Americanism, therefore, was not a viable strategy.

Neither was conservative anti-Americanism. Unlike Panamanians,

Dominican elites were too far from U.S. power to muster much resolve or unity. Those who ended up filling the ranks of political parties after 1961 were moderate, middling groups, not elites. Members of internal resistance groups such as the Democratic Youth (JD) or exile organizations such as the Dominican Revolutionary Party (PRD) led by Juan Bosch mostly belonged to upper-middle-class society. In such a sleepy agrarian country, those who were educated either lived in the capital, away from peasants and from the great U.S. sugar companies, or else abroad, perhaps in Puerto Rico's San Juan, or in New York City. Their fathers had mostly been either "passive anti-Trujillists," as Leandro Guzmán's was, or opponents of the U.S. occupation, like Hugo Tolentino's. Much of the republic's anti-Americanism, as a result, was abstract or cultural. The father of leftist activist Emilio Cordero, for example, was a proponent of "pure and simple" U.S. withdrawal in the 1920s, and Emilio and his peers were "*antiyanqui* from childhood on. We didn't even drink Coca-Cola." Just as they refused to dance to Trujillo's merengues, they rejected rock and roll and sat out the "twist."[21]

The novel *Over* illustrated well the muddled anti-Americanism of that majority of the resistance that was left-leaning but not radical. Published in 1940, Ramón Marrero Aristy's depiction of life on a sugar plantation was widely read among literate Dominicans. Partly because no novel during Trujillo's regime could either denounce the dictator or advance socialist principles, Marrero chose to denounce the United States. *Over* opens with Daniel Comprés taking a job as manager of a supply store on a U.S.-owned plantation. As the story unfolds, Comprés comments on the injustices of the plantation, most notably the underpayment of workers through rigged scales. Though he was in fact illustrating class struggle, said historian Roberto Cassá, Marrero "betrayed a typical motivation of the middle class, which focused on *national* demands against North American imperialism." Indeed, Comprés can feel little more than sympathy for manual workers, who are either Dominican peasants with thick accents from the Cibao (the northern mountain region) or else Haitians or West Indians (*cocolos*)—both social groups outside his own. He sulks away the hours in the store and wastes his time "obeying orders from those I wouldn't want to know and oppressing others I'd rather forget forever."[22] *Over* depicted, unwittingly, a social atomization among Dominicans that carried serious political implications.

By the time of Trujillo's assassination, therefore, Dominican politics still had achieved neither unity nor direction. Rather, from 1961 until the end of 1964, rapid ups and downs in U.S.-Dominican relations taught the U.S. government to expect inconsistent, nonideological hostility that in itself revealed social and political patterns. In the fall of 1961, for example, Santo Domingo was the scene of a spectacular showdown. Since Trujillo's assassination half a year before had unleashed occasional violence in the streets, the U.S. Navy had anchored warships a few times off the Dominican coast. When two of Trujillo's surviving brothers—known as the "Wicked Uncles"—tried to reclaim power in mid-November 1961, Secretary of State Dean Rusk announced that the U.S. government would stand for no such thing. Three U.S. ships reappeared. For a few tense days, the Dominican nation stood waiting, painfully reminded that either *trujillistas* or policymakers on the Potomac were still its masters. On November 20, the brothers left the country.

Dominican responses to this blatant gunboat diplomacy, unsurprisingly, were divided. On one hand, youth groups grew more radical. Leandro Guzmán of the Castro-inspired 14th of June, known as the 1J4, believed that "ordinary people were fooled into thinking that 'the Americans came to help us.'" The appearance of the warships made his friend Manolo Tavárez Justo, the 1J4's leader, "gloomy, crabby, full of ire and indignation."[23] The *catorcistas,* as members of the 1J4 were called, soon broke with the conservative National Civic Union (UCN). Cuba-trained hardliners took over their leadership and laid plans for guerrilla warfare.[24] On the other hand, many Dominicans expressed gratitude for U.S. protection against the "Wicked Uncles." Hundreds cheered in the streets when they saw U.S. warships, and the Dominican foreign minister at the United Nations exclaimed, "Blessed be the moment when the American fleet came to Dominican waters!"[25]

With these extreme displays of anti- and pro-U.S. sentiment, Dominicans confounded U.S. diplomats. While on a fact-finding trip for Kennedy in late 1961, writer and ambassador-to-be John Bartlow Martin happened upon a rally of Dominicans celebrating the anti-Trujillist intervention of the OAS in—of all places—Cordell Hull Plaza. He reported to Kennedy: "Before I knew what was happening, the loudspeaker announced that an OAS representative was on the balcony. Instantly the whole plaza full of people surged over and demonstrated, chanting, cheering, pleading for help. It broke up the meeting, and they would not desist until I had waved to them and got the hell out of sight. All this was embarrassing—but it was the most convincing spontaneous proof imaginable that they still look to us." Martin's first months as ambassador, in contrast, coincided with the other extreme of mass sentiment. Protesting U.S. collaboration with Trujillists, small mobs burned consulate cars and tore up U.S. flags.[26] The beleaguered Martin tried to understand these turnabouts. "Day after day *turbas* [mobs] turned into full-fledged anti-American riots at the Consulate, and on some days it almost seemed to me that the young vice consuls spent more time throwing tear gas out the windows than issuing visas. . . . The disoriented teen-agers of the Republic who had grown up under Trujillo . . . now confused liberty with license. One told my wife he liked the *Americanos* all right—it was the *Yanquis* he hated."[27] Good *americanos* versus bad *yanquis:* the linguistic dissonance was symptomatic of a state of agitation and insecurity among Dominicans who faced a U.S. government deciding the republic's future during a time of political awakening.

The administration of John Kennedy, wishing to bring order to the response to anti-Americanism, saw the Dominican Republic as a good place to try. Kennedy's aides, in contrast to Eisenhower's, asked more specific questions of the republic's politics: Who exactly were these "anti-Americans" abroad? How could they be better reached? As one of the few government entities that could offer fresh answers, the United States Information Agency (USIA) gained political clout under the young president. As a measure of that clout, Kennedy picked Edward R. Murrow, the already legendary journalist, to head the USIA. Murrow got a bigger budget, became a full participant at National Security Council (NSC) meetings, and enjoyed direct access to the Oval Office. Kennedy also minimized bureaucratic wrangling between the CIA and the State Department, sent his own envoys to gather information during crises, and made certain he was apprised of the latest polls, book distributions, and radio programs.[28] The point of all this was to identify pockets of anti-U.S. feeling and to treat them in isolation. By making polling more widespread, specific, and consistent, the Kennedy administration aimed to remove the stigma of inaccuracy from a public relations approach to anti-Americanism.[29]

Partly from these efforts, U.S. analysts learned that anti-U.S. sentiment, in Latin America at least, was most distinct and predictable among intellectuals and students. These two groups were literate and comfortable enough to take note of the intrusion of the U.S. government in their national politics, yet precarious enough to fear instability and to hope for rapid improvement. "We should take into account the traditional prejudices and stereotypes of the intellectual—his attitudes and motivations," went a typical State Department report, "not only because they represent the view of a highly articulate segment of the Latin American population, but also because they tend to form, as well as reflect, the public image of the United States as it exists in the Latin American mind." One somewhat sympathetic scholar, calling these groups "the angry left," agreed that "what they lack in numbers they make up for in tenacity." U.S. officials were poorly read in Latin American political theory and politicized fiction, but they sensed that works such as José Enrique Rodó's *Ariel* had sown the seeds of the present hostility.[30] Kennedy aides noted that, during the Eisenhower years, "the best-liked gringo in Latin America" was not the president but his "egghead" Democratic foil, Adlai Stevenson. Kennedy's own egghead was Arthur Schlesinger, Jr., who would, as Schlesinger himself suggested, "help persuade the Latinos that the new U.S. Government is not run by money-grubbing materialists."[31]

While engaging in a fair amount of babble, Kennedy reports on anti-Americanism nevertheless stressed social and psychological factors, arguing that intellectuals turned to Marxism not as a result of inductive reasoning, after accumulating evidence of U.S. imperialism, but out of emotional ambivalence. "This real or pseudo intellectual is frequently non-academic," argued one report. "While thirsting for recognition to compensate for feelings of insecurity and inferiority, he has a real and motivating fear of cultural domination by the United States, especially philosophical domination by what he considers to be a materialistic pragmatism which would deny him his spiritual eclecticism in his Marxist absolutism." Despite the breezy analysis, the U.S. government's information programs did lead to new nondidactic approaches that were open to all save unrepentant communists. For example, they gave intellectuals outlets for their work by inviting them to participate in cultural exchanges, television and radio programs, and book discussions.[32]

Students were somewhat more difficult to understand and manage. "What gives with Latin American students?" asked *Parade*. "What makes them behave the way they do? Why do they seem to hate us so deeply?" To find out, the Kennedy approach focused on training information officers and political attachés to be sensitive to the societies out of which anti-U.S. students emerged. It also targeted the more vociferous groups among the students themselves. Reports emphasized that most students were conservative, "pro-Western and noncommunist," and that anti-U.S. sentiment was mostly confined to law, economics, and humanities students. The problem was that these students were uninformed, immature, and parochial. They tended, for instance, "to equate the free enterprise system with robber baron capitalism of the history books." And students, more than intellectuals, gave anti-Americanism a sense of urgency for the narrowest of reasons: "They are prone to feel that only they can make a revolution," wrote one scholar, "and that they must do it before they graduate."[33]

In response, the U.S. government was surprisingly precise and upbeat. It listed the names of leaders and the number of members for even the most insignificant student group in almost every Latin American university. In 1962 an Interagency Youth Committee (IYC) began coordinating activities aimed at forming a greater number of friendly leaders. In January 1964 its members took a twelve-day trip to seven Latin American countries. "Students are the most important group that we must reach in Latin America," said the committee upon its return. These youths were so naïve, it reported, that they were anti-U.S. and often Marxist just because they were anti-establishment or antigovernment. "It is essential that the present student leaders be made aware of the true nature of American institutions and ideals before they become committed to an alternative philosophy." The teams assigned to the various countries were not doing this job, the IYC added.[34]

Polls seemed to suggest that the Dominican Republic was one place where such hopes for the peaceful rollback of anti-Americanism should be directed. The USIA's Murrow sent Kennedy a survey conducted in April 1962 on the "attitudes, hopes and fears" of 814 Dominicans. It announced that "the United States is phenomenally popular with the Dominican people." The numbers were indeed astounding. On a popularity scale of 1 to 10, Dominicans from the city and country gave the United States a 9.1, the highest rating any nation had ever given any other in the history of such polls. Kennedy personally earned a 9.4 rating, and three out of four Dominicans gave him a perfect 10. In contrast, Soviet leader Nikita Khrushchev scored a 1.0 and Fidel Castro a 0.3. Only 1 percent said relations with the United States were "bad," and fewer than 1 percent said they were "very bad." Dominicans also gave sterling marks to the Alliance for Progress, Cold War anticommunism, and the U.S. "political system and way of life."[35]

Yet Murrow's cautious assessment of these polls presaged the rapid disillusion among Kennedy liberals that would soon follow. Murrow noted how this peak in pro-U.S. feeling was tied to fleeting circumstances. It came on the heels of the ouster of Trujillo's brothers and the peaceful election of exiled resistance leader Juan Bosch, both events that boosted Dominican confidence in self-determination. Furthermore, Murrow realized that Dominicans held soaring expectations for material improvement. The U.S. government, he counseled, would be wise not to associate itself too closely with those expectations, lest it be blamed if— and more probably when—they were not met.[36] Murrow proved to be no fool. In 1964, in a now typically disdainful study after Bosch's democratic rule ended seven months later in a coup, the USIA reached the conclusion that Dominicans maintained an "underdeveloped mentality" ruled by emotions that made them "suspicious," "passive," "fatalistic," and subject to "psychological panic."[37]

Ambassador Martin, too, came to share this bleak perspective. He learned (from whom it is not clear) that riots were standardized—they cost from $150 to $500, depending on the stunts performed. And they were less than genuine—rioters had often no idea what they were protesting, or else they mixed cries of "Down with Americans!" with those of "Up with Americans!" Martin lost his patience quickly. After rioters threatened his own children, "I tried to talk to them, but it was no use. They seemed young, brainless, posing as intellectuals but only mouthing canned slogans and speeches." He lectured one protest leader that "teaching teen-age children to go into the streets and throw rocks at other children was doing his country no service. They were untroubled by this." Martin characterized even the pro-U.S. sentiment of Dominicans as a deep-rooted defect of character. "Despite sporadic riots led by leftist agitators, the Dominican people . . . have clung to their somewhat childlike faith in us despite the Marine occupation and what many regard as our support of Trujillo. . . . They tend toward dependency."[38] He wrote Kennedy, "Somewhere somehow there is in this country a fatal flaw. . . . Dominicans time and again have seemed determined to tear their country to pieces or sell it and give it away." "This is a sick destroyed nation," Martin once concluded ominously, "ravaged by a thirty-years war, to be occupied and reconstituted."[39]

U.S. officials were in no mood to occupy or "reconstitute" the Dominican Republic in late 1963. Instead, reflecting the gradual hardening that ushered in the Johnson administration, they acquiesced in the coup against Bosch on September 25 with enough subtlety to minimize anti-U.S. sentiment. While there is no direct evidence that U.S. officials incited or assisted in the overthrow of Bosch, as in other Latin American situations they practiced intervention through nonintervention, in this case by allowing anti-Bosch forces to gather strength. In public Kennedy denounced the coup. But in private he confided to advisers that it would be only a few months before he recognized the military-oligarchy alliance which had overthrown Bosch; this would enable him to continue playing to the middle.[40] Department of State officials, meanwhile, kept Martin purposefully uninformed because he had invested too much of his own prestige in Bosch's survival (he even offered to call in U.S. troops to prevent a coup; Bosch declined).[41]

The strategy worked. There were no street protests. The traditionally conservative residents of Santiago, the country's second city, even celebrated Bosch's downfall. This stood in sharp contrast to the three days of mourning in the Dominican Republic that followed the Kennedy assassination two months later. Embassy officials cabled back that their manipulation of anti-Americanism had revived *entreguismo* in their favor: "We do not believe events of last two days have united country in nationalistic, anti-US sympathies. . . . US prestige has never been higher."[42]

Some anti-Americanism, no matter how unfocused, was bound to emerge from such a volatile situation. Bosch's incorruptible pluralism shaped a post-coup radicalization, and this in two ways. First, it fostered a freedom of expression and political activity that allowed the increasingly revolutionary 1J4 as well as the PSP and the MPD to function openly (although Bosch's security maintained the proscription against burning the U.S. flag). UCN or 1J4 rallies simultaneously denounced Bosch and "Yankee imperialism."[43] One State Department official who interviewed "communists" during Bosch's tenure reported that, to them, "all Americans were considered CIA and FBI men who were out to betray any Dominican they met."[44] Second, Bosch's social democratic views nudged mainstream politics enough to the left to force radical groups to further extremes. If the 1963 constitution espoused land reform, for instance, the next step appeared to be confiscation. The abandonment of Bosch's program after the overthrow only confirmed radicals' belief that moderation was a losing strategy.

By 1965, extreme conditions seemed to lay the groundwork for another episode of anti-Americanism. First, foreign powers still threatened the country: U.S. diplomats hovered over Dominican politics, U.S. capitalists controlled its sugar, and even Dominican exiles and Soviet bloc–trained radicals were its most active political leaders. The popular support on which modern anti-Americanism depended for its legitimacy as an indigenous, noncommunist phenomenon still did not exist. Second, in the early 1960s, Dominican leaders still embodied deep social divisions—between city and country, rich and poor, exiles and dissidents, democrats and would-be autocrats—that inhibited anti-U.S. political alliances. The U.S. response only grew harder as these conditions worsened. Confirming the contempt that U.S. policymakers had long had for Dominican leaders, Kennedy abandoned his crusade to make the Dominican Republic a success story in the struggle against anti-Americanism, and Johnson made no plans to revive it.

Stumbling into Anti-Americanism: The Intervention

In April 1965, armed U.S. intervention in a Dominican civil conflict caused an unprecedented and sudden surge in anti-U.S. resentment. The condemnation that the intervention sparked was so virulent that it seemed anti-Americanism would for once spread to the entire nation, persist for years, and possibly turn all of Latin America against Washington. Lyndon Johnson's government had virtually created anti-Americanism out of nothing and stirred up a largely avoidable resentment. Theodore Draper contrasted the Dominican intervention with the Cuban Revolution by calling the former "a self-inflicted wound." He was right. Johnson's men initially proved misinformed, reactionary, and oblivious to the subtleties of Dominican conflicts and ambivalences.[45]

The Dominican crisis began as a largely internal affair. On one side were the "rebels," mostly members of the PRD, Bosch's party, now led by José Rafael Molina Ureña. They declared themselves "Constitutionalists" because they demanded the return of Bosch from exile and the restoration of his 1963 constitution. On the other side were reactionary military leaders, concentrated around the "Loyalist" Elias Wessin y Wessin, director of the Armed Forces Training Center (CEFA) and leader of the 1963 coup against Bosch.[46] Wessin's men protected the ruling triumvirate, now largely controlled by pro-U.S. businessman Donald Reid Cabral. In the spring of 1965, rumors of coup attempts wafted through Santo Domingo like furtive Caribbean winds. Suddenly, on April 24, pro-Bosch junior officers rose up against Reid and Wessin. Lack of preparation on all sides, including among the perpetrators of the coup, led within hours to a revolt with many leaders and few clear aims, but with real potential to destroy the unmotivated military. Constitutionalists established themselves at the downtown presidential palace, and Loyalists gathered at the San Isidro air force base outside Santo Domingo. Each side issued its own radio broadcasts claiming that it enjoyed the support of the people.[47]

Until the U.S. military intervened on April 28, anti-Americanism had not been part of any side's rhetoric. Radical groups especially, though deeply hostile to the United States, refrained from speaking of imperialism and focused on the struggle of the "people" against Wessin and Reid. But as mobs chased down policemen in the streets, U.S. officials increasingly feared a takeover from groups on the far left. Small to tiny organizations such as the 1J4, the PSP, and the MPD passed out weapons and set up roadblocks downtown, an area that contained critical infrastructure as well as government, financial, and press buildings.[48]

Except for these most radical groups, Dominicans on both sides suggested that the U.S. government intercede in their favor. It was predictable, of course, that Loyalists would ask for U.S. help. At noon on April 25, before Reid stepped down under Constitutionalist pressure, he asked U.S. embassy officials to "intervene." Throughout that afternoon, right-wing parties and military leaders requested meetings with embassy officials and wondered what sort of support they could expect from them. The following day Wessin and Air Force chief of staff Juan de los Santos flatly asked for U.S. troops.[49] U.S. officials made no commitments.

More surprising, Constitutionalists also gave signals that a U.S. intervention would be welcome—provided it was in support of Bosch. The initial leader of the pro-Bosch officers, Lieutenant Colonel Miguel Ángel Hernando Ramírez, was aware that U.S. officials knew of the conspiracies against Wessin. He hoped they would at least not intervene if presented with a fait accompli. When U.S. troops started landing, other rebels still believed that a U.S. intervention might restore Bosch and the 1963 constitution. Captain Lorenzo Galvá, for instance, like Hernando Ramírez, believed that the revolt was in no way anti-U.S. because it aimed to purge the military of corruption and in fact attain U.S.-type military professionalism. A U.S. intervention placing Bosch back in office "would have been applauded by the people," said Galvá.[50] Even Bosch himself equivocated in the first days of the revolt. "People are disappointed by the neutrality of the U.S. government," he fumed. "The Dominican people are fighting . . . for something they learned from American history. They are fighting the same fight Washington and Jefferson fought."[51] None of these statements was an open invitation for landing U.S. troops, but they suggested that Dominicans on the left were ambivalent about intervention and held out hope that the U.S. embassy might defend democracy and constitutionality.

Ambassador William Tapley Bennett failed to appreciate such delicate *entreguismo* during a fateful meeting with Constitutionalist leaders on April 27. By this time, Loyalist ships and planes had been shelling the rebels for twenty-four hours. The rebels thought it was only a matter of time—indeed, hours—before Wessin's tanks rolled into the city from San Isidro and crushed them. Intending to ask the U.S. ambassador to mediate his surrender, rebel-proclaimed President Molina Ureña walked up the embassy steps with all the dignity he could muster. As one U.S. observer noted, Molina was about to commit "the cardinal political crime for Santo Domingo"—negotiation—and he knew it.[52]

"Tap" Bennett, however, was anathema to Constitutionalist sensitivities. The ambassador was a gentleman-diplomat from Georgia with a reputation for mixing only with the crème of Dominican society, business leaders, and military officers. Bennett did make some trips to the countryside, as Martin had, but not many. With the most unfortunate timing, just before the coup broke out the ambassador had been summoned to Washington to talk about how to handle all the coup rumors. Rushing back to Santo Domingo on April 27, Bennett agreed to meet with Molina that same day.[53]

U.S. versions of the meeting suggest that Bennett enraged Dominican leaders by committing—again—intervention through nonintervention. The State Department gave Bennett room for interpreting instructions. He was to contact "military leaders of contending forces and suggest to them [the] establishment of [a] military junta to act as [the] provisional government." But he was not to "become involved in [the] details of [the] formation of [a] junta." Bennett swore he followed the guidelines to the letter, suggesting only that the political leaders "approach [the] other side for talks" and that military counterparts "get together." Bennett declined to attend those talks and considered himself magnanimous, since Molina had walked in looking "nervous and dejected."[54] A few months later, when U.S. Senator William Fulbright grilled Bennett during hearings, the ambassador explained that the rebels had "wanted us to negotiate for them a victory which they hadn't won." A little irritated, he told Fulbright, "I don't see why it is always our fault when other people don't act responsibly." Fulbright pressed him further, charging that instructions had not enjoined Bennett from being present at talks but only directed him to avoid forming a new government. "All right, sir, I will take that," said Bennett.[55]

Constitutionalists considered Bennett's conduct at the meeting inexcusably "rude" (grosero), and the episode showed how U.S. officials who misunderstood cultural sore spots could set off anti-Americanism.[56] The Dominicans were not so much bothered by Bennett's refusal to mediate as they were by his cavalier dismissal of their chances for success. They agreed that these chances were low, but in the highly gendered social code of the Dominican military, it was a great insult to disparage a soldier's ability—or worse, his willingness—to fight.

All Dominican accounts concur that it was a emotional meeting. "I will never forget that moment of shame. It was the decisive moment of the war," recalled Constitutionalist chief of security Luis Lajara. Lajara refused to check his weapon at the embassy door and so missed the meeting. Yet he quoted Bennett lecturing the Dominicans: "Before you launched the revolution, you should have known you couldn't win it. Now it's too late. You started this, and you're responsible for everything that's happened. You hold in your hands the key. Go see Wessin yourselves. You are finished." "Tears of shame" welled up in rebel eyes, said Lajara, adding that Bennett had missed "the opportunity to save his country from the loss of prestige it would then suffer in the eyes of the world."[57]

The man who most embodied the ambivalence and instability of episodic anti-Americanism was Francisco Caamaño Deño, a colonel who took over rebel military leadership right before the April 27 meeting. Some saw in Caamaño another Fidel Castro because he was a good orator and a willful leader. But Caamaño lacked the strong desire for social justice, the ability to sustain contradictory views, and the sheer physical and intellectual stamina of Castro. Also, as his nephew and confidant Claudio Caamaño later recalled, "Francis never had an anti–North American feeling before North Americans invaded the country."[58]

The United States, however, had helped breed in Caamaño a great conflict: his experience there made him a military man but also reinforced his distaste for authority. During the 1916–1924 occupation, the Marines had made Caamaño's father a member of the National Police. After that, Fausto Caamaño rose to become one of Trujillo's right-hand men. Francisco resented his distant, authoritarian father, yet desired to impress him. A friend remembered that Francisco grew up hearing Trujillo atrocity stories and "lived in frustration, bitterness, and guilt, which were reflected in his unstable and rebellious military career."[59] To discipline a son who preferred cockfighting to studying, his father gave Francisco what Dominicans considered punishment—Marine training in the United States. It worked. Caamaño came back a loyal officer. In the early 1960s he was a *casco blanco,* a member of the republic's white-helmeted riot squads trained by Los Angeles policemen. He participated in the repression of *catorcistas* with whom he would later make alliances. As *Life* magazine explained, Caamaño's "own inner turmoil seems to symbolize that of the country itself."[60]

Caamaño's version of the embassy meeting made the key accusation that Bennett not only refused to intervene but maintained "that we should capitulate." One rebel wrote that Bennett's remarks enraged Caamaño, who banged his fist on the table before he marched out, pledging to fight to the death. His nephew remembered that Francisco was equally ashamed of the subservience of Molina. "You must understand that that [capitulation] is not an honorable course for men like us," Caamaño explained to a Puerto Rican radio station. "Naturally, I very much regretted that this should have happened, but of course it does not change our opinion concerning the people of the United States." He called the United States "the country that sets the example of democracy for the world," in contrast to Cuba, "a tyrannical regime."[61]

Bennett's interpretation of his instructions allowed rebels to demonize him. Episodic anti-Americanism had emerged from a familiar dynamic: the slightest U.S. arrogance in such a volatile political environment had caused hostility to shoot up. But the shallow roots of that hostility meant that Dominican leaders needed to care for it consistently, which was not likely. U.S. officials, as a result, rarely took such sentiment seriously, thus whipping it up to even greater heights.

As fate would have it, the rest of the day's events completed Caamaño's instant transformation into the Constitutionalists' caudillo.

While Molina and other civilian leaders walked out of the meeting and immediately sought diplomatic asylum, Caamaño's military went on to confront Loyalists with near-suicidal resolve. With miraculous luck, they bottled up Duarte Bridge to keep Wessin's tanks out of downtown Santo Domingo. Caamaño then set aside his ideological differences with socialists and met with 1J4, MPD, and PSP leaders to coordinate a resistance to land invasion. By the next day, April 28, 1965, downtown Santo Domingo was rebel territory. Constitutionalists were hemmed in on all sides, but at least they held the core neighborhood. Caamaño's political star rose to rival Bosch's, who remained in Puerto Rico.[62]

U.S. observers, meanwhile, nervously assessed the level of anti-U.S. sentiment. Bennett heard conservative Dominican friends and overeager CIA operatives tell him chilling tales about Dominicans holding summary executions in the streets and parading decapitated heads on pikes. Bennett believed the reports. In a teleconference with the White House, he and aides warned, "We should bear in mind that we are dealing with mad dogs now as regards leftist forces."[63] He also used stories of snipers shooting at the embassy (which were true) as evidence that communists had taken over (they had not). Both Bennett and Johnson fed this apocryphal material to the press. Tales of terror tapped into several U.S. fears which had become prominent in this period of anti-U.S. rioting: anticommunist and anti-insurrectional paranoia; an obsession with race wars; and a certainty that Latin Americans envied and hated U.S. citizens.[64]

Events at the Embajador Hotel helped cement the perception among U.S. observers that revolutionary anti-Americanism was an alarming possibility at the time. The Embajador was among the most posh of establishments, located next to a polo field in what were then the outskirts of Santo Domingo. U.S. citizens were used to congregating there. On April 27 they rushed to it in large numbers when Dominicans started shooting other Dominicans in the streets. Many U.S. citizens felt they were, as the State Department said, the "logical next target" of violence.[65] The Embajador was the focal point for the evacuation of U.S. citizens, and all went as planned until Constitutionalist bands stormed the hotel. The men with guns were hunting the hated anticommunist Rafael Bonilla Aybar, and rebel radio had announced that he was at the Embajador. The rebels lined up evacuees-in-waiting along the walls and occasionally shot into the ceiling out of frustration at not finding "Bonillita."[66]

The fright of U.S. civilians during the episode was understandable, but they also wrongly jumped to the conclusion that Dominicans had turned their hatred against them. One New York businessman who went through the ordeal in the Embajador lobby concluded that the rebels "knew we were Americans and they were absolutely delighted that we were terrified." As a scholar later noted, however, U.S. witnesses and officials failed to put the episode into perspective "by noting that this kind of incident is endemic to revolutions, by emphasizing that no one had been harmed, and by pointing out that the rebels had not been motivated by anti-Americanism but by factional animosity."[67] The rebels had indeed harmed no one there, and both sides in the conflict reassured U.S. officials that they had ordered troops to avoid endangering U.S. citizens and even to help evacuate them.[68]

Some in the U.S. government eventually realized that there had been an overreaction. In July, Fulbright again dressed down Bennett, this time concerning the Embajador:

> *Bennett:* [The rebels] were shooting all through the crowd. . . . I do not believe that on their arrival they said get out of the way, because they began shooting almost as they arrived.
> *Fulbright:* They didn't shoot at any Americans, did they?
> *Bennett:* Sir, they were shooting all through the crowd . . .
> *Fulbright:* Did they shoot a single American?
> *Bennett:* No, it is miraculous not an American was wounded, but there was—
> *Fulbright:* [interrupting] Someone ventured the view here the other day that in all the numerous Latin American revolutions including the Dominican Republic there were no American civilians, I am not including Marines who are out there fighting, but in these uprisings they never shoot Americans.[69]

The appearance of unrestrained anti-Americanism, however, gave Washington an excuse for political and military intervention the following day. Dean Rusk suggested using the fact that Dominicans had fired on the U.S. embassy as an excuse to control the rest of Santo Domingo and thus act against any communist takeover. The strategy, he said, "would give us intrusion into the city but still on the theory on which we are presently there" (i.e., for the purpose of evacuating U.S. and foreign nationals). On May 2, during a televised address to the nation, President Johnson declared that it was only because of the landing of U.S. troops that no U.S. citizens had been harmed.[70]

"They'll be stoning U.S. Embassies all over," sighed a Latin American diplomat after hearing that Johnson had ordered a massive landing of U.S. forces in Santo Domingo.[71] Indeed, Latin American reaction was "almost wholly negative," according to U.S. monitors of foreign press opinion. Editorials ran ten to one against the intervention, and even many conservative media outlets opposed it. And they—whoever "they" were—*did* stone embassies all over. Almost every Latin American capital in early May was the scene of violent protests. Demonstrations also took place in Tokyo, New Delhi, The Hague, Paris, and Toronto.[72]

Critics throughout the world and especially in the Western Hemisphere condemned the U.S. action on several grounds. First among these was that it violated international laws on nonintervention in civil struggles and, more broadly, the principle of self-determination. Second, anchoring U.S. gunboats off the coast was virtually a parody of an outmoded style of diplomacy. Third, the U.S. government had acted unilaterally, which was against hemispheric agreements, and had consulted the OAS only after it parachuted in troops. Last, Johnson offered little evidence when he claimed that the pro-Bosch rebellion "was taken over and really seized and placed into the hands of a band of Communist conspirators."[73]

After the troops landed, more allegations followed, most notably that the Johnson administration was being disingenuous about ultimate goals. U.S. forces, critics said, pretended to be neutral in the intervention when they were clearly helping Wessin regroup, and spoke of keeping the peace but allowed Loyalists to commit further atrocities. One Santo Domingo waiter upbraided Dan Kurzman of the *Washington Post:* "If the troops hadn't come, Wessin would probably have taken over the whole city. But why did you have to take sides against us?" Such criticism was warranted, since fighting by proxy had long been the U.S. intent. Days into the intervention, Secretary of Defense Robert McNamara suggested that U.S. forces "gradually help Wessin build up his forces during the cease fire—get him a little equipment, a little food, a little medicine—so we have something to offset the Bosch forces during the OAS negotiations." Gregorio Selser, the Argentine chronicler of U.S. "dirty wars" against Latin America, now had enough material to add a third episode to his first two books, on U.S. interventions in Guatemala in 1954 and the Bay of Pigs in 1961.[74]

U.S. officials also faced suddenly polarized impressions of the United States among Dominicans. On the right, as was to be expected, the military and Loyalist civilians wholeheartedly supported U.S. actions.[75] Normally Washington may have been grateful for the vote of confidence, but such blatant *entreguismo* caused discomfort among U.S. policymakers eager to hold up a façade of neutralism. Thomas Mann, now under-secretary of state for inter-American affairs, was embarrassed. On May 2 he wrote to the embassy to get Wessin to abandon the "idea that [the] U.S. government is supporting him." "FYI," he added, "it would be particularly helpful if he could be persuaded to stop playing the 'Star Spangled Banner' over San Isidro Radio Station."[76]

Among many other Dominicans, however, the landing of U.S. troops produced the classic catch-22 of anti-Americanism: it sparked antagonism that forced the troops to stay to help contain that very antagonism. "Two weeks after the first American troop landings in Santo Domingo," wrote Tad Szulc in the *New York Times*, "the United States is facing a surge of anti-American sentiment here. Virtually no such hostility existed here before the landings."[77] Caamaño had warned the U.S. government to withdraw "so that the nationalization of the Dominican people does not transform itself into anti–North Americanism." Because the 82nd Airborne had strayed from its original stated purpose—protecting U.S. lives—the struggle for constitutionality was now a *guerra patria*, a war for the fatherland against an external enemy. Rebels could now portray Loyalists with the imagery of *entreguismo*—as playing the lackey or bootblack of imperialism, selling out the fatherland, and so on. Constitutionalist leader José Francisco Peña Gómez argued that "*antiyanquismo* was a sentiment only among college students and a few leftist parties. Our great masses and even our professional class were definitely pro–North American. This intervention, with its abuses and outrages, had made our people radically anti-Yankee."[78]

With a war for national liberation in mind, many Constitutionalist journalists began to function as military propagandists. Mainstream dailies such as *El Caribe* and *El Listín Diario* abandoned the Colonial Zone (another name for downtown Santo Domingo), which became vulnerable to firebrands who sympathized with Caamaño but operated largely beyond his control. Caamaño therefore had to count on the most vociferous media outlets to broadcast what were often coded instructions to his rebel fighters, while he simultaneously denied that these outlets spoke for him.[79] Among the more radical of these was *El 1J4*. "Yankee

Imperialism Is the Common Enemy of the Peoples of Asia, Africa, and Latin America," ran a typical headline. There were some issues in which all the articles targeted U.S. forces rather than Wessin or the Inter-American Peace Force (IAPF), as the joint U.S.-OAS troops came to be called. Every issue carried a listing of Dominicans killed by IAPF snipers or bazookas, and another of houses occupied or destroyed.[80] Meanwhile, Radio Santo Domingo, the rebel voice countering Wessin's Radio San Isidro, reached the illiterate with broadcasts about "gringos" with "aromatic cigarettes, pockets full of dollars, hard whisky."[81]

Caamaño's unofficial mouthpiece, La Nación, also alleged U.S. atrocities on a daily basis. On one occasion, for instance, it ran an editorial describing how two U.S. paratroopers had killed an eighteen-year-old Dominican for refusing to find prostitutes for them. That same issue accused U.S. snipers of shooting at Dominicans and then at the ambulance that took the wounded away. A week later the paper accused U.S. forces of killing a major rebel leader by shooting him in the back. (According to U.S. columnist Drew Pearson, Bosch had phoned in instructions on the killing of an unnamed rebel leader: "See that he is shot in the back," said Bosch, "and then announce to the press that the Americans shot him.") It once ran a photo of U.S. soldiers with a caption calling them "angels of evil, companions of Lucifer." Another caption termed them "the personification of the plague of the locusts." Rumors that U.S. troops had ransacked an agrarian institute and fouled it with feces made for especially memorable copy. On yet another day, according to La Nación, U.S. forces had traded food to the hungry in exchange for rum and soft drinks, and had withheld food from women unless they washed and ironed the soldiers' clothes.[82]

The radicalized Constitutionalist press also glorified rebel violence. One radio broadcaster entreated his listeners to "fire on Yankee invaders who may be outside of [the] neutral zone; all of [the] people should keep watch on Yankees and all their cunning maneuvers. Yankee troops must leave our country. . . . Kill foreign invaders and their lackeys!"[83] "How beautiful to see fifteen-year-old boys standing behind machine guns!" exclaimed Radio Santo Domingo, even during cease-fires.[84]

Despite their anger, Constitutionalists also stressed that their side was fundamentally pro-U.S. in its values and goals. Rebels, for instance, attempted to conquer the U.S. public by dividing it. "We tried to attack the most radical [U.S.] interventionists," recalled Foreign Minister Jottin

Cury, "and not touch the other, more liberal group."[85] One rebel spokesman, for instance, openly congratulated the U.S. press for criticizing
Johnson's overkill. "You reporters saw through the brainwashing of the
American government. I am recommending that we strike a medal for
the American reporters who covered this story." Others drew up a list of
perceived sympathizers, which included not only Fulbright and journalists Tad Szulc and Dan Kurzman, but also progressives such as Marian
Anderson, Robert Oppenheimer, Marlon Brando, Sidney Poitier, and
even Charlton Heston, known back then as a supporter of Martin Luther
King.[86] Finally, Constitutionalists hoped to point out contradictions between U.S. ideals and actions in the republic. A Radio Santo Domingo
broadcast on July 5 commenting on the Fourth of July, for example, accused the U.S. government of "betraying its own Declaration of Independence" by acting against a revolution that was fighting to defend the
same principles. One rebel editorial bore the title, "Thomas Jefferson
Was a Constitutionalist."[87]

At a broader social level, the intervention strengthened bonds among
Dominicans. It did so because U.S. military strategy centered around
closing off the Colonial Zone from the rest of the city and frisking everyone who went in and out. The unintended result was to foster a rare
sense of unity, civic responsibility, and cultural experimentation among
the enclosed rebel community.[88] Denizens of the Colonial Zone needed
food, water, sanitation, and electricity. The claustrophobia and scarcity
that resulted only heightened creativity and sacrifice, ideal sustenance
for socialist communitarianism. Rebel leader Fidelio Despradel, who
lived within the enclosure, felt he was witnessing nothing less than "a
new type of relation between human beings." Even Peace Corps volunteers living in the Colonial Zone, inspired by its atmosphere, began to
criticize the intervention.[89]

The intervention also restructured and radicalized the politics of anti-
Americanism, as parties weeded out their least committed members.
The three socialist organizations on the Dominican political landscape
—the 1J4, the PSP, and the MPD—all had feared that coup rumors were
an "imperialist trick" or a CIA plot to draw them out and destroy them.[90]
Now that they knew better, they sought to lead the leftward surge in Dominican politics. Right after the coup, on April 25, *catorcistas* vowed to
join the rebellion. The MPD officially aligned its ideology with that of
China in 1965. In August the new young leaders of the PSP rid them-

selves of old guard critics of Castro and changed their name to the Dominican Communist Party (PCD).[91] And most important, on May 3, 1965, a legislative chamber of Constitutionalists, with the blessing of Bosch in Puerto Rico and of many of these far-left groups, elected Caamaño its president. The unity among leftist Dominicans that had been so elusive in the past now seemed an ironic result of Washington's anticommunist zeal.

"How the hell can I get my troops out of this damn mess?" exclaimed a harried Lyndon Johnson a few days into the occupation. The feeling of being beleaguered hung heavy around Washington. With his flair for self-persecution, Johnson called himself "the most denounced man in the world."[92] "I am seeing the pattern and I just cannot be silent," he told National Security Adviser McGeorge Bundy. "What they are doing in La Paz, Bolivia, what they are doing in Mexico City, and what are doing in Vietnam and the Dominican Republic is not totally unrelated." The House Foreign Affairs Committee even felt the need to declare that people all over the world ought to stop assaulting U.S. embassies.[93] U.S. officials were particularly concerned with the connections between the Dominican intervention and their escalating commitment in Southeast Asia. On April 29 Kennedy aide Richard Goodwin expressed the worry to Johnson that Vietnam and the Dominican Republic were both raising fears of U.S. imperialism. He brought up the Caracas incident of 1958: "We can remember the enormous furor that was stirred up when Eisenhower simply announced that troops were on the alert to protect Nixon's life." Suppressing popular revolts anywhere, said Goodwin, aroused anti-imperialism everywhere. "Hostile people will use [the Dominican Republic] as evidence that we are doing the same thing [in Vietnam]."[94]

By the first few weeks of May, the president realized that, whether or not he was right about communism in the Dominican Republic, U.S. troops had stumbled into a civil conflict and turned it into an anti-U.S. war. Johnson's occupation of Santo Domingo allowed the Loyalists to regroup, isolated but fortified the Constitutionalists, and redirected much of the hatred that these groups felt for each other toward Johnson, his ambassador, and his troops. In a classic U.S. response to anti-Americanism, Johnson expressed frustration buoyed by a sense of resilience: "I don't always know what's right," he confided to aide Abe Fortas and McNamara, "and I get misled. Like sending troops in there to Santo Domingo. But the man that misled me was Lyndon *Johnson,* nobody else! I did that! I can't blame a damn human. And I don't want any of them to take credit for it. . . . And I'll ride it out."[95]

Salvaging the Occupation: The Pullout

During the rest of 1965 and through the summer of 1966, Johnson did ride it out—and with relative grace, considering the blundering of the intervention itself. His administration defused the Dominican crisis by making use of the increasingly developed responses that Washington had been revising since 1958. Many of the same players who had teamed up for the Panama crisis of 1964 unlimbered an equally quick and even more multifaceted strategy in 1965—one that placated opponents at home and abroad, yet accomplished the basic goals of avoiding a communist revolution and installing a stable regime. U.S. policymakers understood that radicals and elites in the Dominican Republic were few and divided. They also saw that noncommunist critics harbored ambivalences, had few resources to articulate anti-Americanism, and were growing bitter and disunited as the crisis dragged on. Attrition worked on its own, but U.S. strategy encouraged it, exposing and exploiting flaws in Dominican anti-Americanism.

The earliest and, to Lyndon Johnson, the most crucial victory against anti-Americanism was the safeguarding of support at home. One problem facing the president was that sending troops to the Dominican Republic had more clearly been an "aggression" than had been the situation in Panama, where U.S. troops plausibly claimed self-defense. Also, while the president could act boldly since the 1964 election was behind him, he still feared a domestic backlash if Santo Domingo went the way of Cuba. As Johnson said right before going on national television to explain that U.S. troops were changing their goals from protecting U.S. lives to avoiding social revolution, "When I do what I am about to do, there'll be a lot of people in this hemisphere I can't live with, but if I don't do it there'll be a lot of people in this country I can't live with."[96] Domestic critics trumped foreign ones.

Johnson called together key members of Congress on the evening of April 28, by which time he had already received a written request from Dominicans asking for intervention and had decided to grant it. He avoided confronting reluctant members of Congress with a fait accompli. Yet he conducted the meeting like a sales pitch rather than a discussion. There was "no alternative" to landing troops, he said. "We can't waste one moment in taking action."[97] Possessing only the information that Johnson gave them about communist dangers, all those at the meeting agreed within minutes to send troops. Johnson was proud that "I have just taken an action that will prove that Democratic presidents can deal with Communists as strongly as Republicans."[98]

His political instincts were right. By the first few days of May, Johnson had garnered the blessings of such conservatives as Richard Nixon and Barry Goldwater, and of as many as 76 percent of U.S. citizens polled. Opposition from the *New York Times* and *Washington Post* still bothered Johnson, but supporters such as *Time, Newsweek,* and *U.S. News and World Report* had more than five times the circulation of those liberal dailies. When Fulbright held hearings later in the summer to express his own criticism of the intervention, senators were so divided that no report ever emerged. In fact, in September 1965 the House overwhelmingly passed a resolution that supported the unilateral U.S. use of force (the vote was 312 to 52).[99] Aides wrote of the president's rising star in the Deep South, where "even the rabid racists who hate Johnson for Selma [a site of civil rights protest], etc. acknowledged wryly that they are all for him on this."[100]

Former President Eisenhower, especially, admired the White House's strategy of intervention, in which he noted three components: military, diplomatic, and informational.[101] The man who had faced the Caracas riots and the Cuban upheaval grasped the growing complexity and effectiveness of the U.S. government's responses to foreign hostility. He also correctly identified the three components.

Of these, the military was the first, the most important, and the most successful. The military goal of U.S. planners was to create a plausible equilibrium between Constitutionalists and Loyalists. Initially U.S. troops halted the Constitutionalists and, in the process, any chance of a communist takeover. But they soon also had to prevent Wessin's military from moving in on the Colonial Zone and finishing off the rebels. A total Wessin victory, Johnson feared, would plunge the country into another dictatorship, darken prospects for democracy, or foment an insurrection—and of course make him look bad.[102]

The U.S. forces' General Bruce Palmer thus made what he called "the key military move in the entire Dominican venture." He established the Line of Communication and the International Zone, which together created a nominally neutral cordon of security around Santo Domingo. The Line of Communication, or "LOC," effectively locked 80 percent of Constitutionalists between the cordon and the Caribbean, thus allowing Wessin to make brutal sweeps of the rest of the city and rout out the other 20 percent. Palmer, in other words, kept Wessin from crushing Caamaño's hopes for victory without crushing Caamaño. Scholar Michael Kryzanek noted that the creation of the neutral zone "reveal[ed] a more sophisticated approach to unrest than had previously been seen in the region."[103]

The move also took full advantage of a traditional Dominican weakness: the urban-rural gap. U.S. officials rejoiced that anti-Americanism was largely limited to the capital. In early May, consulate and intelligence staff fanned out around Santiago and La Vega, some on bicycles, others by foot, and reported that all was quiet in the countryside. Sympathies were, according to one CIA report, "apparently pro-Loyalist and pro-U.S." "If the Marines could come through the area," the report even suggested, "it would bolster morale even more and be the finish to any communist sympathy."[104] Palmer noted two features of the countryside. First, "the country [was] tense and wary, watching what was going on in the capital and verifying the saying that 'as Santo Domingo goes, so goes the Dominican Republic.'" And second, people outside Santo Domingo held "a great reservoir of good will and friendship toward the American people. As we were to note later, there was an almost childlike faith in the belief that the United States could accomplish anything and make things right again."[105] Palmer's vision was perhaps too simple, but also oddly reminiscent of John Bartlow Martin's musings about Dominicans' need for guidance. In any case, to U.S. planners, quiescence was good enough for the time being.

Ultimately, the military strategy of enclosure forced Constitutionalists into a waiting game that slowly broke down their morale. The utopian visions of some in the trapped Colonial Zone community seemed like wishful thinking to others, as spring turned into summer without signs of victory. Rebel fighters were often young, poor—and poorly trained— civilians with guns. They served in paramilitary commandos in return for food but, apparently, no pay. Most of the time *catorcistas* headed the commandos, and as Despradel admitted, they were often "inexperienced and naive."[106] Regulars, too, lost their sense of unity. They stole, drank, and fought, and more so as resources grew scarce.[107]

8. These classic photographs capture the tense atmosphere of the U.S. intervention
   in the Dominican Republic, 1965. After a mass meeting in Santo Domingo's
   Parque Independencia, Dominicans gathered in small groups, shouting "Go
   home, Yankees!" and throwing peddlers' fruits on the ground. U.S. soldiers
   demanded that protesters pick up the garbage. One defiant Dominican refused,
   claiming he had not been party to the mess. After these photographs were taken,
   the U.S. soldier apparently struck the man with his rifle and took him into
   custody. Photos taken July 14, 1965, by Juan Pérez Terrero. Reprinted with the
   permission of Juan Pérez Terrero.

At the heart of the rebels' breakdown was a humiliating dilemma, said Jottin Cury: the rebels hated U.S. troops, but those troops were the only thing stopping Loyalist forces from destroying them.[108] Caamaño seemed to have little hold on freewheeling commando groups, and so violence slowly became separated from strategic logic. Some rebels took out their frustrations on the U.S. soldiers who were manning barricades or checkpoints a few feet from them. The U.S. soldiers had orders not to fire unless fired upon, and, later, not to fire unless rebels threatened their position. Tension resulted as Dominican teenagers would walk up to checkpoints and provoke an argument, a fight, or an exchange of gunfire. Snipers broke the cease-fires hundreds of times—a daily occurrence around the embassy. There were even rumors of kidnapping Ambassador Bennett, a gambit that U.S. officials described as "a last final 'back to the wall' measure."[109] When a Dominican refused to pick up garbage after a U.S. soldier ordered him to, the hostility captured in the Dominican's gaze made for the most dramatic photos of the 1965 intervention. Even Caamaño admitted he wanted to lash out against U.S. forces. In a July meeting with U.S. negotiators, he pointed out the window to a hovering U.S. helicopter and said, "Believe me, it's tempting for us to shoot it down."[110]

U.S. diplomats and soldiers, in contrast, steadied their nerves as they settled into routines. U.S. periodicals contrasted the volatility of rebels with the "grace under pressure" of U.S. soldiers. They believed the myth that U.S. soldiers fired only when fired upon, when in fact U.S. troops broke the cease-fires almost as much as the rebels did. (According to Bosch, "one of the Marine Corps jeeps bore the legend 'Rebel Hunter.'") U.S. soldiers, however, did show relative sang froid in the face of anti-Americanism on the ground. As one trooper said in reaction to "Yankee Go Home" graffiti, "I think it's a good idea. I'm ready to go home any time. But I guess we're going to be around awhile, so I just ignore it."[111]

As early as April 30, Mann informed the embassy that the crisis was "entering a political phase"—the second component of the U.S. strategy, as Eisenhower had described it. Mann's mission for this component was similar to the military mission: to rebuild a government with the assent of both sides while avoiding the destruction of either. Specifically, the OAS was to help induce the Constitutionalists and Loyalists to cobble together an interim government that would oversee a presidential election, hopefully sometime in 1966. Theodore Draper early on criticized the Mann approach as "paying lip service" to the goal of constitutional (and not Constitutionalist) government. But more probably, Mann trusted his own determination and capacity to engineer what he called an "apolitical government of technicians" out of a people that he judged to be neither apolitical nor technical when it came to governing.[112]

Since the beginning of the revolt, the horse being backed by the Johnson administration to win the eventual elections was Joaquín Balaguer, Trujillo's president during the dictator's last years. Balaguer was a bona fide conservative and *entreguista* but did not come off as a puppet because he delivered occasional anti-U.S. diatribes for public consumption. Johnson liked that. In the early days of the intervention, when a CIA official mentioned Balaguer as an able noncommunist leader, Johnson answered, "That's it; that's our policy; get this guy in office down there!"[113] Confirmation of Johnson's early choice comes from a Johnson-Mann phone call on April 26, 1965—two days before Johnson even sent troops:

> *Johnson:* We're going to have to really set up that government down there and run it and stabilize it some way or other. This Bosch is no good . . .
> *Mann:* He's no good at all. . . . If we don't get a decent government in there, Mr. President, we get another Bosch. It's just going to be another sinkhole—.
> *Johnson:* Well that's what you ought to do. That's your problem. You better figure it out.
> *Mann:* . . . The man to get back, I think, is Balaguer. He's the one that ran way ahead in the polls.
> *Johnson:* Well, try to do it, try to do it.[114]

Before proceeding with such plans, U.S. officials also needed to create the appearance, however spurious, that Latin American governments supported their intervention. The 1947 Río Treaty allowed multilateral intervention, but only in case of outside aggression. Some countries, such as Mexico and Venezuela, were opposed to any outside intervention. Nevertheless, U.S. officials convinced their Latin American counterparts to support neutral areas in Santo Domingo, reach cease-fires, and mediate talks. Some governments, mostly dictatorships, even provided what Bundy admitted were "token troops" to help form the IAPF. Bundy, showing some knowledge of inter-nation sensitivities, told Johnson not to use troops from Puerto Rico, because "Dominicans are apparently not fond of Puerto Ricans." A Brazilian general amenable to Palmer's "advice" also nominally headed the IAPF, but the overwhelming U.S. control remained obvious to all.[115]

Ambivalence, however, was far more apparent in private conversations. Kurzman could sense it in the streets of Santo Domingo. One young politician told him, "As a man who selfishly wants to live, I am glad the American troops are here. But as a nationalist, I deplore their presence." "We now have a split image of you Americans," explained a businessman. "On one hand, you are generous, peace-loving people who understand freedom. And on the other, you are people with rifles and steel helmets and grenades—symbols of force." Many Latin American diplomats eventually admitted to U.S. colleagues that they supported U.S. ends while opposing the means. Or, as they phrased it, they "understood" the need for action but did not "support" it.[116] A veteran of U.S. foreign policy, Averell Harriman, visited eight Latin American countries in early May. "By and large," he reported to Johnson, "we have real staunch friends in Latin America. Many of them can't express themselves openly, but do, nevertheless, support us." Latin Americans, Harriman concluded, "want to come along with us but they all have some sort of domestic problem."[117] And criticism softened as the Santo Domingo stalemate wore on. In early June a Washington official visited the city for three weeks. "Every local Latin American chief of mission with whom I talked (Argentina, Peru, Guatemala, Colombia, El Salvador, and Ecuador)," he reported, "was emphatic that the arrival of our forces saved Santo Domingo from a major catastrophe, regardless of what their own Foreign Offices might say. Some [Dominican] democratic leaders . . . also admitted this quite readily in private, although for political reasons they did not want to say it publicly."[118]

Mann and his colleagues reacted to this public-private dissonance with typical disdain for ambivalence. Latin Americans were perhaps expressing traditional dualities toward U.S. hegemony or, as scholar Jerome Slater suggested, a desire for the OAS not to be excluded from an important crisis. But to U.S. officials, blessings given behind closed doors seemed hypocritical and hence a sanction for unilateral action behind the OAS veil. Mann, for one, briefed the White House staff on "the Latin American mentality on this sort of operation." He characterized it as wallowing in the contradiction between nonintervention and collective defense, naïve about "the idea of [communist] subversion as aggression," and obsessed with memories of "gunboat diplomacy." "There are, of course, some sophisticated Latin Americans who know what the score is. Privately, they say 'good show,' but politically, they give us no support. The problem is that secret support does us no damn good."[119] Bennett expressed to senators the same exasperation. Latin Americans "will approve what you do but they won't say it publicly." Fulbright asked why. "Well, that is part of being Latin, I suppose," replied Bennett.[120]

To get Constitutionalists and Loyalists to the negotiating table, however, Johnson's advisers reined in their contempt and showed that they had learned something about the political sensibilities in Latin America. They turned to Kennedy liberals such as former ambassador Martin, OAS ambassador Ellsworth Bunker, and former Roosevelt brain-truster Adolf Berle. Martin, for instance, was attuned to Dominican sentiment in the street, and Johnson could use that talent right about then. "There's no gunboat stuff about this," Johnson warned him. "I just think we want to do what's right." The president entreated the former ambassador to avoid "anything that would leave the impression that we're high-handed and arrogant and trying to shove one side."[121] Luckily for Johnson, Martin shared the macho imperiousness of his colleagues: "If we are going to stay in there," he told Johnson, "we're going to need some kind of puppet."[122] Under the close watch of Mann, Bundy, and Johnson, these liberals converted Wessin's military into something resembling a civil government to rival Caamaño's.[123] It named itself the Government of National Reconstruction (GRN) and featured as its president Antonio Imbert Barrera—the "puppet" to whom Martin referred, and a man whose prestige remained high because he had helped kill Trujillo.

For months the talks dragged on, increasingly headed directly by Mann and Bundy. U.S. negotiators made mistakes. Martin, for instance, offered a $300,000 "subsidy" to the rebels, which Caamaño angrily rejected (Imbert took $750,000). But overall, U.S. officials led efforts back to constitutionality, guided by what they considered Dominicans' acquiescence in their hegemony. "We trust you, Mr. Martin," the former ambassador heard crowds chanting as he arrived in Santo Domingo. Like his colleagues, he saw more authenticity in this pro-Americanism than in the clusters yelling at him to "Go home!"[124]

By mid-June, Mann was warning Bunker that the "danger of rapid emergence [of] anti-US nationalistic sentiment in [the] DR increases as time passes." Bennett agreed. He wrote Johnson that an "ugly," "bitter," anti-U.S. mood was taking over Bosch and Caamaño, who felt they had "nothing to lose."[125] Imbert's side was also growing impatient. Johnson, however, realized he had to refrain from applying his "treatment" to this situation and railroading an agreement. Bunker, especially, convinced him to take "a Latin approach to a Latin problem" and allow the slow-moving OAS to form the interim government. Fortunately for Bunker, he was both ambassador to the OAS and chairman of its council, and so he had significant influence over the ad hoc committee that oversaw negotiations. The committee met with Constitutionalists forty-eight times and with Loyalists fifty-three times, and in the end the patient approach worked.[126]

On September 3, 1965, the Caamaño and Imbert groups finally reached two agreements, closing out the "political phase" of the crisis. These agreements—called the Institutional Act and the Act of Reconciliation—entrusted a compromise government headed by Hector García-Godoy with the task of holding a presidential election within nine months. Caamaño resigned reluctantly; Imbert, furiously. Dissenting from the bulk of Loyalists, who accepted the ad hoc committee's proposals, Imbert banged his fist on the table as Caamaño had done in front of Bennett in April. Imbert shouted to Bunker, "You can tell your government, *Presidente* Johnson, and the North American people that Antonio Imbert Barrera will not sell out, will not be humiliated, will not take orders from anyone regarding the internal affairs of his country!" His government, taking orders from the OAS, resigned the following day. Shortly afterward, Bundy congratulated fellow Johnson advisers on saving the country from communism while resisting the efforts of each side to use the U.S. government as a lever against the other.[127]

There was also an important third factor in salvaging the occupation: the informational component. As soon as the Imbert government was up and running, Martin declared that the "politico-propaganda struggle" could begin.[128] Here, Kennedy's optimistic vision for the Dominican Republic lived on. Even in private exchanges, U.S. policymakers expressed concern that Dominican peasants and workers had no voice in the struggle yet tended to desire stability more than did the rabble-rousing intellectuals, students, or soldiers. Top Johnson aides even suggested that U.S. failure to stay connected to public opinion was partly responsible for the civil war. "I feel our people are not in touch with *all* elements of the entire population," Bundy worried aloud to White House staffers.[129]

The informational program, therefore, emphasized reaching the masses with positive U.S. imagery. Adolf Berle wrote to Johnson that Voice of America radio broadcasts in proper Castilian were good only for educated groups. "Flank it with a low-grade service," suggested Berle. "Needed is [the] insistent repetition of a few simple ideas, of which the 'Yankee' is a symbol: better houses, more food, better jobs, a chance for the children; unlimited opportunity. No more killing—and so forth. The Santo Domingo little people want these things." USIA director Carl Rowan agreed. He aimed "to win the support of the Dominican people for a progressive and democratic government" and "mute the cries of 'United States aggression' and 'gunboat diplomacy.'"[130]

With great confidence in their message, officials in the Johnson administration devised one of the most comprehensive two-way informational campaigns in the history of U.S.–Latin American relations. Johnson was furious at the failure of the CIA and the embassy to predict the crisis. Determined not to get caught napping again, the CIA set up a twenty-four-hour crisis operations center. The president also sent twenty-four FBI agents into Santo Domingo and demanded daily (eventually twice-daily) situation reports, or "sitreps."[131] "We must improve the collection of information about what is going on in the countryside," Mann urged. He suggested using medical helicopters to smuggle embassy and military personnel and Peace Corps volunteers into villages. (A handwritten note next to his suggestion said, "Peace Corps doesn't want to do this.") Humanitarian help in the countryside, Mann added, "would be a cover to find out which side controls the major sectors of the population and to improve our intelligence about political activities in the interior. This deserves a high priority." It received it: in early May, Operation Green Chopper dropped CIA agents into the countryside, where they posed as humanitarian workers. Staff from the U.S. embassy, the Agency for International Development (AID), and the USIA, as well as Army Special Forces and Green Berets, soon followed. Most reported little or no rebel activity.[132]

U.S. officials also generated a massive amount of outgoing propaganda. By July 10, a fifty-eight-person psychological warfare team had produced 3 million pieces of printed matter and flown 700 hours in 197 sorties, disseminating information from planes equipped with loudspeakers. The USIA, though it repeatedly failed to jam Radio Santo Domingo, set up radio broadcasts and published *La Voz de la Zona de Seguridad* (The Voice of the Security Zone), which immediately enjoyed the highest circulation up to then of any periodical in Dominican history.[133] The U.S. government also prepared rebuttals to rebel publications, secretly funded a book on the crisis, and highlighted anti-Americanism on Imbert's side to prop up the crumbling U.S. image of neutrality.[134] "Psywar" units ended up broadcasting over 900 hours of locally produced programs, distributing more than 25 million propaganda items, and selling pamphlets at five cents each (which suggests Dominicans' interest in reading them). In June, Bunker's ad hoc committee used already established channels to make its proposals public, without consulting or forewarning either party. It distributed hundreds of thousands of copies all over the country, and the USIA broadcast the proposals. Within days, thousands of supporting telegrams and letters had arrived at the committee's offices.[135]

In contrast, the Constitutionalist information strategy suffered from the lack of sophistication that long characterized episodic anti-Americanism. To be sure, rebels had limited resources. But Caamaño and other Constitutionalists generated plenty of propaganda within Santo Domingo, and they were physically able to go back and forth (unarmed) between Santo Domingo and the countryside. They largely chose not to. Rather, Constitutionalists believed—without evidence—that a majority of Dominicans were as anti-U.S. as the rebels holed up in the Colonial Zone. Bosch, Caamaño, and others dwelled on their encirclement. They reiterated again and again that there were 42,000 U.S. troops in the Dominican Republic, when in fact there were at most 25,000 on the ground and the rest were either offshore or on alert back in the United States.[136] From the entrenched Colonial Zone, the perception was that "logically we had to defend ourselves," according to Caamaño's vice president, Bonaparte Gautreaux Pineyro.[137]

The information that did circulate within the rebel zone suffered from amateurism and runaway propagandizing. Almost none of the stories concerning atrocities committed by U.S. soldiers benefited from objective sources; often there was no source at all. Many people blamed U.S. soldiers for the indiscretions of Latin American IAPF troops, who were reported to be more brutal than their U.S. counterparts.[138] Frequently the stories were just rumors. For example, El 1J4 and La Nación ran stories suggesting that U.S. troops tortured and starved prisoners at the Sans Souci "concentration camp." There was never proof of torture there. Ricardo Espinal, one rebel released from Sans Souci, said U.S. soldiers even slipped him cigarettes during his captivity. "We need to distinguish between the people and government of the United States," he concluded. "The people are fundamentally good."[139] Unfortunately, credible and serious accusations got lost in the din of unsupported allegations. Rebels, for instance, charged that U.S. soldiers raped and killed civilians, that U.S. negotiators ordered bombings on the rebels to pressure them to negotiate, and that U.S. forces provoked a major rollback of Constitutionalist forces in mid-June. Given the lack of evidence and accountability that were hallmarks of the rebel press, few listened.[140]

Ramón Ferreras, the founder-editor of *Patria,* unleashed the most strident anti-Americanism of the crisis and made Caamaño's *La Nación* look moderate in comparison. Dominican journalists and even the 1J4 had banished Ferreras, who, by 1965, was sporting the nickname "Chino" for his admiration of the People's Republic of China. During the intervention, *Patria* specialized in casting blanket indictments over much of U.S. society. Ferreras was not surprised, for instance, to be invaded by people who nurtured a culture of crime. The United States was the "country that produced Al Capone, John Dillinger, Lucky Luciano, Alberto Anastasia, the crime syndicate, Indian reservations, chewing gum, large-scale drug dealing, corrupt politicians, Chicago gangsters, youth gangs, racial discrimination . . . This is how the Yankee invaders plan to introduce into Santo Domingo the '*American way of life.*'"[141] Writer Marcio Veloz admitted that *Patria* "was a little . . . virulent. It was a very denunciatory newspaper." Gautreaux Pineyro agreed that *Patria* was more propaganda than news, but remembered indulging Ferreras as the enemy of his enemy. "When he came to my office I told him, 'Chino, what the hell are you doing? You're telling a bunch of lies.' But he thought he was justified and said it was propaganda against the enemy." Gautreaux supplied him with ink and paper.[142]

Finally, another Constitutionalist propaganda weakness characteristic of episodic anti-Americanism was the inability to capitalize on parallels between this intervention and the 1916–1924 occupation. Dominican oral tradition had built up martyrs of the occupation such as Cayo Báez and had demonized U.S. villains such as Sergeant Charles Backlaw, the infamous "Bacalú." But rebels in 1965 rarely exploited that collective memory. Historian Roberto Cassá lived in the rebel zone and recalled that in the early 1960s the new radical youths had pushed out old-guard leftists. A by-product of this purge was the erasing of these vivid memories of the first occupation. Gregorio Urbano Gilbert, a *gabillero* who had fought Marines in the early years of the century and at Augusto Sandino's side in Nicaragua, only occasionally figured as a living icon of the old anti-Americanism. And only once in a while did older or more educated leaders such as Juan Bosch talk about the "other invasion." The anniversary of the U.S. withdrawal of 1924, July 12, passed with only a few commemorations and a rally where a crowd burned a U.S. flag. It was small fare, considering the urgent need for a usable past.[143]

Humanitarianism was also part of U.S. propaganda against anti-Americanism. For the White House, avoiding mass misery and an economic collapse was not only humane, but also smart politics. Presidential adviser Jack Valenti wrote to Johnson that aid might "cause a great wave of pro-American feeling throughout the Island—and possibly throughout the Hemisphere itself—for instead of firing guns the Marines are distributing food and clothing to people who are desperately in need of both." Mann agreed. He also proposed feeding Loyalists and Constitutionalists as well as neutrals. Some rebels, again isolated from the goings on outside the Colonial Zone, refused to believe that U.S. troops fed anyone at all during the crisis. Yet as photos in *Look* magazine plainly showed, "an American soldier's day in Santo Domingo" consisted of three tasks: "Fight . . . feed . . . frisk." In the end, IAPF troops provided food, clothing, and medicine to more than 2 million of the country's 3.5 million inhabitants.[144]

U.S. citizens on the ground felt good about this. One Peace Corps volunteer was "very proud to be part of a U.S. organization that was totally accepted in a situation where there was such anti-American feeling." A U.S. reverend noted that "for the first time in history, American soldiers had come to help the common people, not to support bond holders or dictators but to preserve peace for the ordinary citizen." General Palmer also thought that "the presence of many black American soldiers . . . , as well as some who spoke Spanish, helped establish friendly relations between our troops and the people of Santo Domingo. This good spirit generally prevailed during the entire period of the U.S. presence, despite the sustained efforts of the rebel opposition to arouse the people against us."[145]

Day-to-day exchanges between U.S. soldiers and hungry Dominicans highlighted much of the ambivalence of ordinary Dominicans. In general, Dominicans seemed to welcome the aid, work, and good cheer of

U.S. soldiers, yet men and women expressed the duality of anti-Americanism according to their gender. Men were often reluctant to relinquish their bread-winning role to foreign troops. A U.S. aid worker once announced over a loudspeaker that the men should get out of a food line and "let only the women stay who are heads of families." "They shouldn't say that to men," opined a Dominican. "It is not respectful." Other men disparaged aid as "the 'gingerbread' method, handing out corn flour, Coca-Cola, and ice cream" or as an invasion of their country by "filthy dollars."[146] Women, on the whole, welcomed the U.S. soldiers more readily. To them, outside intervention seemed to be no worse than Dominican internecine fighting, and at least it allowed a return to stability. Mothers were responsible for the well-being of their families and took whatever help they could get. "I hate to see Yankee soldiers in my country," said one housewife standing in a food line. "But Americans do have a big heart." Here again was the dissonance between the bad "Yankee" and good "American."[147]

As the Institutional Act and the Act of Reconciliation became law in the late summer of 1965, the U.S. government closed its informational phase by containing anti-Americanism where it would most likely persist: among university students. By 1965 the State Department was producing longer and more subtle reports on foreign criticism—reports that married an ethnographic flavor with the polls and lists that were now well established. This allowed analysts, for instance, to distinguish anti-Americanism from neutralism or nationalism, "which are not *per se* attitudes toward the United States." As they had done with travelers years before, reports now provided arguments and facts for "countering negative stereotypes" held specifically by students.[148]

These reports also demonstrated that social scientists were now at the forefront in the effort to identify and isolate anti-Americanism among youths. One of these researchers, Bryant Wedge of the Institute for the Study of National Behavior in Princeton, largely confirmed the episodic and nonrevolutionary nature of Dominican hostility. Since his study concerned a crisis area, it rose to the attention of Bennett, Bundy, and Rusk. The embassy had sponsored Wedge's studies even though he criticized the intervention, and after he conducted 281 interviews with revolutionary youths in September–October 1965, Wedge came to startling conclusions. Yes, there had been a "substantial risk of a communist takeover" in late April, his respondents told him, and moreover they believed that only the U.S. intervention had prevented it; but they had depended on the communists for military rather than political leadership, and so the radicals and even Bosch had quickly disenchanted them. Wedge found that young Dominicans took up arms because of their "great sensitivity concerning Dominican autonomy." They were "realistic," "discriminating," "pragmatic," and "eager to develop democratic political alternatives and to enter into dignified dialogue with acceptable United States persons and representatives." These were not the hate-filled savages who paraded heads on pikes or the terrorists of the Embajador whom Bennett and Johnson had warned about back in April.

Most surprisingly, Wedge found almost no anti-Americanism among the youths he interviewed. Dominicans showed no "displacement of anger" onto the United States, in contrast to people in other Latin American countries. "Dominican students identified, without any serious dissent, the frustrator—the Dominican police and military. Even the young Communists did not very seriously maintain that United States imperialism was a principal problem." Wedge explained: "The reasoning patterns characteristic of Dominican society were pragmatic and case-particularistic in the extreme. In a culture where survival has depended on having one's particular facts correct—as is always true in a police state— there can be little indulgence in theory."[149]

Soon after Wedge's report circulated among policymakers, officials from the State Department, AID, and the USIA began holding frequent discussions about how to address the "new and complex situation with regard to Dominican youth." They ordered further studies and added a "youth affairs officer" to the embassy staff. While many disagreed with Wedge and observed that anti-Americanism was alive and well among youth groups, they were equally confident that it could be contained within universities.[150]

The result of the Wedge study was a project—"the Wedge effort" as it was known, in an unintended double entendre—to open up Dominican universities to pro-U.S. sentiment. U.S. officials in 1966 pledged $400,000 a year for five years to the promotion of new, private universities and the appeasement of the radical, public Autonomous University of Santo Domingo (UASD). They appointed U.S. faculty, promoted exchanges with U.S. students, and developed an apolitical curriculum to, as embassy officials said, "establish American influence and improve [the] quality of instruction."[151]

It is difficult to say if these reforms moderated anti-U.S. protests, especially at the UASD, where fear of "Americanization" continued for decades. But the precision with which U.S. social scientists and policymakers identified the sources and nuances of anti-Americanism was impressive, and the effort at least to isolate anti-Americanism seems to have succeeded. As Hugo Tolentino Dipp, a pro-rebel dean of UASD, later admitted, "The university was a way to corner many of us." Leftist political activity flourished at the UASD, but did not spread to the society at large or even to other universities.[152]

The final U.S. strategy to wear down anti-Americanism was the presidential election. If all went well, the election would provide a tolerable, conservative anti-U.S. government to marginalize Dominican moderates such as Bosch and Caamaño, the same way the youth strategy was boxing in radical students. Luckily for the Johnson administration, U.S. dependence on Balaguer to win the contest rested on better knowledge of Dominican voting patterns than even the Dominicans themselves had. Above all else, polls before, during, and after the U.S. intervention demonstrated that Balaguer doubled the showing of Juan Bosch, who also ran. Balaguer tapped into the timidity of campesinos, and so could win them over as a voting bloc as well as Bosch could.[153]

In contrast, political passions, not polls, motivated those on the left, who hated Balaguer for repressing political freedoms after Trujillo's death. As a result, rather than work concretely to earn Bosch the presidency, Caamaño merely expressed confidence that Bosch would win 95 percent of the vote. "And I am not exaggerating. The Unity of the popular forces is total. Not only in the Capital, but in the country as a whole." Ellsworth Bunker, in response, challenged Constitutionalists to put their votes where their mouths were. "If you have the support of the people, the best thing for you is to have elections and bring the country back to normality." Mann himself reassured U.S. senators that he had confidential polls and that "it has never been very clear on that scene that Bosch was the knight on the white horse who the Dominican people demanded return."[154]

Yet he did return. The day Bosch rode into Santo Domingo—September 25, 1965, the two-year anniversary of his overthrow—was, revealingly, the most anti-American episode of the following nine months. Bosch attracted thousands to the capital city, yet there were signs that fissures in the anti-U.S. constituency had deepened. The ceremonies were rife with contradictions. U.S. soldiers, for example, guarded Bosch as he walked out of his plane to chants of "Yankees no!" and "Give it to the Yankees!" Once in the Colonial Zone, Bosch made what the embassy considered a "rambling, long-winded anti-American speech," while in private he expressed his displeasure at communist slogans and the authority that radical leftists now claimed. He charged that the U.S. government had "ordered" the bombing of Santo Domingo, but refused to enter into power-sharing agreements with those who had actually fought U.S. troops.[155] Weeks later, Bosch demanded personal U.S. protection during the election campaign. One U.S. official called the request "a rather eloquent commentary on the inconsistency of the man."[156]

U.S. officials were quite unruffled about intervening in the election. They set aside their dislike of Bosch in favor of their need to have him lend legitimacy to a free contest. The word around the State Department was to "clam up" about U.S. favorites, but their preference for Balaguer rather than Bosch was obvious. Evidence suggests that the Johnson administration even financed Balaguer's campaign.[157] The resulting paradox was that while Bosch berated the U.S. government for thwarting the will of "the people," the White House planned to "get out a big vote because this favors Balaguer."[158]

On June 1, 1966, the U.S. gamble paid off. Balaguer won by about the same margin that the secret polls had predicted. The campaign may have been unfair, because Bosch's life was threatened on a daily basis. But, as independent observers noted and even PRD leaders admitted, the vote itself was free. An insecure electorate had chosen the confident Balaguer rather than an opponent who displayed astounding pessimism. As the periodical *Army* noted with self-congratulation, "The vindication of the force came with the elections of June 1." Over the rest of the summer of 1966, IAPF troops withdrew from the Dominican Republic.[159]

After the pullout, Joaquín Balaguer began a brutal, autocratic twelve-year rule with full U.S. acquiescence. While one top Johnson aide thought that "the Dominican Republic is prospering . . . it has a good democratic government," Balaguer was recasting the country in the role of a subservient U.S. ally.[160] After the election, Johnson showered Balaguer with financial aid and sugar purchases. Holding up his end, Balaguer repressed anti-U.S. rallies. Over the years, allegedly with the help of U.S. military attachés and CIA operatives, he secretly sponsored terrorism against an already imploding left. He also modified laws to benefit U.S. investors, froze wages, instituted anti-union measures, and restructured the Dominican economy as a haven for sweatshops. (He died in 2002 after presiding over the country for more than twenty of his ninety-five years.) Scholar Howard Wiarda observed that Dominican society and politics after 1965 were even more "fragmented, dissentious, fissured, divided, unintegrated, and imbalanced" than they had been before.[161]

For the Johnson administration, the behind-the-scenes engineering of the election and the extrication of the troops had all the virtues of a cinematic happy ending. U.S. gunslingers had ridden into a sleepy Latin locale, defended the natives against communist bandits, and taken off into the sunset without a thought for themselves. While the credits rolled, Johnson's aides regarded the intervention as an unmitigated success. Under Secretary of State George Ball offered the typical assessment: Johnson's "exaggerated Dominican reaction did little harm." Even Kennedy aide Richard Goodwin, who had opposed the intervention, found it "relatively peaceful and short-lived . . . [and] virtually without harmful consequence."[162] Before U.S. troops pulled out, Bundy predicted that the U.S. government would achieve all its goals in the Dominican Republic: saving U.S. lives, checking communism, avoiding a social revolution, and restoring the electoral process. After the troops did pull out, several analysts concluded that Bundy had been right.[163]

Indeed, episodic anti-Americanism in the Dominican Republic proved no match for the U.S. counter-strategy of containment. To be sure, hostility toward the U.S. government in the spring and summer of 1965 was massive, violent, and unifying for the Constitutionalists. But it peaked sharply. By the end of the summer, the republic's weaknesses—collaboration with foreign powers and atomization—resurfaced. Dominicans expressed significant positive sentiment toward U.S. influence. The Johnson administration restrained itself after an overly forceful armed intervention and resolved to chip away resentment. Anti-Americanism again proved to be an elusive sentiment and strategy, contained most effectively with a patient, pragmatic approach.

For the U.S. handling of anti-Americanism, the Dominican experience signified the passing of an era rather than a return to the complacency of 1958. A learning process had occurred since the Eisenhower years. Johnson's team spoke with caution rather than hubris. Mann judged that the "moralistic rhetoric that was used in attempts to justify [Woodrow] Wilson's interventions in the past" no longer applied in the Western Hemisphere.[164] U.S. policymakers accepted that they could not please all the world's peoples all the time. When they could prevent hostility, U.S. officials figured, they should do so with aid and propaganda that focused on the institutions most likely to produce it. When they could not prevent it, they would listen carefully and answer with a coordinated, multifaceted, country-specific strategy. The lessons of the Dominican Republic provided a modicum of satisfaction to a U.S. government that only a few years earlier had felt beleaguered in the hemisphere.

Epilogue
Toward Global Anti-Americanism

"Yankee go home" [is] not very original advice.
—*The Economist*, 2000

The Economist's opinion[1] on the alleged banality of anti-Americanism—offered a full century after the comment by Rodó that opened this study—prompts two observations. The first is that the source was not a parochial or Cold War–obsessed U.S. publication but a British one, read the world over and respected in much of it. The second is that it concerned a protest in South Korea, a U.S. ally on the other side of the planet, not in a Soviet-backed regime ninety miles from U.S. shores. Together, these observations suggest that in the early twenty-first century both anti-Americanism and defenders of U.S. influence have become pervasive across the globe. Following September 11, 2001, those dueling sets of voices created a veritable cacophony on the world stage. One element in this noise seemed to be an impulse on the part of the defenders of the United States to ignore foreign critics of U.S. power, a collective rolling of the eyes—call it forbearance fatigue—with deleterious effects on international affairs. These effects might be mitigated by looking more closely at anti-Americanism as a historical phenomenon.

The similarities between the protest-response dynamics of Latin American anti-Americanism on one hand and global anti-Americanism on the other since the pullout of U.S. troops from the Dominican Republic suggest a possible universality. In the upheavals of 1958 to 1966, previously estranged groups banded in the thousands, sometimes in the millions, to denounce, attack, or overturn U.S. hegemony in Latin

163

America and the attitude of contempt that infused it. The Dominican "happy ending" provided only a short respite from these dynamics, as anti-U.S. strategies shifted to other parts of the world. Tension over the Vietnam War, in fact, was becoming the dominant motif in anti-U.S. discourse and demonstrations in *every* region of the world.

Around 1966, as one of the most anxious eras in the history of U.S.-Latin American relations drew to a close, many U.S. observers refused to breathe easy. They braced for the worst from a foreign public opinion increasingly literate, urban, organized, and angry at U.S. power. Their warnings emphasized the scope of the discontent: middle-class rebels, poor peasants, urban workers, liberal reformers, law students, housewives, social conservatives, military officers, and even wealthy elites could be anti-American when the right circumstances arose. U.S. journalists noted the boldness of recently empowered peoples. "If you're a gringo in Bolivia now, they'll push you off the pavement," observed a mining engineer in 1966. Attitude was easy to grasp; cause, less so. "Probe for the motives of anti-Americans and you are . . . confronted by the chaos of the human condition," sighed journalist Thomas Morgan after he traveled the world in the mid-1960s and returned with a sketch of life "among the anti-Americans."[2] Fearing that various groups now identified an array of problems with the United States—issues as abstract as nationalism and as concrete as hunger—John Bartlow Martin predicted in his 1966 memoir, "We shall almost surely encounter a new and more genuine and more potent kind of anti-Americanism than we have faced in the past. Nobody likes big brother."[3] The three features of anti-Americanism—variability, ambivalence, and U.S. resilience—turned out to be alive and well.

Since 1966, variability has been, of course, the most noticeable feature on a global scale. When speaking of anti-Americanism, wrote *Le Monde's* Alain Frachon, "one should use the plural form. There are anti-Americanisms." A special study by the French paper following September 11 demonstrated that there were not only partly independent political, economic, and cultural anti-Americanisms, but also variations of those in different countries and regions.[4] Just as anti-U.S. sentiment in Cuba, Panama, and the Dominican Republic long reflected the diversity of grievances against U.S. power and a range of social configurations, it did so elsewhere as well. Whether sweeping, self-protective, or short-lived, anti-Americanism showed that it could serve many masters. It was a deep-seated sentiment and a viable political strategy in fundamentally dissimilar societies across the world.

A French variant of anti-Americanism, to mention just one example, has stood out over the years. Part criticism of U.S. unilateralism from the left, part cultural snobbery from the elite, and part spokesmanship for the developing world, French anti-Americanism has reflected a desire to compete against the United States for the right to define dominant Western-based values. A U.S. ambassador to France explained that "anti-Americanism today encompasses not a specific policy . . . but a feeling that globalization has an American face on it and is a danger to the European and French view of society." That many scholars of anti-Americanism have focused on France is not surprising; France's alternative universalism has expressed much of the world's frustration.[5]

The French may be distinctive in their anti-Americanism, but they are not alone. Global U.S. power now touches every society. It compels both change within other countries and resistance to that change, with the seeming inevitability that U.S. policymakers perceived in the late 1960s. As a result of the pervasiveness of U.S. power—and its facile equation with globalization and modernity—"almost everyone who is not an American is, in some sense, an anti-American," in the words of one expatriate Canadian.[6] The so-called American century—the twentieth—was also an anti-American century.

Yet scholars need not fear the dilution of anti-Americanism—its irritating tendency to be opaque but clearly evident. They simply need to make it more concrete. "What is normally pointed to as 'anti-Americanism' is difficult to find as hard evidence of the ideas in peoples' minds," reported the USIA in 1979 when faced with the example of the recent Iranian Revolution, which largely expressed the Islamic fundamentalist variant of anti-Americanism and in so doing gave the Middle East a potent political model. "It exists, instead, in the form of campaigns and communications, as policy of parties and themes of speeches."[7] Here was U.S. pragmatism once again showing up as a measured response to a seemingly unrestrained hatred of the "Great Satan": USIA officials knew that the payoff in the study of anti-Americanism remained its ability to reveal as much about specific domestic politics abroad as it did about U.S. power—perhaps even more. Many scholars in the past few decades have likewise used anti-Americanism as a wedge to understand the complexities of sweeping revolutions such as Iran's or of brief but fiery protest movements in allied countries such as South Korea (echoes of Cuba and the Dominican Republic, respectively).[8]

While anti-Americanism existed everywhere, so did pro-Americanism. Ambivalence, the second feature highlighted in this book, also survived the turmoil of the 1960s. Latin Americans in the late 1960s continued to send mixed messages. Irreverent graffiti spoke loudly: "Yankee go home—and take me with you!" or "Yankee go home—via Pan Am!"[9] Many citizens of other countries who denounced political or economic U.S. power also embraced U.S. culture or political ideology, or else they made separate compartments in their hearts and minds for the U.S. "people" and the U.S. government. Certainly in Latin America, such distinctions had positive consequences. Since the 1920s, noted one scholar in 1967, not one U.S. life had yet been lost in a change of government. Even Fidel Castro, the only Latin American political figure able to sustain a revolution predicated on the myth of moral U.S. society and immoral U.S. government, never killed a U.S. citizen to achieve his goals. (Similarly, in the early twenty-first century U.S. citizens have generally felt safe in, say, Venezuelan upheavals against U.S. political meddling or Argentine riots over U.S.-influenced financial debacles.) And so by the late 1960s, while some U.S. visitors abroad resented being pushed off pavements, others commented on the steady, even improving intimacy between individual U.S. citizens and Latin Americans.[10]

Evidence from various nations after September 11 confirmed that pro-U.S. sentiment remained healthy amid the most profound diplomatic crises. "We are all Americans," declared *Le Monde,* which noted the continuing popularity of U.S. movies even in the Middle East and described anti-Americanism as "fueled by a contradictory mixture of hatred and fascination, repulsion and attraction." Worldwide polls confirmed a "familiar love-hate relationship with America" in *all* regions of the world following the attacks. In France perhaps more than anywhere, ambivalence remained strong: the French felt that the effects of U.S. policies on their country were more negative than positive, yet in late 2001 only 5 percent expressed antipathy to the United States and 73 percent felt that France should take part in the military action against the Taliban regime in Afghanistan—a higher percentage than in Germany, Italy, even Israel.[11]

The poor have continued to surprise world leaders by being the least responsive to anti-U.S. strategies. In fact, from the 1960s on, these strategies have highlighted the wide gap between rich and poor, rulers and ruled. By the late 1960s, the Alliance for Progress had failed in large part because elites had resisted redistributing land and paying their fair share of taxes. Feeling their isolation, they had virtually ceased trying to make anti-U.S. speeches or devise anti-U.S. policies, lest they alienate Washington, their only supporter in the hemisphere. To the extent that anti-U.S. sentiment did motivate the economically disfranchised, resentment of things U.S.—such as that found in Mexico's Zapatista movement—was often an expression of the shame they felt because of the obsequiousness of elites toward Washington.[12] After the Cold War especially, as Mexico's Jorge Castañeda argued, the revolutionary focus on external causes of poverty transformed itself into a far less ideological grassroots insistence on specific internal or transnational issues. Castañeda quoted the regretful comment of an aging Brazilian communist in 1989: "The biggest problem, the most serious mistake, lay in our identification of the United States as the principal enemy, in placing all our emphasis on the external factor."[13]

U.S. observers have thus grown irritated at what they perceive to be elite opportunism all over the world. "In case after case," scholars wrote in 1988, "anti-Americanism appears mainly as the preserve of the upper classes while the mass of the population is more tolerant of American shortcomings or even seeks to make American culture, if not values, its own."[14] In France some have noted that anti-Americanism often stems from an elite-driven, conservative desire to ward off the leveling effects of U.S.-driven popular tastes. "In culture, diplomacy and political culture," wrote one scholar in 2001, elites "looked ever more beleaguered, overtaken and outpaced by the appeal of American dress-styles to their children, of fast food to their youth, and of Hollywood to the cinema audiences."[15] This class divide—and the substantial disingenuousness it encouraged—only fueled the patriotic fire of the U.S. right, which delighted in branding anti-Americanism as anti-democratic intemperance.

Finally, the third feature of anti-U.S. diplomacy—U.S. resilience—has also persisted and somewhat solidified. By 1966, U.S. policymakers believed they had acquired a certain maturity that permitted them to question the wisdom of trying to change the opinions of foreigners. Most who had dealt with Latin America seemed to feel that, rather than having ignored criticism abroad since 1958, they had listened to the new urban masses over the heads of those who claimed to speak for them. They had found both groups lacking. Some of the harshest experiences of the postwar period had bred in U.S. officials a toughened faith in the righteousness of U.S. foreign policy, not a crisis of conscience.[16] Some people "simply do not like Americans," concluded former USIA director George Allen in 1966. "At times, Americans show too much sensitivity to their image abroad, giving the impression that their primary concern is how they appear to others. Nevertheless, their concern for world opinion is in keeping with the American tradition." In early 1967, Howard Smith, a CBS correspondent to the White House from 1957 to 1961, looked back and said, "People hate us, and they're going to go on hating us." Like Allen, Smith was oddly flattered. The very existence of anti-Americanism proved that the U.S. government could withstand criticism from its allies: "I think actually we behaved very generously throughout those years."[17]

The rise of the USIA itself and the broader trust in social-science approaches within the U.S. government had contributed to such conclusions. Both had promoted the acceptance of anti-Americanism as indigenous, substantive, widespread, and integrated within knowable social and cultural patterns. The Kennedy administration, especially, took anti-Americanism seriously. It gave it its due as a mass-based, noncommunist phenomenon. For a while, the U.S. government was determined to understand and accept the fact that anti-Americanism would not go away. "I think it's a very dangerous, untidy world. I think we will have to live with it," said Kennedy.[18]

But after the mid-1960s, U.S. policymakers—and, to a certain extent, the U.S. public—also demonstrated a growing weariness in the face of relentless criticism by foreigners. After the Dominican pullout, some seemed to feel that a weight had been lifted. One editorialist in 1966 even envisioned "an end to 'Yankee No!'" Soon, however, more waves of worldwide protest crashed down on the United States—for instance in 1968, when the Tet offensive in Vietnam, racial strife at home, and the assassinations of Martin Luther King and Robert Kennedy all shook the U.S. political establishment. (Sympathies across the globe, it turned out, peaked right before John F. Kennedy's assassination in 1963.)[19]

In response, most U.S. policymakers seemed resigned to the fact that anti-Americanism had become part of the modern condition. They blamed unchanging cultural differences. They dismissed hostility as the "price" to be paid for world power or as a "spin-off" of it. Latin America, wrote one disheartened commentator, "is too different to conform [but] it is too weak to ignore us. . . . Thus our intervention in the Dominican Republic must seem a banal confrontation. . . . The debate within the United States . . . is only over the character of the American intervention," not the intervention itself.[20]

There was something disarmingly optimistic in the substantial innocence that remained despite the vanishing naïveté. That something resurfaced following September 11. President George W. Bush was not alone in asking, "Why do they hate us?" More than seven thousand Web sites contained that exact phrase. Answers to this question-of-the-moment reflected every part of the political spectrum, from Republicans to antiglobalization protesters, from mainstream dailies to "e-zines," from libertarians to newly arrived Arab immigrants. In a prime-time White House press conference, Bush pondered the question out loud: "How do I respond when I see that in some Islamic countries there is vitriolic hatred for America? I'll tell you how I respond: I'm amazed. I'm amazed that there is such misunderstanding of what our country is about that people would hate us. I am—like most Americans, I just can't believe it, because I know how good we are." Good or not, Bush was right about being like most of his compatriots in one way: fewer than one in five thought that U.S. policies were to blame.[21]

In a now-familiar loop, one of the most galling aspects of U.S. resilience, for foreign observers, was precisely the lack of self-criticism. "You cannot conceive of yourself as a conquered people," was a rebuke from India in the 1950s, expressing much of the world's frustration at U.S. citizens' sense of invulnerability. After September 11, when some vulnerability finally seemed to appear, polls revealed that—in sharp contrast to U.S. citizens—three out of five respondents outside the United States felt that "U.S. policy caused [the] attacks" of that year and that seven out of ten believed it was "good" for the United States "to feel vulnerable."[22] The world, unable to get U.S. citizens to accept some responsibility for its pain, clearly wanted them to share it. As events in the Spanish Caribbean during the 1950s and 1960s had already suggested, arrogance in the face of aggression eventually produced more aggression.

The search for answers following the events of 2001 demonstrated more than ever the need to understand that anti-Americanism has not been a pathological prejudice but a complex cultural and political concept that merits serious treatment by historians. It is capacious, to be sure. But it is also a rich source of understanding that can help investigators move beyond traditional concerns about revolution and communism that so monopolized scholarship during the Cold War. Anti-Americanism existed long before the Cold War, and has survived its demise. In the meantime, the United States has become even more of a universal presence, both rejected and admired. This book is a call to turn to history as a means of illuminating both the sources of this rejection and the ways in which admiration has often tempered that rejection. It will also, one hopes, move policymakers and other caring readers—in the United States and elsewhere—to help prevent hostility from inciting violence and destroying the goodwill that does exist between nations.

Abbreviations

1J4	14 de Junio, Dominican Republic (a.k.a. *catorcistas*)
AGNC	Archivo General de la Nación, Cuba
AGNDR	Archivo General de la Nación, Dominican Republic
AHT	Archives of Hugo Tolentino, Dominican Republic
AID	Agency for International Development, United States
ANRP	Archivo Nacional, Republic of Panama
APRA	Alianza Popular Revolucionaria Americana, Peru
ARC	Archives of Roberto Cassá, Dominican Republic
BHS	Balboa High School, Canal Zone
CEFA	Centro de Enseñanza de las Fuerzas Armadas, Dominican Republic
CIA	Central Intelligence Agency, United States
CINCSO	Commander-In-Chief, Southern Command
CNRE	Consejo Nacional de Relaciones Exteriores, Panama
COAS	Council of the Organization of American States
DDEL	Dwight D. Eisenhower Library, Abilene, Kansas
DFE	Directorio de la Federación de Estudiantes, Cuba
FBI	Federal Bureau of Investigation, United States
FRUS	*Foreign Relations of the United States* (Washington, D.C.: Government Printing Office)
GN	Guardia Nacional, Panama
GRN	Gobierno de Reconstrucción Nacional, Dominican Republic
IAPC	Inter-American Peace Commission, Organization of American States
IAPF	Inter-American Peace Force, Organization of American States
IN	Instituto Nacional, Panama
INRA	Instituto Nacional de Reforma Agraria, Cuba
IYC	Interagency Youth Committee, United States
JCS	Joint Chiefs of Staff, United States
JD	Juventud Democrática, Dominican Republic
JFKL	John F. Kennedy Library, Boston, Massachusetts
LBJL	Lyndon B. Johnson Library, Austin, Texas
LCong	Library of Congress, Washington, D.C.

LOC	Line of Communication, Dominican Republic
MPD	Movimiento Popular Dominicano
NARA	National Archives and Records Administration, College Park, Maryland
NSAM	National Security Action Memorandum, United States
NSC	National Security Council, United States
OAS	Organization of American States
OC	Organ of Consultation, Organization of American States
OCB	Operations Coordinating Board, United States
PAMINREX	Archivo del Ministerio de Relaciones Exteriores, Panama
PCC	Panama Canal Company
PCD	Partido Comunista Dominicano (PSP until 1965)
PRD	Partido Revolucionario Dominicano
PSP	Partido Socialista del Pueblo, Cuba and Dominican Republic
RG 59	Records of the Department of State, United States
RG 84	Records of the Foreign Service Posts of the Department of State, United States
RG 111	Records of the Office of the Chief Signal Officer, United States
RG 185	Records of the Panama Canal, United States
RG 306	Records of the United States Information Agency, United States
SOUTHCOM	U.S. Southern Command, Panama
UASD	Universidad Autónoma de Santo Domingo, Dominican Republic
UCN	Unión Cívica Nacional, Dominican Republic (a.k.a. *cívicos*)
UFCO	United Fruit Company, United States
UP	Universidad de Panamá, Panama City
USIA	United States Information Agency
USIS	United States Information Service (foreign offices of the USIA)
WH	White House, United States

Notes

Introduction

1. Apart from "anti-Americanism," I will not use the words "America," "American," or "Americans" with reference to the United States or its citizens. Neither will I use "North American" unless I include Canadians (but not necessarily Mexicans). "North American" and "American" will appear only in quoted passages. I choose to use "anti-American" to mean "anti-U.S." (and to use these terms interchangeably) because they are common parlance and because they obviously refer only to the United States.

2. George W. Bush, "Address to a Joint Session of Congress and the American People," 20 September 2001, *Weekly Compilation of Presidential Documents,* 24 September 2001, 37 (Washington, D.C.: GPO), pp. 1347–1351. A Lexis-Nexis search comparing the frequency of the term "anti-Americanism" in the four months following September 11 with that in the eight months preceding it turned up, respectively, 108 articles against 43, or about five times more articles per month. For examples of these analyses, see Fareed Zakaria, "Why They Hate Us," *Newsweek,* 15 October 2001; and Mary Cooper, "Hating America," *CQ Researcher,* 23 November 2001. More examples are given in the Epilogue.

3. "How Deep 'Hate-America'" *Newsweek,* 26 May 1958, p. 29; Nuri Eren, "Why Is America Misunderstood?" *Reader's Digest* 78 (April 1961): 75–78; "Anti-Americanism Sweeps World," *U.S. News and World Report,* 8 April 1968, pp. 51–52; John Sheerin, "Do They Like Us?" *Catholic World* 177 (June 1953): 161–165; Harold Martin, "Why Do They *Hate* Us?" *Saturday Evening Post,* 23 April 1960, pp. 24–25.

4. "The Anatomy of Anti-Americanism," *Senior Scholastic,* 11 February 1966, p. 6.

5. William Pfaff, "Yankees vs. Latins," *Commonweal,* 28 May 1965, pp. 309–310.

6. Tai Chong-Soo, Erick Peterson, and Ted Robert Gurr, "Internal versus External Sources of Anti-Americanism: Two Comparative Studies," *Journal of Conflict Resolution* 17 (September 1973): 463.

7. Paul Hollander, *Anti-Americanism: Critiques at Home and Abroad, 1965–1990* (New York: Oxford University Press, 1992), pp. viii–x. Alvin Rubinstein and Donald Smith defined anti-Americanism as "any hostile action or expression that becomes part and parcel of an undifferentiated attack on the foreign policy, society, culture, and values of the United States"; see Rubinstein and Smith, "Anti-Americanism in the Third World," *Annals of the American Academy of Political and Social Science* 497 (May 1988): 35. Richard Kuisel gave a more European-centered definition: "A descriptive category signifying a pattern of attitudes, predominantly, if not systematically or permanently, critical. What counts is disdain for American society and American institutions as well as for the celebrated 'American way of life.' So does hostility toward an American conception of Western security." Kuisel, "Was de Gaulle an Anti-American?" *La Revue Tocqueville / The Tocqueville Review* 13 (1992): 22. For "anatomies," see Marcus Cunliffe, "The Anatomy of Anti-Americanism," in Rob Kroes and Maarten van Rossem, eds., *Anti-Americanism in Europe* (Amsterdam: Free University Press, 1986), pp. 20–36; and Rubinstein and Smith, "Anti-Americanism: Anatomy of a Phenomenon," in Rubinstein and Smith, eds., *Anti-Americanism in the Third World: Implications for U.S. Foreign Policy* (New York: Praeger, 1985), pp. 1–30. Kim Jinwung, in "The Nature of South Korean Anti-Americanism," *Korea Journal* 34 (Spring 1994): 36–47, compares several definitions.

8. Franklin Franco, interview with the author. Irving Louis Horowitz called anti-Americanism an "ideology" and an "ideological concept"; see Horowitz, "Latin America, Anti-Americanism, and Intellectual Hubris," in Rubinstein and Smith, eds., *Anti-Americanism in the Third World*, p. 63. Paul Hollander lists ideologies that overlap with anti-Americanism, such as nationalism, anticapitalism, and fear of modernization (*Anti-Americanism: Critiques at Home and Abroad*, p. 7).

9. For examples, see Robert Palkowski, "An Empirical Analysis of Anti-Americanism" (master's thesis, University of Alberta, 1972); Lars Schoultz, "The Nature of Anti-U.S. Sentiment in Latin America: A Preliminary Analysis with Argentine Data," *Comparative Politics* 11 (July 1979): 467–481; and Chong-Soo, Peterson, and Gurr, "Two Comparative Studies," pp. 455–488.

10. Rob Kroes, "The Great Satan versus the Evil Empire: Anti-Americanism in the Netherlands," in Kroes and van Rossem, eds., *Anti-Americanism in Europe*, p. 40.

11. Hollander, *Anti-Americanism: Critiques at Home and Abroad*, p. viii. See also the introduction in Paul Hollander, *Anti-Americanism: Irrational and Rational* (New Brunswick, N.J.: Transaction Publishers, 1995); and Stephen

Haseler, *The Varieties of Anti-Americanism: Reflex and Response* (Washington, D.C.: Ethics and Public Policy Center, 1985), especially the introduction by Midge Decter. Among the more fair-minded on the right are Mark Falcoff, *A Culture of Its Own: Taking Latin America Seriously* (New Brunswick, N.J.: Transaction Publishers, 1998), especially p. 2; Lawrence Harrison, *The Pan-American Dream: Do Latin America's Cultural Values Discourage True Partnership with the United States and Canada?* (New York: Basic Books, 1997); idem, *Underdevelopment Is a State of Mind* (Lanham, Md.: Madison Books, 2000); Horowitz, "Latin America"; and Carlos Rangel, *The Latin Americans: Their Love-Hate Relationship with the United States*, trans. Ivan Kats (New York: Harcourt Brace Jovanovich, 1977).

12. Hollander, *Anti-Americanism: Irrational and Rational*, pp. xiii–xiv.

13. For such language, see Juan Gualberto Gómez et al., *La lucha antimperialista en Cuba* (Havana: Instituto Cubano del Libro, 1976); Mariano Aguirre and Ana Montes, eds., *De Bolívar al Frente Sandinista: Antología del pensamiento anti-imperialista latinoamericano* (Madrid: Ediciones de la Torre, 1979); Instituto de Estudio del Sandinismo, *Pensamiento antimperialista en Nicaragua: Antología* (Managua: Nueva Nicaragua, 1982); and Olga Cabrera, ed., *El antimperialismo en la historia de Cuba* (Havana: Editorial de Ciencias Sociales, 1985). Rebecca Scott, a leading historian of Cuba, finds the term "anti-Americanism" "too capacious" and "not useful as an analytical concept" (remarks made during a conference on U.S.-Cuban relations at the University of North Carolina, Chapel Hill, 27–28 October 2000).

14. On Latin America, the best analyses are Rangel, *The Latin-Americans;* and John Reid, *Spanish American Images of the United States, 1790–1960* (Gainesville: University Presses of Florida, 1977). Anthologies of "great texts" include Carlos Rama, *La imagen de los Estados Unidos en la América Latina, de Simón Bolívar a Allende* (Mexico City: Secretaría de Educación Pública, 1975); F. Toscano and James Hiester, *Anti-Yankee Feelings in Latin America: An Anthology of Latin American Writings from Colonial to Modern Times in Their Historical Perspective* (Washington, D.C.: University Press of America, 1982); and all the books in note 13. Anti-Americanism as an intellectual movement has also shaped the study of this phenomenon in other countries. See, for example, David Strauss, *Menace in the West: The Rise of French Anti-Americanism in Modern Times* (Westport, Conn.: Greenwood Press, 1978); Richard Kuisel, *Seducing the French: The Dilemma of Americanization* (Berkeley: University of California Press, 1993); Gi-Wook Shin, "Marxism, Anti-Americanism, and Democracy in South Korea: An Examination of Nationalist Intellectual Discourse," *Positions: East Asia Cultures Critique* 3 (Fall 1995): 508–534; Dan Diner, *America in the Eyes of*

the Germans: An Essay on Anti-Americanism, trans. Allison Brown (Princeton: Marcus Wiener Publishers, 1996); and J. L. Granatstein, *Yankee Go Home? Canadians and Anti-Americanism* (Toronto: Harper Collins, 1996).

15. Russell Fitzgibbon, "Measurement of Latin-American Political Phenomena: A Statistical Experiment," *American Political Science Review* 45 (June 1951): 517.

16. Compare with Kuisel, *Seducing the French,* pp. 6–9.

17. Richard Bissell, "Implications of Anti-Americanism for U.S. Foreign Policy," in Rubinstein and Smith, eds., *Anti-Americanism in the Third World,* p. 249. Similar observations can be found in Milton Barall, "The United States Government Responds," *Annals of the American Academy of Political and Social Science* 334 (March 1961): 133–142; Rhodri Jeffreys-Jones, "The CIA and the Demise of Anti-Anti-Americanism: Some Evidence and Reflections," in Kroes and van Rossem, eds., *Anti-Americanism in Europe,* pp. 121–136; and W. Scott Thompson, "Anti-Americanism and the U.S. Government," *Annals of the American Academy of Political and Social Science* 497 (May 1988): 20–34. A mere handful of scholars have focused on U.S. responses to anti-Americanism in Latin America, and they have taken anti-Americanism mostly as an offshoot of nationalism, revolution, or communism. See Cole Blasier, *The Hovering Giant: U.S. Responses to Revolutionary Change in Latin America, 1910–1985,* rev. ed. (Pittsburgh, Pa.: University of Pittsburgh Press, 1985); Richard Welch, *Response to Revolution: The United States and the Cuban Revolution, 1959–1961* (Chapel Hill: University of North Carolina Press, 1985); Michael Krenn, *U.S. Policy toward Economic Nationalism in Latin America, 1917–1929* (Wilmington, Del.: SR Books, 1990); John Britton, *Revolution and Ideology: Images of the Mexican Revolution in the United States* (Lexington: University Press of Kentucky, 1995); and Charles Bergquist, "Latin American Revolution, U.S. Response," in Bergquist, *Labor and the Course of American Democracy: U.S. History in Latin American Perspective* (New York: Verso, 1996), pp. 81–115.

18. On the adjective "anti-American," see Sir Vincent Troubridge, "Note on *DAE,* I: Words on the Colonial and Revolutionary Periods," *American Speech* 20 (December 1945): 269.

1. The Road to Caracas

1. Figueres cited in Thomas Paterson, *Contesting Castro: The United States and the Triumph of the Cuban Revolution* (New York: Oxford University Press, 1994), p. 151; William Snow to Dulles, 15 May 1958, folder Vice President Nixon's Trip to South America, April 27–May 15, 1958, box 25, lot 61D411, Office Files of Snow, 1956–1959, RG 59, NARA; Henry Hoyt

to Snow, 15 May 1958, folder Nixon Trip Follow-up 1958, box 8, lot 60D513, Office Files of Hoyt, 1956–1958, RG 59, NARA.

2. Juan José Arévalo, *The Shark and the Sardines,* trans. June Cobb and Raúl Osegueda (New York: Lyle Stuart, 1961); see also Juan José Arévalo, *Anti-Komunism in Latin America,* trans. Carleton Beals (New York: Lyle Stuart, 1963).

3. Richard Nixon, *Six Crises* (New York: Warner Books, 1979; orig. pub. 1962), p. 270.

4. The very first Latin American criticisms are perhaps impossible to pinpoint and this chapter will not attempt to do so. One scholar in 1950 noted "the absence of any thorough research into the historical beginnings of Yankeephobia"; Mary Patricia Chapman, "Yankeephobia: An Analysis of Anti–United States Bias of Certain Spanish South American Intellectuals, 1898–1928" (Ph.D. diss., Stanford University, 1950), p. 4.

5. Unless otherwise indicated, all translations from Spanish and French are the author's. Sarmiento cited in Pablo Pozzi, "Estado Unidos y Sarmiento: Una visión para el desarollo nacional," *Estados Unidos desde América Latina: Sociedad, política y cultura,* comp. Victor Arriaga Weiss and Ana Rosa Suárez Argüello (Mexico City: Colegio de México, 1995), p. 144.

6. Cited in Lester Langley, *America and the Americas: The United States in the Western Hemisphere* (Athens: University of Georgia Press, 1989), p. 82; Lawrence Harrison, *The Pan-American Dream: Do Latin America's Cultural Values Discourage True Partnership with the United States and Canada?* (New York: Basic Books, 1997), p. 29; John Reid, *Spanish American Images of the United States, 1790–1960* (Gainesville: University Presses of Florida, 1977), pp. 32, 46–51, 66.

7. John Quincy Adams from 1821 in Piero Gleijeses, "The Limits of Sympathy: The United States and the Independence of Spanish America," *Journal of Latin American Studies* 24 (October 1992): 482; John Adams from 1815 in Lars Schoultz, *Beneath the United States: A History of U.S. Policy toward Latin America* (Cambridge, Mass.: Harvard University Press, 1998), p. 5; George Black, *The Good Neighbor: How the United States Wrote the History of Central America and the Caribbean* (New York: Pantheon Books, 1988), p. 7; Langley, *America and the Americas,* p. 69; and Alvin Goffin, "Nationalism and Mexican Interpretations on the War of the North American Invasion, 1846–1848," *Canadian Review of Studies in Nationalism* 19 (1992): 129–138.

Walker, called "The Grey-Eyed Man of Destiny," was a native of Tennessee who, leading small armies, failed to take over Baja California in 1853–1854 but then seized control of Nicaragua from 1855 to 1857. At various times, he drew on support from U.S. entrepreneurs, U.S. politicians, and the Nicaraguan Liberal Party. He notably got himself elected president of Nicaragua and declared the country open to slavery. By mid-1857 he was forced to abandon Nicaragua. In 1860 the British captured him and handed him over to the Hondurans, who shot him. In response to Walker's adventurism, delegates from several Latin American countries held a conference to insist on the territorial integrity of nations. See William Walker, *The War in Nicaragua* (Mobile, Ala.: S. H. Goetzel, 1860; Karl Bermann, *Under the Big Stick: Nicaragua and the United States since 1848* (Boston: South End Press, 1986); especially ch. 4; and Frederic Rosengarten, Jr., *Freebooters Must Die! The Life and Death of William Walker, the Most Notorious Filibuster of the Nineteenth Century* (Wayne, Pa.: Haverford House, 1976).

8. Minister in Schoultz, *Beneath,* pp. 18, 19; Bolívar in Carlos Rama, *La imagen de los Estados Unidos en la América Latina, de Simón Bolívar a Allende* (Mexico City: Secretaría de Educación Pública, 1975), p. 53; Victorino Lastarria in José Martí, *Martí on the U.S.A.* (Carbondale: Southern Illinois University Press, 1966), p. 125, n. 3; Bilbao in F. Toscano and James Hiester, *Anti-Yankee Feelings in Latin America: An Anthology of Latin American Writings from Colonial to Modern Times in Their Historical Perspective* (Washington, D.C.: University Press of America, 1982), p. 17. Gordon Brotherson charges Sarmiento with "heavy racism"; see "Rodó Views His Continent," in Gustavo San Ramón, ed., *This America We Dream Of: Rodó and "Ariel" One Hundred Years On* (London: Institute of Latin American Studies, 2001), p. 36.

9. Rodó, *Ariel,* trans. Margaret Sayers Peden (Austin: University of Texas Press, 1988; orig. pub. 1900); see also San Ramón, ed., *This America.*

10. Lars Schoultz, "The Nature of Anti-U.S. Sentiment in Latin America: A Preliminary Analysis with Argentine Data," *Comparative Politics* 11 (July 1979): 467; Peter Smith, *Talons of the Eagle: Dynamics of U.S.–Latin American Relations* (New York: Oxford University Press, 1996), pp. 96–97. Carlos Rangel, among other Latin Americans, has been resentful of Arielism, saying, "It has provided the intellectuals with the psychological compensation they craved"; see Rangel, *The Latin Americans: Their Love-Hate Relationship with the United States,* trans. Ivan Kats (New York: Harcourt Brace Jovanovich, 1977), p. 95. See also Pablo Mella, "La crisis de *Ariel* y la juventud dominicana," *Estudios Sociales* (Dominican Republic) 60 (April–June 1985): 79–95. San Román, "Introduction," in *This America,* p. 4.

11. Cited in Rama, *La imagen,* p. 95 (see also pp. 91–97); William Stokes, "Cultural Anti-Americanism in Latin America," *Issues and Conflicts: Studies in Twentieth Century American Diplomacy,* ed. George Anderson (Lawrence: University of Kansas Press, 1959), pp. 318–319.

12. David Whisnant, "Rubén Darío as a Focal Cultural Figure in Nicaragua," *Latin American Research Review* 22 (1992): 18; idem, *Rascally Signs in Sacred Places: The Politics of Culture in Nicaragua* (Chapel Hill: University of North Carolina Press, 1995), pp. 321–323; Reid, *Spanish American Images,* p. 195; Jason Wilson, "Replay of Plato: Rodó, Darío and Poetry," in *This America,* p. 23.

13. Schoultz, *Beneath,* pp. 179–80, 192. Excellent monographs on economic growth and its social and political consequences include Paul Dosal, *Doing Business with the Dictators: A Political History of United Fruit in Guatemala, 1899–1944* (Wilmington, Del.: Scholarly Resources, 1993); Darío Euraque, *Reinterpreting the Banana Republic: Region and State in Honduras, 1870–1972* (Chapel Hill: University of North Carolina Press, 1996); and César Ayala, *American Sugar Kingdom: The Plantation Economy in the Spanish Caribbean, 1898–1934* (Chapel Hill: University of North Carolina Press, 1999).

14. Pablo Riguzzi, "¿Arte o comercio, poesía o industria? La impresa económica de EU en América Latina, 1870–1914: Visiones y actitudes latinoamericanas," *Estados Unidos desde América Latina,* pp. 159–182. For more on workers and resistance, see Thomas O'Brien, *The Revolutionary Mission: American Enterprise in Latin America, 1900–1945* (Cambridge: Cambridge University Press, 1996).

15. Nancy Mitchell, *The Danger of Dreams: German and American Imperialism in Latin America* (Chapel Hill: University of North Carolina Press, 1999).

16. José Vasconcelos, *The Cosmic Race / La raza cósmica,* trans. Didier Jaén (Baltimore, Md.: Johns Hopkins University Press, 1997; orig. pub. 1925), pp. xiv, 19, ix. Stokes, "Cultural Anti-Americanism," p. 321. Indigenism inspired various writers. José Santos Chocano of Peru dreamed of a revived Inca spirit rising to conquer "the man with blue eyes," "the race with blond hair"; Miguel Ángel Asturias of Guatemala, who wrote novels about U.S. banana plantations, was influenced by the *Chilam Balam,* the Mayan text that inspired resistance to the Spaniards; and Costa Rican Carlos Luis Fallas admitted being moved by *La raza cósmica* to write the classic *Mamita Yunai* (Mommy United [Fruit Company]) (Havana: Editorial de Arte y Literatura, 1975; orig. pub. 1941). See Toscano and Hiester, *Anti-Yankee Feelings,* pp. 55, 183.

17. John Britton, *Revolution and Ideology: Images of the Mexican Revolution in the United States* (Lexington: University Press of Kentucky, 1995), pp. 63, 111.

18. Consul Samuel Magill at Guadalajara to Secretary of State Philander Knox, 1911; and Charles Freeman at Durango, both in Frederick Turner, "Anti-Americanism in Mexico, 1910–1913," *Hispanic American Historical Review*

47 (1967): 502, 503. Banking and mining operator M. S. Largey, 1913, in Smith, *Talons*, p. 106.

19. Sandino to Francisco Paguaga and others, 21 October 1927, in Augusto Sandino, *El pensamiento vivo*, vol. 1 (Managua: Nueva Nicaragua, 1984), pp. 163–164.

20. Similar movements arose in the Dominican Republic, Haiti, and elsewhere, and in the end they were all defeated in battle or by betrayal. See Lester Langley, *The United States and the Caribbean in the Twentieth Century*, rev. ed. (Athens: University of Georgia Press, 1985); idem, *The Banana Wars: United States Intervention in the Caribbean, 1898–1934*, rev. ed. (Wilmington, Del.: Scholarly Resources, 2002); Hans Schmidt, *The United States Occupation of Haiti, 1915–1934* (New Brunswick, N.J.: Rutgers University Press, 1995); and Bruce Calder, *The Impact of Intervention: The Dominican Republic during the U.S. Occupation of 1916–1924* (Austin: University of Texas Press, 1984).

21. Cited in Karl Bermann, *Under the Big Stick: Nicaragua and the United States since 1848* (Boston: South End Press, 1986), p. 210; for other *cortes*, see Eduardo Crawley, *Nicaragua in Perspective* (New York: St. Martin's Press, 1984), p. 72.

22. "A cantarles voy, señores" (n.d.), Instituto del Sandinismo, *El sandinismo: Documentos básicos* (Managua: Nueva Nicaragua, 1983), p. 141.

23. Humberto Ortega Saavedra, *50 años de lucha sandinista* (Havana: Editorial de Ciencias Sociales, 1980), p. 128.

24. Michelle Dospital, *Siempre más allá . . . El movimiento en Nicaragua, 1927–1934*, trans. Verónica Kugel (Mexico: IHN/CEMCA, 1996), p. 52. On Sandino see also Volker Wünderich, *Sandino: Una biografía política* (Managua: Nueva Nicaragua, 1995); Michael Schroeder, "The Sandino Rebellion Revisited: Civil War, Imperialism, Popular Nationalism, and State Formation Muddied Up Together in the Segovias of Nicaragua, 1926–1934," in Gilbert Joseph, Catherine LeGrand, and Ricardo Salvatore, eds., *Close Encounters of Empire: Writing the Cultural History of U.S.–Latin American Relations* (Durham, N.C.: Duke University Press, 1998), pp. 208–268; and Alejandro Bendaña, *La mística de Sandino* (Managua: Centro de Estudios Internacionales, 1994).

25. Cited in Bermann, *Big Stick*, p. 216. See also pp. 196–217.

26. Smith, *Talons*, p. 105. Of these "codes" Smith writes: "This was not a strategic option or policy guideline so much as an expression of popular feeling, the adoption of a general stance, and the construction of a national and regional discourse." See also his periodization of Latin American resistance movements, pp. 88–104.

27. Mariátegui quotations in Chapman, "Yankeephobia," p. 124; Diego Rivera,

Portrait of America (New York: Covici, Friede, 1934), pp. 192–195; Rama, *La imagen*, pp. 36, 120; Smith, *Talons*, p. 113; Cuesta, *El imperialismo yanqui y la revolución en el Caribe* (San Juan, Puerto Rico: Campos, 1936); Saenz, *Hispanoamérica contra el coloniaje* (Mexico City: Unión Democrática Centroamericana, 1949). See also William Stokes, "Economic Anti-Americanism in Latin America," *Inter-American Economic Affairs* 11 (Autumn 1957): 3–22.

28. Alan Angell, "The Left in Latin America since c. 1920," in Leslie Bethell, ed., *Latin America: Politics and Society since 1930* (Cambridge: Cambridge University Press, 1998), pp. 75–107.

29. Smith, *Talons*, pp. 132, 134.

30. An early analysis of these "middle sector" political agendas is John Johnson, "The Political Role of the Latin-American Middle Sectors," *Annals of the American Academy of Political and Social Science* 334 (March 1961): 20–29.

31. Laura Ruiz Jiménez, "Peronism and Anti-Imperialism in the Argentine Press: 'Braden or Perón' Was Also 'Perón Is Roosevelt,'" *Journal of Latin American Studies* 30 (October 1998): 551–571.

32. Cited in Toscano and Hiester, *Anti-Yankee Feelings,* p. 96.

33. Charles Ameringer, *The Caribbean Legion: Patriots, Politicians, Soldiers of Fortune, 1946–1950* (University Park: Pennsylvania State University Press, 1996).

34. Víctor Raúl Haya de la Torre, *¿A dónde va Indoamérica?* 2nd ed. (Santiago, Chile: Biblioteca América, 1935), p. 75; Bendaña, *La mística de Sandino,* p. 83; Víctor Alba, *Nationalists without Nations: The Oligarchy versus the People in Latin America* (New York: Praeger, 1968), p. 71.

35. Frederick Pike, *The Politics of the Miraculous in Peru: Haya de la Torre and the Spiritualist Tradition* (Lincoln: University of Nebraska Press, 1986), pp. 142, 241.

36. Juan Acevedo, "Anti-Americanism in Latin America; or, Why the Ill-Feeling toward the United States" (master's thesis, Boston University, 1927), p. 38.

37. Chapman, "Yankeephobia," p. 18.

38. Samuel Huntington, "American Ideals versus American Institutions," *Political Science Quarterly* 97 (March 1982): 15, 16, 21–22. Worsthorne in Henry Fairlie, "Anti-Americanism at Home and Abroad," *Commentary* 60 (December 1975): 34; the scholar is Thomas Perry Thornton, "Preface," *Annals of the American Academy of Political and Social Science* 497 (May 1988): 9. On power and "the American conception of world opinion," see Frank Ninkovich, *Modernity and Power* (Chicago: University of Chicago Press, 1994), pp. xiii–xvi; and Gertrude Himmelfarb, "American Democ-

racy and Its European Critics," *Twentieth-Century* 151 (April 1952): 320–
327. Wilson himself had said, in a wildly successful tour of Europe after
World War I, that "the great working classes of the world . . . have by their
conscience of community of interests . . . done perhaps more than any
other influence to establish a world opinion" and that diplomats "must
think and act and confer in the presence of that opinion"; quoted in
Thomas Knock, *To End All Wars: Woodrow Wilson and the Quest for a New
World Order* (Princeton, N.J.: Princeton University Press, 1992), p. 196.

39. For an overview of scholarship on this issue, see Ole Holsti, "Public Opin-
ion and Foreign Policy: Challenges to the Almond-Lippman Consensus
Mershon Series: Research Programs and Debates," *International Studies
Quarterly* 36 (1992): 439–466.

40. Acheson in Lloyd Free and Hadley Cantril, *The Political Beliefs of Americans: A Study of Public Opinion* (New York: Simon and Schuster, 1968),
p. 78; Richard Wightman Fox, *Reinhold Niebuhr: A Biography* (San Francisco: Harper and Row, 1987), p. 245; Reston, "Why We Irritate Our
Allies," *Harper's,* May 1951, p. 30.

41. David Strauss, *Menace in the West: The Rise of French Anti-Americanism in
Modern Times* (Westport, Conn.: Greenwood Press, 1978); Leo Winston
Hindsley, "In Search of an Ally: French Attitudes toward America, 1919–
1929" (Ph.D. diss., Michigan State University, 1980). On the impact of Eu-
ropean socialism, conservatism, and fascism on the developing world, see
Stephen Haseler, *The Varieties of Anti-Americanism: Reflex and Response*
(Washington, D.C.: Ethics and Public Policy Center, 1985), pp. 19–38;
and Nils Wessell, foreword, in Alvin Rubinstein and Donald Smith, eds.,
Anti-Americanism in the Third World: Implications for U.S. Foreign Policy
(New York: Praeger, 1985), p. ix.

42. Editorial, "Why Is U.S. Prestige Declining?" *New Republic* 23 (August
1954): 8.

43. Anonymous Europeans quoted in "How We Appear to Others," *Life,* 23
December 1957, pp. 150–154.

44. William Buchanan, "As Others See Us," *Annals of the American Academy of
Political and Social Science* 295 (September 1954): 9. The United Nations
Economic, Social and Cultural Organization conducted this poll in Aus-
tralia, Britain, France, Germany, Italy, the Netherlands, Norway, and the
United States. For similar results in later polls, see "In the Mirror," *Time* 21
(April 1952): 31; and Andrew Henry Ziegler, Jr., "The West European Pub-
lic and the Atlantic Alliance (NATO)" (Ph.D. diss., University of Florida,
1987).

45. Circumscribing anti-Americanism in France, for example, Richard Kuisel
writes that "anti-Americanism during the Cold War, in my interpretation,

did not represent the French and was in its most polemical form essentially the product of leftist Parisian, especially *marxisant* and Christian, literati and of the Communist Party." See Kuisel, *Seducing the French: The Dilemma of Americanization* (Berkeley: University of California Press, 1993), p. 16.

46. Reston, "Why We Irritate Our Allies," p. 29.

47. "'Liberal' Horror Stories about U.S.A. Aren't Helping Our Reputation Abroad," *Saturday Evening Post*, 16 January 1954, p. 12; D. W. Brogan, "America through British Eyes," *Saturday Review*, 13 October 1951, p. 19.

48. Editorial, "Learning about 'Anti-Americanism,'" *America*, 26 December 1953, p. 330.

49. John B. Sheerin, "Do They Like Us?" *Catholic World* 177 (June 1953): 161.

50. Raymond Cartier, "Pourquoi les Américains sont-ils détestés aujourd'hui dans le monde entier?" *Paris-Match*, 24 March 1956, p. 21.

51. "Fighting Anti-Americanism Abroad," *Newsweek*, 30 April 1956, p. 94.

52. William Lederer and Eugene Burdick, *The Ugly American* (New York: Fawcett Crest, 1958); Michael Hunt, *Lyndon Johnson's War: America's Cold War Crusade in Vietnam, 1945–1968* (New York: Hill and Wang, 1996), p. 3.

53. Mark Haefele, "John F. Kennedy, USIA, and World Public Opinion," *Diplomatic History* 25 (Winter 2001): 63, 66.

54. Robert Knopp, "How We Look to Latin Americans," *America* 7 (March 1959): 662–664.

55. "'Liberal' Horror Stories," p. 12; "Fighting Anti-Americanism," p. 94.

56. "Anti-Americanism," *Commonweal* 66 (7 June 1957): 245; "'Anti-Americanism' Abroad," *Newsweek*, 10 June 1957, pp. 51–53. Examples of protests in East Asia are in Buel Patch, *Anti-Americanism and Soldiers Overseas*, Editorial Research Reports (Washington, D.C.), vol. 2, no. 1, 3 July 1957.

57. "Argentina's Anti-U.S. Barrage," *Newsweek*, 19 May 1952, p. 56; Irwin Edman, "No Culture in the USA?" *Americas* 3 (November 1951): 3, 4, 5.

58. USIA poll, 1957, folder LA-12, box 2, Latin America, Public Opinion Barometer Reports, 1955–1962, Office of Research, RG 306, NARA; Adolf Berle, "Communist Thunder to the South," *New York Times Magazine*, 4 July 1954, p. 8; Cartier, "Pourquoi les Américains," pp. 20–23.

59. R. D. Murphy, "Review of Recent Anti-American Demonstrations," *U.S. Department of State Bulletin*, 9 June 1958, p. 954.

60. Nixon, *Six Crises*, pp. 215, 219.

61. Marvin Zahnister, "A Diplomatic Pearl Harbor? Richard Nixon's Goodwill Mission to Latin America in 1958," *Diplomatic History* 13 (March 1989): 179. The most complete public reporting at the time was William Hines, "The Venezuela Story," *Washington Evening Star*, 25–29 May 1958. For in-

ternal government narratives, see J. M. Perry to Terry Sanders; Viron Vaky to Sanders; and Jackson Wilson to Sanders, all 14 May 1958, folder Vice President Nixon's Trip—General, box 24, lot 62D31, RG 59, NARA.

62. Rubottom interview by Luter, 22 December 1969.

63. Nixon, *Six Crises,* p. 238.

64. Nixon trip briefing papers, April 1958, folder Bernbaum—Briefing Papers for Vice President's South American Tour, box 23, lot 61D332, Office Files of Maurice M. Bernbaum, 1954–1959, RG 59, NARA; Juan de Onís, "Caracas Annoyed by U.S. Oil Curbs," *New York Times,* 14 May 1958.

65. Quotation is from Rubottom interview by Luter, 22 December 1969; Rubottom interview by Challener, 12 June 1966; Russ Olson, "'You Can't Spit on a Foreign Policy,'" *SHAFR Newsletter* (September 2000): pp. 31–33.

66. Unattributed quotation from Hines, "The Venezuela Story," 25 May 1958, p. A-1.

67. Olson, "'You Can't Spit,'" p. 33.

68. Quotations from "The Venezuelan Story," 25 May 1958, p. A-19.

69. Unnamed correspondent cited in Bill Brammer to Senator Lyndon Johnson, 18 June 1958, folder Reaction to Nixon's South American Trip, box 602, Subject Files 1958, Senate Papers, LBJL. Other quotations are from Nixon, *Six Crises,* pp. 255, 256–257.

70. "When Reds Tried to Kill Nixon: A Close-Up," *U.S. News and World Report,* 30 May 1958, p. 51; "What's Wrong Now in South America?" *U.S. News and World Report,* 23 May 1958, p. 44.

71. Quotation from NSC meeting notes, 19 June 1958, *FRUS 1958–1960,* 5: 29; compare Cabinet meeting handwritten notes by Art Minnich, 16 May 1958, folder C-45 (1) May 16 and 23, 1958, box 5, Cabinet Series, Office of the Staff Secretary: Records 1952–1961, White House Office, DDEL; see also Dulles telephone conversation with Andrew Goodpaster, 13 May 1958, folder Memoranda of Tel. Conv.—W.H. April 1, 1958 to July 31, 1958 (3), box 13, Telephone Calls Series, Dulles Papers, DDEL.

72. Cushman interview by Soapes.

73. Whitman Diary, 13 May 1958, folder May, 1958—ACW Diary (1), box 10, Ann Whitman Diary Series, Eisenhower Papers as President, 1953–1961, DDEL.

74. "How Deep 'Hate-America,'" *Newsweek,* 26 May 1958, p. 29.

75. William Snow to Dulles, 15 May 1958, folder Vice President Nixon's Trip —General, box 24, lot 62D31, RG 59, NARA. The statements themselves are in "Remarks by the President and the Vice President at Mats Terminal on the Return of the Vice President from his South American Tour," 15 May 1958, folder Vice President's Return 5/15/58, box 26, Speech Series, Eisenhower Papers as President, 1953–1961, DDEL. Senator Homer Cape-

heart (Republican from Indiana) blamed "a 100 percent Russian penetration." Senator Bourke Hickenlooper (Republican from Iowa) said the trip revealed a "world-wide pattern of Communist stimulus." Both are cited in Peter Smith, *Talons,* p. 140.

76. Henry Hoyt to Rubottom, Snow, and Bernbaum, 19 June 1958, folder Nixon Trip—Follow-up 1958, box 8, Office Files of Henry Hoyt, lot 60D513, RG 59, NARA.

77. Murphy, "Review," p. 953. See also U.S. Senate, Judiciary Committee, Internal Security Subcommittee, *Communist Anti-American Riots: Mob Violence as an Instrument of Red Diplomacy,* 26 August 1960 (Washington, D.C.: GPO, 1960).

78. Nixon telephone conversation with Christian Herter, 16 May 1958, folder CAH Telephone Calls 4/1/58 to 6/30/58 (1), box 11, Herter Papers, 1957–1961, DDEL; Nixon, *Six Crises,* p. 273.

79. Maurice Bernbaum memorandum to Rubottom and Snow, 16 May 1958, folder Nixon Trip—Follow-Up 1958, box 8, lot 60D513 Office Files of Henry A. Hoyt, 1956–1958, RG 59, NARA; Olson, "'You Can't Spit,'" p. 32.

80. Berle, *The Adolf A. Berle Diary* (Hyde Park, N.Y.: Franklin D. Roosevelt Library, 1978), 22 May 1958; Zahnister, "A Diplomatic Pearl Harbor?" pp. 184–185; John Dreier to Rubottom, 27 May 1958, folder NSC Miscellaneous 1958, box 8, Office Files of Henry A. Hoyt, 1956–1958, lot 60D513, RG 59, NARA.

81. Editorial, "Anti-Americanism," *Des Moines Register,* 15 May 1958; editorial, "Beirut, Algiers and Caracas," *New York Times,* 14 May 1958; Carey McWilliams, "Anti-Americanism Updated," *The Nation,* 31 May 1958, p. 488.

82. Nixon speech to National Press Club, 21 May 1958, folder The Vice President 1957–1958, box 353, lot 62D92, Public Affairs Subject Files, Executive Office, Office of the Assistant Secretary for Public Affairs, RG 59, NARA.

83. OCB special report to NSC, 28 November 1958, *FRUS* 1958–1960, 5: 54; NSC meeting notes, folder 396th Meeting of NSC February 12, 1959, box 11, NSC Series, Eisenhower Papers as President, 1953–1961, DDEL.

84. National Intelligence Estimate 80/90–58, "Latin American Attitudes toward the U.S.," *FRUS* 1958–1960, 5: 69, 70.

85. For example, USIA, "Prevalent Opinions Held by Latin Americans about the People of the US," 10 April 1962, and USIA, "Some Contemporary Prevalent Attitudes of Latin Americans toward the US," 16 April 1962, both in folder RO/LA 1962 1/38, box 2, Requestor Only Reports, 1956–1962, Office of Research, RG 306, NARA; USIA, "Latin American Opin-

ion—A Current Assessment," 1 July 1959, folder P-32-59, box 7, Production Division Research Reports, 1956–1959, Office of Research, RG 306, NARA.

86. Joseph Silberstein to Terry Sanders, 14 May 1958, folder Vice President Nixon's Trip—General, box 24, lot 62D31, RG 59, NARA; John Dreier to Rubottom, 27 May 1958, folder NSC Miscellaneous 1958, box 8, Office Files of Henry A. Hoyt, 1956–58, lot 60D513, RG 59, NARA.

87. "How Deep 'Hate-America,'" p. 34; McWilliams, "Anti-Americanism Updated," p. 489.

88. Examples include USIA, "Free World Opinion on Selected International Issues," 14 June 1960, folder RN-25-60, box 3, Research Notes, 1958–1962, Office of Research, RG 306, NARA; see also Washburn interview by Edwin.

89. Allen cited in "Image of America," 23 October 1958, folder Image of America, box 3, Subject Subseries, OCB Series; and in a presentation to the Planning Board, 30 September 1958, folder United States Information Agency (1) [1954–1960], box 18, Briefing Notes Subseries, NSC Series, both in Office of the Special Assistant for National Security Affairs: Records, 1952–1961, White House Office, DDEL. Eisenhower in NSC meeting notes, folder 381st Meeting of NSC October 2, 1958, box 10, NSC Series, Eisenhower Papers as President, 1953–1961, DDEL.

90. Haefele, "John F. Kennedy," 67.

91. "Major Findings of Latin American 'Flash' Survey on Nixon Trip," folder Multi L. American May 1958 General Attitudes (LA7) ZP5801, box 5, Multi Country (Area) Project Files, 1952–1963, Latin America, 1958–1961, RG 306, NARA; "Attitudes toward America in Recent Surveys," 18 July 1958, folder S-11-58, box 15, Office of Research Special Reports, 1953–1963, RG 306, NARA.

92. International Research Associates poll for *Life en español: A Survey of Latin American Public Opinion* (New York: Time, Inc., 1958), p. 1; "Antiamericanismo en Colombia," *Revista de la Universidad de los Andes* (1959): 105; USIA overview of the *Revista* article, 22 July 1959, folder S-51-59, box 17, 1959, Special Reports, 1953–1963, Office of Research, RG 306, NARA; the results also appeared in "Survey on Anti-Americanism," *Times of Havana*, 3 August 1959, p. 15; Division of Research and Analysis for American Republics, "Latin American Attitudes toward the United States," 19 January 1959, *OSS / State Department Intelligence and Research Reports, 15: Latin America: 1941–1961*, ed. Paul Kesaris (Washington, D.C.: UPA, n.d.), 4: 0463.

93. *Life en español* poll, p. 1. Similar responses were obtained in USIA poll, "Recent Trends in Latin American Opinion toward the United States and

the Soviet Union," October 1958, folder LA-16, box 2, Latin America, Public Barometer Reports, 1955–1962, Office of Research, RG 306, NARA.

94. Cabinet meeting handwritten notes by Art Minnich, 16 May 1958, folder C-45 (1) May 16 and 23, 1958, box 5, Cabinet Series, Office of the Staff Secretary: Records 1952–1961, White House Office, DDEL.

95. NSC meeting notes, 23 May 1958, folder 366th Meeting of NSC May 22, 1958, box 10, NSC Series, Eisenhower Papers as President, 1953–1961, DDEL. For details on what was done, see Stephen Rabe, *Eisenhower and Latin America: The Foreign Policy of Anti-Communism* (Chapel Hill: University of North Carolina, 1988), pp. 111–112; Rubottom interview by Luter, 22 December 1969; and Snow to Cushman, 22 September 1958, folder 1958 Nixon Trip to South America, box 7, lot 60D553, Subject Files, Records of Roy Rubottom, RG 59, NARA; Joseph Tulchin, "The United States and Latin America in the 1960s," *Journal of Inter-American Studies and World Affairs* 30 (March 1988): 10.

96. Emphasis in original; Rubottom to Gerard Smith, 11 August 1958, folder Latin America—General 1958, box 7, Office Files of Henry A. Hoyt, 1956–1958, lot 60D513, RG 59, NARA.

2. Cuba, 1959

1. Emphasis in original; Carlos Rangel, *The Latin-Americans: Their Love-Hate Relationship with the United States,* trans. Ivan Kats (New York: Harcourt Brace Jovanovich, 1977), p. 53.

2. Louis Pérez, Jr., *Cuba and the United States: Ties of Singular Intimacy* (Athens: University of Georgia Press, 1990), p. xvi. Cole Blasier affirmed that by 1958 "Cuba had fallen under U.S. influence more than almost any other Latin American country, with the possible exception of Panama." See Blasier, "The Elimination of United States Influence," in Carmelo Mesa-Lago, ed., *Revolutionary Change in Cuba* (Pittsburgh, Pa.: University of Pittsburgh Press, 1971), p. 54.

3. Cited in Louis Pérez, Jr., *The War of 1898: The United States and Cuba in History and Historiography* (Chapel Hill: University of North Carolina Press, 1998), p. 23; Carlos Alberto Montaner, "The Roots of Anti-Americanism in Cuba: Sovereignty in an Age of World Cultural Hegemony," trans. Nelson Durán, *Caribbean Review* 13 (March 1984): 13; Pérez, *Ties,* p. 98.

4. Montaner, "Roots," 13.

5. Thomas O'Brien, *The Revolutionary Mission: American Enterprise in Latin America, 1900–1945* (Cambridge: Cambridge University Press, 1996), pp. 208–210; Pérez, *Ties,* p. 144.

6. Louis Pérez, Jr., *Cuba: Between Reform and Revolution* (New York: Oxford University Press, 1988), p. ix; Susan Schroeder, ed., *Cuba: A Handbook of Historical Statistics* (Boston: G. K. Hall, 1982), pp. 413, 261, 190.

7. Ramón Ruiz, *Cuba: The Making of a Revolution* (Boston: University of Massachusetts Press, 1968), pp. 9–10; Thomas Paterson, *Contesting Castro: The United States and the Triumph of the Cuban Revolution* (New York: Oxford University Press, 1994), pp. 34, 35, 41; on cultural influences, see pp. 46–57.

8. Montaner, "Roots," pp. 14, 15. Louis Pérez made a similar claim the central thesis of his *On Becoming Cuban: Identity, Nationality, and Culture* (Chapel Hill: University of North Carolina Press, 1999), p. 9: the U.S. presence "was most obviously economic and political, but it was most decisively cultural, whereby the influence of North American institutions, ideas, values, and norms took hold not through compulsion or coercion but by way of assent and acquiescence."

9. Boris Goldenberg, *The Cuban Revolution and Latin America* (New York: Praeger, 1965), p. 101; Pérez, *War of 1898*, p. 33. See the essays by Sanguily, Varona, and Portuondo in Juan Gualberto Gómez et al., *La lucha antimperialista en Cuba* (Havana: Instituto Cubano del Libro, 1976); and Sheldon Liss, *Roots of Revolution: Radical Thought in Cuba* (Lincoln: University of Nebraska Press, 1987), p. 59.

10. The term is from Thomas Schoonover, *The United States in Central America, 1860–1911: Episodes of Social Imperialism and Imperial Rivalry in the World-System* (Durham, N.C.: Duke University Press, 1991). On José Martí, see Martí, *Martí on the U.S.A.*, ed. and trans. Luis Baralt (Carbondale: Southern Illinois University Press, 1966); and Emilio Roig de Leuchsenring, *Martí Anti-Imperialist* (Havana: Book Institute, 1967).

11. Alfred Melon, *L'anti-impérialisme dans la poésie cubaine: R. Pedroso, N. Guillén, M. Navarro Luna* (Publications de l'Equipe de Recherche de l'Université de Paris VIII, 1980), pp. 24–25.

12. Julio César Gandarilla cited in Pérez, *Ties*, p. 146. See also pp. 149–169.

13. Alfred Padula, Jr., "The Fall of the Bourgeoisie: Cuba, 1959–1961" (Ph.D. diss., University of New Mexico, 1974), pp. vii, 7.

14. Jorge Domínguez, "Culture: Is It the Key to the Troubles in U.S.-Cuban Relations?" review of *On Becoming Cuban*, by Louis Pérez, Jr., *Diplomatic History* 25 (Summer 2001): 514; Hugh Thomas, "Middle-Class Politics and the Cuban Revolution," in Claudio Veliz, ed., *The Politics of Conformity in Latin America* (New York: Oxford University Press, 1967), pp. 249–277; Pérez, *On Becoming Cuban*, pp. 446–448. On the Ortodoxos (the Partido del Pueblo Cubano) see Elena Alavez Martín, *Eduardo Chibás en la hora de la ortodoxia* (Havana: Editorial de Ciencias Sociales, 1994). On

1950s resistance to Batista, see Gladys Marel García, *Memoria e identidad: Un estudio específico, 1952–1958* (Havana: Editorial de Ciencias Sociales, 1996). For similar arguments about rich land and poor people, see Lowry Nelson, *Rural Cuba* (Minneapolis: University of Minnesota Press, 1950); and Ruiz, *Cuba.*

15. Núñez Jiménez interview by Szulc, 4 April 1985, Szulc Papers, JFKL.

16. Robert Freeman Smith, "Twentieth-Century Cuban Historiography," *Hispanic American Historical Review* 44 (February 1964): 48, n. 19.

17. Gandarilla, *Contra el yanqui: Obra de protesta contra la enmienda Platt y contra la absorción y el maquiavelismo norteamericanos* (Havana: Rambla, Bouza, 1913), pp. 10, 8.

18. Blas Roca Calderío interview by Szulc, 4 June 1985, Szulc Papers, JFKL. For more on Gandarilla, see Olga Cabrera, *El antimperialismo en la historia de Cuba* (Havana: Editorial de Ciencias Sociales, 1985), p. 102.

19. Alavez Martín, *Eduardo Chibás,* p. 5.

20. Raúl Roa, *La revolución del 30 se fue a bolina* (Havana: Instituto Cubano del Libro, 1973), p. 364.

21. Quotation is from Roa, *La revolución del 30 se fue a bolina,* p. 100. Jaime Suchlicki, *Cuba: From Columbus to Castro,* 2nd ed. (Washington, D.C.: Pergramm-Brassey, 1986), pp. 96–98; Cabrera, *El antimperialismo,* p. 135; José Tabares del Real, *La revolución del 30: Sus dos últimos años* (Havana: Instituto Cubano del Libro, 1973), pp. 70–73; Melon, *L'anti-impérialisme,* p. 43; Sheldon Liss, *Fidel! Castro's Political and Social Thought* (Boulder, Colo.: Westview Press, 1994), p. 31.

22. Kierkegaard cited in Joan Stambaugh, "On the Meaning of Ambivalence," *Philosophy Today* 24 (Summer 1980): 165.

23. Emphasis in original; Wickham-Crowley, *Guerrillas and Revolution in Latin America; A Comparative Study of Insurgents and Regimes since 1956* (Princeton, N.J.: Princeton University Press, 1992), p. 152.

24. Max Lesnick interview by Szulc, 10 August 1984, Szulc Papers, JFKL.

25. CIA Psychiatric Staff, "Psychiatric Personality Study of Fidel Castro," December 1961, folder Cuba 2 of 5, box WH-31 to WH-48, Classified Subject Files, 1961–1964, White House Files, Schlesinger Papers, JFKL; Paterson, *Contesting Castro,* p. 32; Peter Bourne, *Fidel: A Biography of Fidel Castro* (New York: Dodd, Mead, 1986), p. 17.

26. Castro to Roosevelt, 6 November 1940, Cuba: Havana Consulate General: Confidential File, 1935–1940, RG 84, NARA; Georgie Anne Geyer, *Guerrilla Prince: The Untold Story of Fidel Castro* (Boston: Little, Brown, 1991), p. 37; Bourne, *Fidel,* pp. 23, 47; Van Gosse, *Where the Boys Are: Cuba, Cold War America and the Making of a New Left* (New York: Verso, 1993), p. 63; Lesnick interview.

27. Geyer, *Guerrilla Prince,* p. 66; Enrique Ovares interview by Szulc, 23 October 1984, Szulc Papers, JFKL.
28. Guillermo García Frías interview by Szulc, 24 May 1985, Szulc Papers, JFKL.
29. Cited in Paterson, *Contesting Castro,* p. 156.
30. Sweig made the point about the urban resistance after interviewing several of its members and reviewing Cuban archives, in *Inside the Cuban Revolution: Fidel Castro and the Urban Underground* (Cambridge, Mass.: Harvard University Press, 2002). Cole Blasier has noted that all the rebel movements he studied in Latin America muted their anti-U.S. rhetoric while struggling against foreign influence, in *The Hovering Giant: U.S. Responses to Revolutionary Change in Latin America, 1910–1985* (Pittsburgh, Pa.: University of Pittsburgh Press, 1985), p. 31.
31. Castro cited in George Black, *The Good Neighbor: How the United States Wrote the History of Central America and the Caribbean* (New York: Pantheon Books, 1988), p. 103. See also Paterson, *Contesting Castro,* p. 78; and Andrew St. George, "A Visit with a Revolutionary," *Coronet,* February 1958, pp. 74–80.
32. Paterson, *Contesting Castro,* p. 44; U.S. embassy in Havana to State, 3 July 1958, *FRUS* 1958–1960, 6: 127–129; Robert Murphy to Herter, 8 July 1958, *FRUS* 1958–1960, 6: 133.
33. Paterson, *Contesting Castro,* p. 164.
34. William Wieland to Rubottom, 10 October 1958, *FRUS* 1958–1960, 6: 240. Also in *FRUS* 1958–1960, vol. 6, see U.S. consulate in Santiago de Cuba to State, 21 February 1958, pp. 32, 33; Allan Stewart, 24 July 1958, p. 165; and U.S. consulate in Santiago de Cuba to State, 30 September 1958, p. 232.
35. Húber Matos interview by author.
36. "Gambits and Taboos," 1 April 1957, folder Secret Briefing Material—Cuba, box 1, lots 62D418 and 64D15, Subject Files of the Assistant Secretary, 1959–1962, RG 59, NARA.
37. "The 26th of July Movement since the Abortive General Strike of April 9, 1958," 15 August 1958, *O.S.S / State Department Intelligence and Research Reports 14: Latin America, 1941–1961,* ed. Paul Kesaris (Washington, D.C.: UPA, n.d.), 8: 0425–0418.
38. U.S. embassy in Havana to State, 28 February 1958, *FRUS* 1958–1960, 6: 39.
39. Paterson, *Contesting Castro,* ch. 16; quotation is from p. 186.
40. Rubottom's handwritten remark on "Communism in the Cuban Situation," 28 March 1958, folder Cuba Jan.–Aug. 1958, box 7, Office Files of Henry A. Hoyt, 1956–1958, lot 60D513, RG 59, NARA.

41. "U.S./Cuban Relations—January 2, 1959 to January 3, 1961," folder Plank/ Chase Report on US-Cuban Relations, 1959–60, box 4, Files of Gordon Chase, National Security File, LBJL.

42. NSC meeting, 14 April 1958, folder 362nd Meeting of NSC April 14, 1958, box 10, NSC Series, Eisenhower Papers as President, 1953–1961, DDEL; NSC meeting, 18 December 1958, *FRUS* 1958–1960, 6: 300.

43. Herter to Eisenhower, 23 December 1958, folder Herter Christian L. [*sic*] (1), box 18, Administration Series, Eisenhower Papers as President, 1953– 1961, DDEL.

44. Dulles in Frederick Marks III, *Power and Peace: The Diplomacy of John Foster Dulles* (Westport, Conn.: Praeger, 1993), p. 152; Núñez Jiménez, *En marcha con Fidel, 1959* (Havana: Editorial Letras Cubanas, 1982), p. 56.

45. The gradualism and Castro's mix of strategy and improvisation argued here contributes to a running debate among scholars regarding the "stages" of the first year or so of the Castro regime. To some, Castro planned a communist revolution from the very beginning and "betrayed" the reformist goals he had set before 1959. To others, he found its true essence after being provoked by the United States and set whole new goals as the year progressed. See Theodore Draper, "The Runaway Revolution," *The Reporter,* 12 May 1960, pp. 14–20; Rufo López-Fresquet, *My Fourteen Months with Castro* (Cleveland: World Publishing Company, 1966); Nelson Amaro Victoria, "Mass and Class in the Origins of the Cuban Revolution," in Irving Louis Horowitz, ed., *Masses in Latin America* (New York: Oxford University Press, 1970), pp. 562–576; Lynn Darrell Bender, *The Politics of Hostility: Castro's Revolution and United States Policy* (Hato Rey, Puerto Rico: Inter-American University Press, 1975), pp. 15–20; Richard Welch, *Response to Revolution: The United States and the Cuban Revolution, 1959–1961* (Chapel Hill: University of North Carolina Press, 1985), p. 13; and Alan Luxenberg, "Did Eisenhower Push Castro into the Arms of the Soviets?" *Journal of Inter-American Studies and World Affairs* 30 (March 1988): 37–71.

46. Castro to *Havana Post,* 20 January 1959, p. 1; Jules Benjamin called this first stage the "honeymoon"; see Benjamin, *The United States and the Origins of the Cuban Revolution: An Empire of Liberty in an Age of National Liberation* (Princeton, N.J.: Princeton University Press, 1990), p. 182.

47. Urrutia speech, 3 March 1959, expediente 159, legajo 9, Fondo Minrex, AGNC; *Times of Havana,* 5 January 1959.

48. Castro speech to Lions' Club, *Revolución,* 14 January 1959, pp. 1, 2; "Briefing Paper for Castro Visit," folder Cuba 1959, box 16, lot 61D248, Subject Files Relating to Regional Economic Affairs, 1951–1961, RG 59, NARA.

49. Braddock to State, 20 January 1959, *Confidential U.S. State Department Central Files: Cuba 1955–1959* (Frederick, Md.: University Publications of America, 1987), 25: 437.

50. Castro paraphrased in "Briefing Paper for Castro Visit," folder Cuba 1959, box 16, lot 61D248, Subject Files Relating to Regional Economic Affairs, 1951–1961, RG 59, NARA.

51. Braddock to State, 15 January 1959, *Central Files,* 4: 877; Rosalie Schwartz, *Pleasure Island: Tourism and Temptation in Cuba* (Lincoln: University of Nebraska Press, 1997), pp. 196, 197–198; Bonsal to Dulles, 20 February 1959, *Central Files,* 5: 395–397; Paterson, *Contesting Castro,* p. 235; Vicente Martínez, "Fidel Castro vuelve a la Sierra," *Carteles,* 15 February 1959, p. 21.

52. Braddock to State, 18 February 1959, *Central Files,* 25: 459–461; E. T. Smith to State, 16 January 1959, *Central Files,* 25: 435.

53. Braddock to Dulles, 22 January 1959, *Central Files,* 25: 443.

54. Memorandum of conversation, 12 February 1959, *Central Files,* 5: 347; U.S. embassy in Havana to State, 19 February 1959, *Central Files,* 9: 569.

55. John Hill memorandum, 6 February 1959, *FRUS 1958–1960,* 6: 396; U.S. consulate in Santiago to State, 26 January 1959, *Central Files,* 5: 141–146; Pérez, *On Becoming Cuban,* p. 495; Braddock to State, 16 February 1959, *Central Files,* 5: 357–358.

56. NSC meeting, folder 396th Meeting of NSC February 12, 1959, box 11, NSC Series, Eisenhower Papers as President, 1953–1961, DDEL.

57. Bonsal to State, 17 April 1959, *FRUS 1958–1960,* 6: 474; remarks by Rubottom in Chile, 7 May 1959, *FRUS 1958–1960,* 6: 507, 508.

58. Evaluation of visit of Castro, 23 April 1959, folder Cuba (1), box 8, International Series, Eisenhower Papers as President, 1953–1961, DDEL; conversation between Herter and Eisenhower, 18 April 1959, *FRUS 1958–1960,* 6: 475.

59. Oscar Pino Santos, "El nivel de vida del pueblo cubano," *Carteles,* 26 April 1959, pp. 36–37, 67 (reproducing 1958 and 1953 findings about Cuban poverty); Núñez Jiménez, "Un año de liberación agraria," August 1960. On the lack of campesino organization, see Amaro Victoria, "Mass and Class," pp. 547–548. See also Raj Desai and Harry Eckstein, "Insurgency: The Transformation of Peasant Rebellion," *World Politics* 42 (July 1990): 441–465.

60. Juan Valdés Paz, *Procesos agrarios en Cuba, 1959–1995* (Havana: Editorial de Ciencias Sociales, 1997), pp. 36, 38–46; José Mayo, *Dos décadas de lucha contra el latifundismo: Breve historia de la asociación nacional campesina* (Havana: Editora Política, 1980), p. 11; U.S. embassy in Havana to State, 2 June 1959, *Central Files,* 17: 206.

61. Tannenbaum, "Castro and Social Change," *Political Science Quarterly* 77 (June 1962): 190; Nelson cited in Gil Carl Alroy, "The Peasantry in the Cuban Revolution," in Rolando Bonachea and Nelson Valdés, eds., *Cuba in Revolution* (Garden City, N.Y.: Anchor Books, 1972), p. 6; Cole Blasier, "Social Revolution: The Origins in Mexico, Bolivia, and Cuba," in *Cuba in Revolution,* pp. 5, 23, 42. See also Maurice Zeitlin, "Economic Insecurity and the Political Attitudes of Cuban Workers," *American Sociological Review* 31 (February 1966): 35–51.

62. Gregorio Ortega, "El latifundio de la United Fruit," *Revolución,* 16 March 1959, p. 24, and 17 March 1959, p. 8; Black, *The Good Neighbor,* p. 36.

63. Alroy, "The Peasantry," p. 12.

64. José Soler Puig, *Bertillón 166* (Havana: Editorial de Arte y Literatura, 1975; orig. pub 1959), p. 32.

65. "¡Bienvenidos, hermanos!" and "Los guajiros en la Habana," *Carteles,* 2 August 1959, pp. 21 and 30–31, respectively (quotation from p. 31); *Revolución,* 29 June 1959, p. 1; *The Times of Havana,* 27 July 1959, p. 1.

66. Mario Parajón, "La verdadera reforma agraria," *El Mundo,* 31 March 1959, p. A-4; also on guilt, see Carlos Franqui, *Family Portrait with Fidel,* trans. Alfred MacAdam (New York: Vintage, 1985), p. 36; Efren Cordova, "Fidel Castro and the Cuban Labor Movement, 1959–1961" (Ph.D. diss., Cornell University, 1973), p. 75.

67. The peso was on par with the U.S. dollar. Núñez Jiménez, *En marcha con Fidel,* p. 134. *Revolución,* 16 May 1959, p. 15, explains the founding of the Fund for the Institute for Agrarian Reform; *Revolución,* 14 April 1959, p. 12.

68. In *Revolución,* see Armando Florez Ibarra, "Hacia la independencia económica," 3 March 1959, p. 2; Núñez Jiménez, 31 July 1959, p. 19; Carlos Franqui, 11 September 1959; and Guevara, 18 September 1959, p. 1; Guevara cited in Braddock to State, 13 August 1959, *Central Files,* 6: 640; Castro speech at Harvard University, 27 April 1959, sound recording, ENH-T-3757A-B, RG 306, NARA.

69. Castro speech to the United Nations Press Corps, 20 April 1959, sound recording, ENH-T-3553, RG 306, NARA.

70. Núñez Jiménez, *La liberación de las islas* (Havana: Editorial Lex, 1959), n.p.; U.S. embassy in Havana to State, 27 July 1959, *Central Files,* 6: 423–424; epigraph, *Obra revolucionaria,* 27 May 1960; Núñez Jiménez, *En marcha con Fidel,* pp. 98–99. See also *Revolución,* 16 February 1959, p. 21.

71. Haydée Santamaría interview by Szulc, 5 June 1986, Szulc Papers, JFKL; Mann interview by Burg.

72. Alfredo Guevara interview by Szulc, 30 April 1985, Szulc Papers, JFKL; other members were Che Guevara, Vilma Espín, Antonio Nuñez Jiménez,

Segundo Ceballos, and Oscar Pino Santos. See Szulc, "Fidel Castro's Years as a Secret Communist," *New York Times Magazine,* 19 October 1986, pp. 47–48, 70–74, 121; Goldenberg, *The Cuban Revolution,* p. 220.

73. Cited first in Goldenberg, *The Cuban Revolution,* p. 220, and then in Lee Lockwood, *Castro's Cuba, Cuba's Fidel* (Random House, 1967; rpt. New York: Vintage, 1969), p. 161.

74. Memorandum of conversation, 2 June 1959, *Central Files,* 17: 219.

75. Núñez Jiménez, *En marcha con Fidel,* pp. 149–155; Edward Scott, "The Glorious Mud and Famine of the Sierra," *Havana Post,* 22 May 1959, p. 4. See also *Revolución,* 18 May 1959, p. 12.

76. Rafael Menjivar, *Reforma agraria: Guatemala-Bolivia-Cuba* (San Salvador: Editorial Universitario de El Salvador, 1969), p. 406. There is disagreement over whether campesinos took over lands before the enactment of the law in May. Núñez painted the law as a measure to appease land-hungry peasants (*En marcha con Fidel,* p. 62). But others said campesinos were in no great hurry to take over large lands that were technically challenging. See James O'Connor, "On Cuban Political Economy," *Political Science Quarterly* 79 (June 1964): 237.

77. Núñez Jiménez interview.

78. "U.S./Cuban Relations—January 2, 1959, to January 3, 1961," folder Plank/Chase Report on US-Cuban Relations, 1959–60, box 4, Files of Gordon Chase, National Security File, LBJL.

79. "Impressions of Recent Trip—Communism, Propaganda and Anti-Americanism," 8 December 1959, *Central Files,* 7: 237; Draper, "The Runaway Revolution," p. 17. For another description of an intervention, see Oscar Zanetti et al., *United Fruit Company: Un caso del dominio imperialista en Cuba* (Havana: Editorial de Ciencias Sociales, 1976), pp. 358, 362–364.

80. Castro cited in Núñez Jiménez, *En marcha con Fidel,* p. 246.

81. R. Hart Phillips, "Cuban Farm Law Imperils U.S. Sugar Concerns' Land," *New York Times,* 19 May 1959, p. 12; U.S. embassy in Havana to State, 23 May 1959, *FRUS* 1958–1960, 6: 511.

82. "Synopsis of State and Intelligence Material Reported to the President," 25 May 1959, folder Intelligence Briefing Notes, vol. I (7) [May 1959], box 14, Alphabetical Subseries, Subject Series, Office of the Staff Secretary, 1952–1961, White House Office, DDEL; memorandum of conversation, 26 May 1959, folder CU-445.2311 (1), box 16, lot 75D242, Records of the Component Offices of the Bureau of Intelligence and Research, 1947–1963, RG 59, NARA; Braga telephone conversation with Rubottom, 26 June 1959, folder Cuba Agrarian Reform Law + Sugar thru 6/30/1959, box 1, lot 63D67, Subject Files, 1957–1962, Office of Caribbean and Mexican Affairs, RG 59, NARA.

83. Memorandum of conversation, 12 February 1959, *Central Files,* 5: 346.

84. Rubottom interview by Luter; memorandum of conversation between Braddock, Bonsal, and Agramonte, 1 June 1959, *Central Files,* 17: 217.

85. Memorandum of conversation, 10 June 1959, *Central Files,* 17: 271; Eisenhower to Kleberg, 6 July 1959, folder OF 171 (s), box 857, Official File, White House Central Files, DDEL.

86. Memorandum of conversation, 15 June 1959, *Central Files,* 6: 125.

87. Rubottom to Herter, 2 July 1959, *Central Files,* 6: 411; Bonsal suggested consulting with sugar executives before drafting a key U.S. response, in his letter to Robert Stevenson, 11 September 1959, *Central Files,* 17: 603; Rubottom interview by Luter.

88. Núñez Jiménez, *En marcha con Fidel,* p. 320; Bonsal to State, 23 October 1959, *Central Files,* 6: 953–956; "Cuba: Boiling Up," *Newsweek,* 2 November 1959, p. 45.

89. U.S. Navy in Havana to State, 24 October 1959, *Central Files,* 6: 965–966; this argument about dropping grenades appeared in *Revolución,* 10 November 1959, pp. 1, 16; *Havana Post,* 22 October 1959, p. 1; Norm McLean's description of events, 24 October 1959, folder 320 U.S./Cuba 1959, box 3, lot 60F102, Havana Embassy Classified Records, 1959–1961, Cuba, RG 84, NARA; State to U.S. embassy in Havana, 24 October 1959, *Central Files,* 25: 727; see also R. Hart Phillips, "Castro Arrests Aide Who Quit after Charging Red Infiltration," *New York Times,* 22 October 1959, p. 1; and idem, "Cuban Crowd Assails U.S. after Attack by Terrorists," *New York Times,* 23 October 1959, p. 1.

90. Núñez Jiménez, *En marcha con Fidel,* pp. 423, 335; *Havana Post,* 22 October 1959, p. 1.

91. Cited in Richard Fagen, "Mass Mobilization in Cuba: The Symbolism of Struggle," in *Cuba in Revolution,* p. 201.

92. *Sierra Maestra* cited in U.S. Consulate in Santiago to State, 22 October 1959, *Central Files,* 6: 950; Goldenberg, *The Cuban Revolution,* p. 190; "Agenda: Trouble," *Time,* 23 November 1959, p. 39; Cuba, Ministerio de Estado, Departamento de Relaciones Públicas, *¡Cuba denuncia ante el mundo!* (1959); *Noticias de hoy,* 23 October 1959, p. 1; U.S. Navy in Havana to State, 24 October 1959, *Central Files,* 6: 965–966.

93. State to U.S. embassy in Havana, 24 October 1959, *Central Files,* 25: 727; Bonsal to State 16 November 1959, *Central Files,* 25: 827.

94. Unnamed businessman cited in *Newsweek,* 2 November 1959, p. 45; Rubottom to Ernesto Dihigo, 9 November 1959, *Central Files,* 25: 803; R. Hart Phillips, "F.B.I. Names Cuban Flier," *New York Times,* 24 October 1959, p. 4.

95. "Action with Respect to Cuban Pamphlet on 'Bombing' of Habana," 4 De-

cember 1959, folder Cuba 1959, box 2, lot 64D24, Records of the Special Assistant on Communism, 1958–1961, RG 59, NARA; *Times of Havana,* 9 November 1959, p. 16; Goldenberg, *The Cuban Revolution,* p. 190, n. 1; *Life en español,* 22 February 1960.

96. *Times of Havana,* 26 October 1959, p. 1; Bonsal to State, 23 October 1959, *Central Files,* 6: 953–956; B. E. Aguirre, "The Conventionalization of Collective Behavior in Cuba," *American Journal of Sociology* 90 (November 1984): 541–566.

97. Bonsal to State, 26 October 1959, *Central Files,* 6: 798–799.

98. Matos interview; David Reed, "The Man Who Defied Castro," *Reader's Digest* (reprint), April 1960; Benjamin, *The United States,* p. 185. Since Castro arrested Matos before the late-afternoon Díaz Lanz "bombing," he was more likely reacting to the accelerated pace of real bombings of canefields, the last of which was on 19 October.

99. Edward González, "Castro's Revolution, Cuban Communist Appeals, and the Soviet Response," *World Politics* 21 (October 1968): 48; Teresa Casuso in NBC, *Meet the Press,* 4, 30 October 1960, p. 2; "Conversation with Victor Moreno, INRA official," Braddock to State, 18 September 1959, *Central Files,* 17: 673–676.

100. "Agrarian Reform Developments," 27 November 1959, folder Cuba 1959 Aug.–Dec., box 1, Bonsal Papers, Manuscript Division, LCong.

101. "Revolution Is Religious, Says Castro," *Havana Post,* 28 November 1959, p. 1.

102. Bonsal to State, 16 November 1959, *Central Files,* 25: 827; Henry Hoyt to Rubottom, 28 July 1959, *Central Files,* 6: 457; Marvin Gettleman cited in "A CCNY Instructor Reports," *Student Council: Fair Play for Cuba,* 4 November 1960, p. 3. See also Edward Scott, "U.S. Church Leader Says People Are for Fidel," *Havana Post,* 18 December 1959, p. 4.

103. U.S. embassy in Havana to State, 30 October 1959, *FRUS 1958–1960,* 6: 649; Henry Goethals, "Deep Concern Expressed over U.S.-Cuba Relations," *Times of Havana,* 29 October 1959, p. 1; "Anti-American Propaganda in Oriente," U.S. Consulate in Santiago to State, *Central Files,* 25: 674.

104. "Impressions of Recent Trip—Communism, Propaganda and Anti-Americanism," 8 December 1959, *Central Files,* 7: 237–239; Goethals, "Deep Concern," p. 1.

105. Powell cited in memorandum of conversation, 12 March 1959, *FRUS 1958–1960,* 6: 425; Braddock draft attached to memorandum to Bonsal, 12 September 1959, folder Cuba 1959, box 16, lot 61D248, Subject Files Relating to Regional Economic Affairs, 1951–1961, RG 59, NARA.

106. Conversation between U.S. officials, 18 September 1959, folder Cuba

1959, box 2, lot 64D24, Records of the Special Assistant on Communism, 1958–1961, RG 59, NARA; Bonsal to Rubottom, 6 November 1959, *Central Files,* 25: 797; Bonsal, *Cuba, Castro, and the United States* (Pittsburgh, Pa.: University of Pittsburgh Press, 1971), p. 37.

107. Rubottom telephone conversation with Standard Oil representative, 25 November 1959, folder Cuba—General 1959, box, lot 63D67, Subject Files, 1957–1962, Office of Caribbean and Mexican Affairs, RG 59, NARA; NSC meeting, folder 429th Meeting of NSC December 16, 1959, box 12, NSC Series, Eisenhower Papers as President, 1953–1961, DDEL. See also John Correll to Rubottom, 24 November 1959, folder Cuba (September–December) 1959, box 1, lots 62D418 and 64D15, Subject Files of the Assistant Secretary 1959–1962, RG 59, NARA; Paarlberg interview.

108. John Hill to Rubottom, 24 April 1959, *FRUS* 1958–1960, 6: 489; NSC meeting, folder 441st Meeting of NSC April 14, 1960, box 13, NSC Series, Eisenhower Papers as President, 1952–1961, DDEL; for polling efforts, see John Williams to USIA, 24 April 1959, Paul Phillips to USIA/Washington, 9 July 1959, and Elmo Wilson to Leo Crespi, 27 July 1959, all in folder Cuba—Correspondence 1959, box 3, Country Project Correspondence, 1952–1963, Office of Research, RG 306, NARA.

109. Wieland to Rubottom, 4 December 1959, folder Cuba—General 1959, box 1, lot 63D67, Subject Files, 1957–1962, Office of Caribbean and Mexican Affairs, RG 59, NARA.

110. Domínguez, "Culture," p. 515; U.S. embassy in Havana to State/USIA, 9 August 1960, folder Cuba Correspondence 1960, box 3, Country Project Correspondence, 1952–1963, Office of Research, RG 306, NARA; Castro took over or closed the last remaining free presses, with *Diario de la Marina* on 10 May and *Prensa Libre* on 16 May 1960. See "Current Intelligence Weekly Summary," 19 May 1960, folder Cuban Situation (1) [1959–60], box 6, Briefing Notes Subseries, NSC Series, Office of the Special Assistant for National Security Affairs Records, 1952–1961, White House Office, DDEL; Goldenberg, *The Cuban Revolution,* p. 211.

111. "Current Basic United States Policy towards Cuba," 15 October, folder Cuba—General 1959, box 1, lot 63D67, Subject Files, 1957–1962, Office of Caribbean and Mexican Affairs, RG 59, NARA.

112. "Current Basic Policy," 29 October 1959, folder Cuba (September–December) 1959, box 1, lot 62D418, Subject Files of the Assistant Secretary, 1959–1962, RG 59, NARA. The final draft was Herter to Eisenhower, 5 November 1959, folder Cuba (1) [1959], box 4, International Series, Office of the Staff Secretary, White House Office, DDEL. Paterson also noted this important idea of a progression in anti-Americanism, of a series of "tests" (*Contesting Castro,* p. 255).

113. NSC meetings, 10 and 16 December 1959, *FRUS 1958–1960*, 6: 698–700, 703–706; Dulles cited in NSC meeting, 18 February 1960, *FRUS 1958–1960*, 6: 792; Rubottom cited in John Hickey, "The Role of the Congress in Foreign Policy: Case—The Cuban Disaster," *Inter-American Economic Affairs* 14 (March 1961): 77.

114. The document approved was "A Program of Covert Action against the Castro Regime," 16 March 1960, folder CIA Policy Paper re Cuba [March 17, 1960], box 4, International Series, Office of the Staff Secretary, 1952–1961, White House Office, DDEL; NSC meeting, 14 January 1960, *FRUS 1958–1960*, 6: 742.

115. For a study of U.S. criticisms of Eisenhower policy toward Cuba, see David Robert Jenkins, "Initial American Responses to Fidel Castro, 1957–1959" (Ph.D. diss., University of Texas at Austin, 1992).

116. Dulles cited in NSC meeting, 17 November 1960, *FRUS 1958–1960*, 5: 453; Herbert Garrettson Schoonmaker, *Military Crisis Management: U.S. Intervention in the Caribbean* (Westport, Conn.: Greenwood Press, 1990), p. 49.

117. Richard Gott, *Guerrilla Movements in Latin America* (London: Nelson and Sons, 1970), p. 7; Kubitschek cited in *Time,* 23 November 1959, p. 39.

118. C. Wright Mills, *Listen, Yankee: The Revolution in Cuba* (New York: Ballantine Books, 1960), p. 34; Baiocchi Armando to Castro, 5 August 1960, expediente 8, legajo 1, Fondo Minrex, AGNC.

119. "Bolivia: The Fanned Spark," *Time,* 16 March 1959, pp. 10, 40, 42. Herter telephone conversation with Allen Grover, folder March 59 (4), box 7, Chron. File, Herter Papers, DDEL.

120. Mills, *Listen, Yankee,* p. 148; D. H. Radler, *El Gringo: The Yankee Image in Latin America* (Philadelphia, Pa.: Chilton, 1962), p. 3; Robert Burr, "Foreword," *Annals of the American Academy of Political and Social Science* 334 (March 1961): vii–viii.

121. Edmund W. Janss, *Yankee Si! The Story of Dr. J. Calvitt Clarke and His 36,000 Children* (William Morrow, 1961), p. 1.

122. Radler, *El Gringo,* p. 48; Radler, "Our National Talent for Offending People," *Harper's* 223 (April 1961), quotations from pp. 65, 69.

123. Mario Pei, "Why Do So Many Americans Apologize for Their Country?" *Saturday Evening Post,* 17 September 1960, p. 10; Boorstin, *The Image: A Guide to Pseudo-Events in America* (New York: Atheneum, 1972; orig. pub. 1962), pp. 243, 246.

124. Kennedy speech in San Juan, Puerto Rico, 15 December 1958, folder Latin America, box 35, Subject Files 1961–1964, Sorensen Papers, JFKL.

125. Wilton Persons, 18 January 1961, folder USIA (1), box 37, Administration

Series, Eisenhower Papers as President, 1953–1961, DDEL; Allen interview.

126. Kennedy speech in San Juan, Puerto Rico, 15 December 1958, folder Latin America, box 35, Subject Files 1961–1964, Sorensen Papers, JFKL.

127. Kennedy cited in Goodwin, *Remembering America: A Voice from the Sixties* (Boston: Little, Brown, 1988), p. 147; Smathers to Kennedy, undated, folder USIA 1960 and 1/61–6/61, box 91, Departments & Agencies, President's Office Files, Kennedy Papers, JFKL.

128. Figueres to Schlesinger, 15 February 1960, folder José Figueres (1953–1961), box P-13, Private Files, Schlesinger Papers, JFKL.

129. John Daniel Coats, "A Matter of Perspective: U.S. Policy toward the Caribbean during the Kennedy and Johnson Administrations, 1961–1965" (Ph.D. diss., Texas A&M University, 1996), pp. 40, 43; Piero Gleijeses, *The Dominican Crisis: The 1965 Constitutionalist Revolt and American Intervention*, trans. Lawrence Lipson (Baltimore, Md.: Johns Hopkins University Press, 1978), p. 36; Edwin McCammon Martin, *Kennedy and Latin America* (Lanham, Md.: University Press of America, 1994), p. 29.

130. Samuel Baily, *The United States and the Development of South America, 1945–1975* (New York: New Viewpoints, 1976), p. 87; Stephen Rabe, *The Most Dangerous Area in the World: John F. Kennedy Confronts Communist Revolution in Latin America* (Chapel Hill: University of North Carolina, 1999), p. 16.

131. Schlesinger to Goodwin, 8 March 1961, folder Latin America 3/8/61–4/30/61, box WH-13, White House Files, Schlesinger Papers, JFKL.

132. USIA, "Revised List of Terms Suitable for Use Abroad," 21 August 1961, folder USIA, box 355, lot 62D187, Public Affairs Subject Files, 1957 to 1961, Executive Office, Office of the Assistant Secretary for Public Affairs, RG 59, NARA; Bundy to NSC staff, 26 July 1961, folder Bundy, McGeorge 5/61–7/61, box 62, Staff Memoranda, President's Office Files, Kennedy Papers, JFKL.

133. Frank Devine to Thomas Mann, 16 March 1961, folder Task Force—Mr. Wollam, box 2, Office Files of the Deputy Assistant Secretary for Inter-American Affairs, lot 64D369, RG 59, NARA.

134. Lester Langley, *The United States and the Caribbean in the Twentieth Century* (Athens: University of Georgia Press, 1985), p. 234; Stephen Rabe, *Eisenhower and Latin America: The Foreign Policy of Anti-Communism* (Chapel Hill: University of North Carolina, 1988), p. 142; on the Alliance for Progress, see Jerome Levinson and Juan de Onís, *The Alliance That Lost Its Way: A Critical Report on the Alliance for Progress* (Chicago: Quadrangle Books, 1970); and L. Ronald Scheman, ed., *The Alliance for Progress: A Retro-*

spective (New York: Praeger, 1988); Baily, *Development of South America,* pp. 94–95.

135. Elizabeth Cobbs Hoffman, *All You Need Is Love: The Peace Corps and the Spirit of the 1960s* (Cambridge, Mass.: Harvard University Press, 1998), p. 1.

136. Edward Murrow to Kennedy, 21 March 1961, folder USIA 1960 and 1/61–6/61, box 91, Departments & Agencies, President's Office Files, Kennedy Papers, JFKL.

137. Donald Wilson to Kennedy, 20 October 1961, folder USIA 7/61–12/61, box 91, Departments & Agencies, President's Office Files, Kennedy Papers, JFKL; USIA, "Castro's Standing in Five Latin American Cities during 1961," folder 2nd Series LA-5, box 2, Latin America, Public Opinion Barometer Reports, 1955–1962, Office of Research, RG 306, NARA; see also USIA, "the Impact of Castro upon Latin American Public Opinion," February 1961, folder S-6–61, box 20, 1961, Special Reports, 1953–1963, Office of Research, RG 306, NARA; "Latin American Attitudes toward the Alliance for Progress," 1962, folder Oct. 1961–1963, box 5, Latin America, 1958–1961, Multi Country (Area) Project Files, 1952–1963, RG 306, NARA.

138. Norman A. Bailey, "The United States as Caudillo," *Journal of Inter-American Studies* 5 (July 1963): 313–324; Martin, *Kennedy and Latin America,* p. 29. For polls done during the Cuban Missile Crisis, see 27 and 30 October 1962, folder RO/LA 1962 71–100 incomplete, box 2, Requestor Only Reports, 1956–1962, Office of Research, RG 306, NARA.

139. Edwin Lahey, "In 18 Months, 30 Anti-American Attacks," *Miami Herald,* 27 April 1964; Ron Robin, *Enclaves of America: The Rhetoric of American Political Architecture Abroad, 1900–1965* (Princeton, N.J.: Princeton University Press, 1992), p. 137; Venezuelan cited in Gerassi, *The Great Fear: The Reconquest of Latin America by Latin Americans* (New York: Macmillan, 1963), p. 27.

3. Panama, 1964

1. Neil Richardson, *Foreign Policy and Economic Dependence* (Austin: University of Texas Press, 1978), pp. 94–111. See also Xabier Gorostiaga, "La Zona del Canal y el subdesarollo panameño," *Tareas* 29 (November–December 1974): 45–62; and José Torres Abrego, "En torno a la Zona del Canal y el subdesarollo panameño," *Tareas* 31 (May–June 1975): 91–126.

2. Juan Antonio Tack, *Ilusiones y realidades en las negociaciones con los Estados Unidos de América* (Panama City: Manfer, 1995), pp. 24–25.

3. Michael Conniff, *Panama and the United States: The Forced Alliance* (Ath-

ens: University of Georgia Press, 1992), pp. 24–30, 35–37; Denis Javier Chávez, *Autonomía, nacionalidad y antiyanquismo en Justo Arosemena* (Panama City: Editorial Portebelo, 1997), p. 15.

4. The Watermelon Riot was only the most brutal of several such incidents. See, for instance, Alfredo Castillero, "Un antecedente de la 'Tajada de Sandía,'" *Lotería* 69 (August 1961): 20–23.

5. *Frank Leslie's Illustrated Newspaper,* 17 May 1856, p. 1.

6. Mercedes Chen Daley, "The Watermelon Riot: Cultural Encounters in Panama City, April 15, 1856," *Hispanic American Historical Review* 70 (February 1990): 85–108, offers the most complete description and analysis of the riots; Conniff, *Panama and the United States,* pp. 24–39.

7. *Leslie's,* 17 May 1856, p. 1. Panamanians have embraced the riots as anti-U.S. heroism but ignored the elite's acquiescence in the violence. Those celebrating the riot include David Acosta, *Influencia decisiva de la opinión pública en el rechazo del Convenio Filos-Hines de 1947,* 4th ed. (Panama City: Editorial Universitaria, 1994), p. 5; and Ricaurte Soler, *Cuatro ensayos de historia sobre Panamá y nuestra América,* 2nd ed. (Panama City: Ediciones Mariano Arosemena–INAC, 1985), p. 29. Autoridad del Canal, *Los sucesos del 9 de enero de 1964* (Panama City: Autoridad del Canal, 1999) contains Ernesto Castillero's recounting of the riots, usually considered the definitive Panamanian version. Castillero emphasized white Panamanians' innocence: the "pillagers" were all West Indians, and he did not mention that almost all the victims were U.S. citizens. On West Indians, see Celestino Andrés Araúz, *Panamá y sus relaciones internacionales: Estudio introductorio,* vol. 1 (Panama City: Editorial Universitaria, 1994), pp. 38, 40–42. Marco Gandásegui et al., *Las luchas obreras en Panamá, 1850–1978,* 2nd ed. (Panama City: CELA, 1990), p. 17, note how Panama—formerly the "Isthmus of Jamaica"—became the "Isthmus of New York" at the turn of the twentieth century.

8. Conniff, *Panama and the United States,* p. 33; Walter LaFeber, *The Panama Canal: The Crisis in Historical Perspective* (New York: Oxford University Press, 1978), p. 70; Gandásegui et al., *Las luchas obreras en Panamá,* p. 80; Carlos Cuestas Gómez, *Soldados americanos en Chiriquí* (Panama City: n.p., 1990).

9. Squiers cited in John Major, *Prize Possession: The United States and the Panama Canal, 1903–1979* (Cambridge: Cambridge University Press, 1993), p. 124; on disarming, see Víctor Ávila, "Del tratado colonialista de 1903 a la insurrección patriótica de 1964," *Tareas* 97 (September 1997): 38; on fights, Marta Chiari, *Historia de las relaciones de Panama con los Estados Unidos: Material de apoyo docente* (Panama City: Universidad de Panama, 1983); Maggali Carreiro Ordoñez, "Teoría política en la diplomacia pana-

meña durante el período 1903–77" (thesis, Universidad de Panamá, 1982), pp. 30–31; and Tack, *Ilusiones y realidades,* p. 143; Cuestas, *Soldados americanos,* pp. 140–143.

10. Isaias García, *Naturaleza y forma de lo panameño* (Panama City: Ministerio de Educación, 1956), pp. 85, 86; Mercer Tate, "The Panama Canal and Political Partnership," *Journal of Politics* 25 (1963): 124; Steve Ropp, "Military Reformism in Panama: New Directions or Old Inclinations," *Caribbean Studies* 12 (October 1972): 55; Luisita Aguilera Patiño, *El panameño visto a través de su lenguaje* (Panama City: Ferguson and Ferguson, n.d.); USIA, "Panama: A Communications Fact Book," 27 September 1960, folder R-58–60, box 3, Office of Research "R" Reports, 1960–1963, 1960, RG 306, NARA; Michael Conniff, *Black Labor on a White Canal: Panama, 1904–1981* (Pittsburgh, Pa.: University of Pittsburgh Press, 1985).

11. John Biesanz and Mavis Biesanz, *The People of Panama* (New York: Columbia University Press, 1955), pp. 92, 222–225, 229. While outsiders saw a ratio of two mulattos (a mixed black-and-white person) to one mestizo (a mixed indigenous-and-white person), Panamanians saw the opposite; see LaFeber, *The Panama Canal,* p. 63.

12. Gil Blas Tejeira, "En busca del panameño," *Siete,* 21 March 1953; Ricaurte Soler, *Formas ideológicas de la nación* (Panama City: Editorial Universitaria, 1971), p. 19.

13. Quotation is from Guillermo Patterson, Jr., *Panama-U.S. Relations* (Panama City: Excelsior, 1962), p. 13; Julio Ortega interview by author.

14. Joaquín Beleño, *Luna verde* (Panama City: Manfer, [1950]); interview with Beleño, 2 May 1987, in Rosa Itzel De Beermann and Ernestina Orocú S., "La preocupación político-social en la novela canalera de Joaquín Beleño C." (thesis, Universidad de Panamá, 1989). Beleño died in 1988.

15. Cited in Biesanz and Biesanz, *The People of Panama,* 189; Torrijos interview by Jorden, 24 April 1979, Jorden Papers, LBJL.

16. Ricaurte Soler, *Panama: Nación y oligarquía, 1925–1975* (Panama City: Ediciones Tareas, 1976), pp. 31–33; LaFeber, *The Panama Canal,* p. 80; Thomas Pearcy, *La generación del 31: Patriotas y pretorianos,* trans. M. A. Pantaleón García (Panama City: Universidad de Panamá, 1997), pp. 6–7.

17. Victor Manuel Perez and Rodrigo Oscar de León Lerma, *El movimiento de Acción Comunal en Panamá* (Panama City: n.p., n.d.), pp. 21, 29; R. M. Koster and Guillermo Sánchez, *In the Time of the Tyrants: Panama, 1968–1990* (New York: W. W. Norton, 1990), p. 59; Conniff, *Panama and the United States,* pp. 86–87.

18. The man cited went by the nickname "Flacco" according to Thomas Wright, in Wright to Merchant, 23 April 1960, folder Policy 1960 Panama, box 1, Records Relating to Panama, 1959–1965, Office of Central Ameri-

can and Panamanian Affairs, RG 59, NARA; Jorge Conte Porras, *Arnulfo Arias Madrid* (Panama City: n.p., 1980); José Díaz to Kennedy, 17 January 1963, folder Panama General 11/62–1/63, box 150, Countries, National Security File, Kennedy Papers, JFKL; LaFeber, *The Panama Canal,* pp. 93–98.

19. Conte Porras, *Arnulfo Arias Madrid,* p. 24.
20. Lester Langley, *The United States and the Caribbean in the Twentieth Century,* rev. ed. (Athens: University of Georgia Press, 1985), pp. 171–176; John Biesanz and Luke Smith, "Panamanian Politics," *Journal of Politics* 14 (August 1952): 399; Carreiro Ordoñez, "Teoría política," pp. 66–89; Thomas Leonard, *Panama, the Canal, and the United States: A Guide to Issues and References* (Claremont, Calif.: Regina Books, 1993), pp. 23–26; Koster and Sánchez, *Tyrants,* pp. 58–62.
21. César Villareal interview by author; Luis Vergara interview by author.
22. Edward Scott, Jr., "The Political Orientations of Panamanian and Canal Zone Students: A Comparative Case Study in the Political Socialization of Latin American and American Youth" (master's thesis, Michigan State University, 1964); José Ignacio Martínez interview by author; U.S. embassy in Panama City to State, 23 July 1965, folder POL 13–3 PAN 1/1/66, box 2559, Central Files 1964–1966, RG 59, NARA; Conniff, *Panama and the United States,* p. 107.
23. Daniel Goldrich, *Radical Nationalism: The Political Orientation of Panamanian Law Students* (East Lansing: Bureau of Social and Political Research, College of Business and Public Service, Michigan State University, 1961), p. 9; Mary Alice Abrego Hayward, "Political Opinions of Panamanian Elite High School Youth: A Comparison of 1961–63 Students to 1989 Students" (master's thesis, University of Texas at Austin, 1990).
24. Conniff, *Panama and the United States,* pp. 80–81; Koster and Sánchez, *Tyrants,* pp. 48–49; LaFeber, *The Panama Canal,* p. 92. Around 1967, of the sixty largest companies in Panama, forty-five dealt with commerce and fifteen with manufacturing. About twenty families held almost all economic power in Panama, based on import-export businesses: Marco Antonio Gandásegui, Jr., *La concentración del poder económico en Panamá* (Panama City: Tareas, 1967), pp. 7, 11.
25. Alfredo Figueroa Navarro, *Dominio y sociedad en el Panamá colombiano, 1821–1903* (Panama City: Impresora Panamá, 1978), pp. 215–237.
26. Langley, *The United States and the Caribbean,* pp. 154–155; Pearcy, *La generación del 31,* pp. 13–14; Ricardo J. Alfaro et al., *Panamá y los Estados Unidos de América ante el problema del Canal* (Panama City: Imprenta Nacional, 1966), p. 128; Conniff, *Panama and the United States,* p. 91; LaFeber, *The Panama Canal,* p. 85.

27. Harold Martin, "Why Do They *Hate* Us?" *Saturday Evening Post,* 23 April 1960, p. 118; Conniff, *Panama and the United States,* pp. 107–108.

28. Universidad de Panamá, Instituto Panameño de la Opinión Pública, *Bulletin,* Panama City, 5 (November 1949), "Problems of Panama."

29. Moreno to Ernesto de la Guardia, 12 July 1958, Visitas Oficiales a Panamá, 1958–1959, vol. 2, PAMINREX.

30. Rusk in Senate Committee on Foreign Relations, *Report of Proceedings: Briefing by Secretary of State Dean Rusk on the World Situation,* Washington, D.C., 16 January 1964, 5: 36; Major, *Prize Possession,* pp. 47–48; Langley, *The United States and the Caribbean,* pp. 67–68; Thelma King, *El problema de la soberanía en las relaciones entre Panamá y los Estados Unidos de América* (Panama City: Ministerio de Educación, 1961), p. 52.

31. "Resumen de los puntos planteados por el señor Presidente de la República de Panamá al Dr. Milton Eisenhower," 16 July 1958, Visitas Oficiales a Panamá, 1958–1959, vol. 2, PAMINREX.

32. See Presciliano Barrios, *Identidad nacional: Fantasía y verdad* (Panama City: Editorial Mariano Arosemena, 1993), p. 13; Carlos Arosemena Arias, "Una visión sociológica de nuestras relaciones con los Estados Unidos," *Lotería* 16 (March 1957): 14; and José Isaac Fábrega, "Se va produciendo un cambio en la psicología del panameño," *Lotería* 366 (May–June 1987): 104.

33. García, *Naturaleza y forma,* pp. 18, 21, 83; Juan Materno Vásquez, *Sobre el hombre cultural panameño* (Panama City: Impresora Panamá, 1971), p. 37; Allen Patiño, "Xenofilia, pecado capital de la sociedad panameña," *Lotería* 415 (November–December 1997): 29–39; Goldrich, *Radical Nationalism,* p. 4.

34. Biesanz and Biesanz, *The People of Panama,* p. 156; Diego Domínguez Caballero, "Motivo y sentido de una investigación de lo panameño," *Presente* 7 (July–September 1966): 10.

35. Diamantina de Calzadilla and Etna de Martínez, *Educación cívica,* 4th ed. (Panama City: n.p., 1964–1965); Autoridad del Canal, *Los sucesos del 9 de enero de 1964,* p. 109.

36. King, *El problema de la soberanía,* p. 18; Beleño, *Luna verde,* p. 42; *El Día,* 12 December 1960.

37. *Panama Canal Review,* 3 December 1954; Selden Rodman, *The Road to Panama* (New York: Hawthorne Books, 1966), p. 207; J. Michael Hogan, *The Panama Canal in American Politics: Domestic Advocacy and the Evolution of Policy* (Carbondale: Southern Illinois University Press, 1986), p. 36.

38. Quotations from "US Citizens Eye Zonians' Attitude," *Panama American,* 24 February 1960; Ralph Skinner, "'Double Wage Scale' Aired in Anti-U.S. Panama Riots," *Christian Science Monitor,* 30 November 1959. In 1959 the

company claimed to have eliminated discrimination by tacking the "silver" to the bottom of the "gold" roll and thus making one continuous pay scale, but the modification was largely cosmetic.

39. Jhan Robbins, "The Children Who Caused a Crisis," *Redbook,* August 1964, p. 111; see also Herbert Knapp and Mary Knapp, *Red, White, and Blue Paradise: The American Canal Zone in Panama* (San Diego, Calif.: Harcourt, Brace, Jovanovich, 1984).

40. *Panama American,* 5 May 1958, p. 2.

41. Conniff, *Panama and the United States,* pp. 108–109.

42. Rocco Siciliano to Andrew Goodpaster, 14 July 1959, folder OF209 (2) Panama, box 884, Official File, White House Central Files, DDEL; "Memorandum of conference with the president," 27 November 1959, folder State Department: October 1959–February 1960 (2), box 3, Subject Series, State Department Subseries, Office of the Staff Secretary 1952–1961, White House Office, DDEL; República de Panamá, Ministerio de Relaciones Exteriores, *Memoria* (1959), pp. 5–6.

43. Milton Eisenhower, *The Wine Is Bitter* (Garden City, N.Y.: Doubleday, 1965), p. 217.

44. U.S. embassy in Panama City to State, 15 July 1959, folder Panama Vol. 2, box 4, Panama City Embassy Classified General Records, 1959–1963, Panama, RG 84, NARA. Harmodio Arias apparently also led the march; see Sheldon Liss, *The Canal: Aspects of United States–Panamanian Relations* (Notre Dame, Ind.: University of Notre Dame Press, 1967), p. 61.

45. "Background information concerning recent incidents in Panama," 13 November 1959, folder Panama (4) [November–December 1959], box 12, International Series, Office of the Staff Secretary, 1952–1961, White House Office, DDEL.

46. Martin, "Why Do They *Hate* Us?" p. 23.

47. Boy cited in "Army Guards Canal Zone Border," *Panama American,* 4 November 1959, p. 10; "The Anti–United States Riots of November 1959," Canal Zone, [1960?]. For an official Panamanian version, see República de Panamá, Ministerio de Relaciones Exteriores, *Memoria* (1960).

48. Quotations from 102nd session, 5 November 1959, Actas del Consejo Nacional de Relaciones Exteriores, PAMINREX; "New Anti-U.S. Demonstrations in Panama Analyzed," 30 November 1959, folder 320—U.S./Panama Includes Correspondence Nov. 3–28 + Merchant's Visit 1959 (1 of 2), box 2, Panama City Embassy General Records 1959–1963, Panama, RG 84, NARA.

49. Lester Langley, "U.S.-Panamanian Relations since 1941," *Journal of Inter-American Studies and World Affairs* 12 (1970): 352; "Memorandum of conference with the president," 27 November 1959, folder State Department:

October 1959–February 1960 (2), box 3, Subject Series, State Department Subseries, Office of the Staff Secretary 1952–1961, White House Office, DDEL; Eisenhower press conference, 2 December 1959, folder Press and Radio Conference 12/2/59, box 9, Press Conference Series, Eisenhower Papers as President, 1953–1961, DDEL.

50. "Background information," DDEL; U.S. embassy in Panama City to State, 4 May 1960 and 23 May 1960, both folder Panama Vol. 3, box 4, Panama City Embassy Classified General Records, 1959–1963, Panama, RG 84, NARA.

51. República de Panamá, Ministerio de Relaciones Exteriores, *Memoria* (1960), p. xiii.

52. Rubottom to Robert Murphy, 27 November 1959, in *FRUS* 1958–1960, 5: 1351–1352.

53. Chelf to Eisenhower, 16 November 1959, folder 52 (4), box 237, Official File, White House Central Files, DDEL; Wynne to [Eisenhower?], 9 December 1959, folder 320—U.S./Panama Includes Correspondence Nov. 3–28 Merchant's Visit, box 1, lot 65F33, Panama City Embassy General Records 1959–1963, Panama, RG 84, NARA.

54. Francis Dorn to Eisenhower, 7 January 1960, folder OF 209 (2) Panama, box 884, White House Central Files, Official File, DDEL; Reed to Eisenhower, 9 January 1960, folder 52 (4), box 237, Official File, White House Central Files, DDEL.

55. State position paper, 8 December 1959, folder Panama, box 20, lot 61D473, RG 59, NARA; Rubottom to Rusk, 15 February 1960, folder Panama (Jan.–Mar.) 1960, box 2, lot 63D127, Subject and Country Files, 1955–1963, Office of Central American and Panamanian Affairs, RG 59, NARA; "Panama's Flag Ordered Flown over Canal Zone by Eisenhower," *New York Times,* 18 September 1960, p. 1; on Flood, McPherson interview by Jorden, 28 March 1979, Jorden Papers, LBJL.

56. "Memorandum of conference with the president," 1 September 1960, folder Staff Notes—September 1960 (4), box 53, DDE Diary Series, Eisenhower Papers as President, 1953–1961, DDEL; Langley, "U.S.-Panamanian Relations since 1941."

57. Stephen Rabe, *The Most Dangerous Area in the World: John F. Kennedy Confronts Communist Revolution in Latin America* (Chapel Hill: University of North Carolina, 1999), p. 18; Kennedy to Chiari, 2 November 1961, and U.S. embassy in Panama City to State, 22 November 1961, both in folder Panama General 10/61–3/62, box 149, Countries, National Security File, Kennedy Papers, JFKL; "Visit of President Chiari," 7 June 1962, folder Panama Subjects Chiari Briefing Book 6/12/62, box 150, Countries, National Security File, Kennedy Papers, JFKL.

58. Conversation involving Chiari, Kennedy, and others, *FRUS* 1961–1963, 12: 833; Katherine Bracken, 15 June 1962, folder Panama General 6/62, box 149, Countries, National Security File, Kennedy Papers, JFKL; Rusk to U.S. embassy in Panama City, 14 May 1963, folder Panama 5/63–7/63, box 150, Countries, National Security File, Kennedy Papers, JFKL; NSAM 152, 30 April 1962, available from www.cs.umb.edu/jfklibrary/nsam152a .jpg; NSAM 164, 15 June 1962, available from www.cs.umb.edu/jfklibrary/ nsam164a.jpg.

59. For a study of the political socialization of the BHS students, see Alan McPherson, "From 'Punks' to Geopoliticians: U.S. and Panamanian Teenagers and the 1964 Canal Zone Riots," *The Americas* 58 (January 2002): 395–418.

60. Napoleón de Bernard interview by author. The best published account of the Balboa side is William Jorden, *Panama Odyssey* (Austin: University of Texas Press, 1984), pp. 35–37. A fairly complete and accurate account of the riots can be found in "United States Presentation: Background and Chronology of the Events in Panama and the Canal Zone on the Ninth, Tenth, and Subsequent Days in January 1964 for the Committee Established under the Resolution of the OAS/OC, February 6, 1964," box 15, Declassified General Correspondence, 1945–1979, Internal Security Office, RG 185, NARA. See also *Transcript of the United States Oral Presentation on February 14th and 15th, 1964, to the Committee Established under the Resolution of the OAS/OC, February 6, 1964,* Technical Resources Center, Balboa, Republic of Panama; and affidavits by César Villareal and Amarilis Estela Ponce, both 10 February 1964, and Alejandro Julio Jaen Palma, 12 February 1964, all in Serie 9 de enero 1964, Expedientes No. 8 Fiscalia Auxiliar 1964, PAMINREX.

61. David Parker, "Chronology of Events Involving the Acting Governor of the Canal Zone," 18 January 1964, folder C/DEF 3-1 Operational Plan for Civil Disturbances Vol. 1 January 1964 to December 1964, box 4, Declassified General Correspondence, 1945–1979, Internal Security Office, RG 185, NARA.

62. Arias cited in *El Día*, 13 January 1964, p. 2; "Background and Chronology"; USCINCSO to State, 10 January 1964, folder POL—Political Affairs & Rel. PAN-US 1/1/64, box 2561, Central Files 1964–1966, RG 59, NARA; "'Je Suis Français' Saves American," *New York Herald Tribune,* 13 January 1964; "Riot Incidents as Reported by Radio and TV Broadcasts from the Republic of Panama, January 9–10, 1964," box 15, Declassified General Correspondence, 1945–1979, Internal Security Office, RG 185, NARA; "Lack of RP Action Caused Riots, US Alleges to Jurists," *Panama American,* 21 March 1964, p. 1. A photo of Club 27 is in *El Día*, 15 January 1964, p. 1.

The legend states, "This sign clearly demonstrates the anti–North American sentiment that has awakened in Panama."

63. Jules Dubois, *Danger over Panama* (New York: Bobbs-Merrill, 1964), p. 251; Roberto Méndez, *Panamá, 9 de enero de 1964: "Qué pasó y por qué"* (Panama City: Imprenta de la Universidad de Panamá, 1999), p. 104; affidavit by Panamanian Adrian Wright, 24 January 1964, in Serie 9 de enero, Expedientes No. 7 Fiscalia Auxiliar 1964, PAMINREX; De Bernard interview. The United States ventured outside the Zone in the Colón corridor by closing it and the Bridge of the Americas, thereby shutting off any land connection. Otherwise some U.S. soldiers were often as unsure as Panamanians about the exact limits of the Zone (John Sheffey interview by Jorden, 8 May 1979, Jorden Papers, LBJL).

64. Affidavit by Inocencio Garibaldi, 27 January 1964, Serie 9 de enero 1964, Expedientes No. 7 Fiscalia Auxiliar 1964, PAMINREX; Richard Eder, "Violence a Shock to Panama; Radio Continues Attacks on U.S.," *New York Times*, 13 January 1964. Canal Zone Police Chief Gaddis Wall said his police only shot at a wall or into the ground to ward off approaching crowds; see *Hearings of the Committee of the International Commission of Jurists in Panama, Republic of Panama* (6–13 March 1964), 10 March.

65. Both cited in "Women Tell of Panama Escape," *Miami Herald*, 21 January 1964; Jorden, *Panama Odyssey*, p. 50.

66. USCINCSO to State, 13 January 1964, folder Political Affairs & Rel. PAN-US 1/12/64, box 2561, Central Files 1964–1966, RG 59, NARA; Waldron, "'I Was the Only American in the Town,'" *Miami Herald*, 21 January 1964.

67. The number of Panamanian dead still cited by historians is improbably high (twenty-four). See Stephen Rabe, *Eisenhower and Latin America: The Foreign Policy of Anti-Communism* (Chapel Hill: University of North Carolina, 1988), p. 187, and Walter LaFeber, *The Panama Canal: The Crisis in Historical Perspective* (New York: Oxford University Press, 1978), p. vii.

68. Panama Ministry of Health final statistics are in U.S. consulate in Panama City to State, 2 March 1964, folder POL 2 General Reports & Statistics PAN 1/1/64, Box 2557, Central Files 1964–1966, RG 59, NARA; U.S. presentation to the OAS/OC, 12 February 1964, Panama Canal Company and the Canal Zone Government Vol. II, Administrative Histories, LBJL; Judge Guthrie Crowe testimony, *Hearings of the Committee*, 10 March 1964; "Panama," 8 February 1964, folder P10g9 Country Background—Panama, box 209, Country Files 1955–1964, Planning and Development Staff, Bureau of Cultural Affairs, RG 59, NARA; Méndez, *Panamá, 9 de enero de 1964*, p. 205.

69. There could be several reasons for Panamanians' shooting other Panamanians: by accident, to settle scores, to produce martyrs, or to draw out the

GN against U.S. forces. For examples, see Richard Baxter and Doris Carroll, *The Panama Canal: Background Papers and Proceedings of the Sixth Hammarskjöld Forum* (Dobbs Ferry, N.Y.: Oceana Publications, 1965), p. 53; *Hearings of the Committee,* 11 March 1964; and Eugene Methvin, "The Anatomy of a Riot: Panama 1964," *Orbis* 14 (June 1970): 479, 484. In 1972 a former Guard member (unnamed) argued that "if anyone was shot they were shot by Panamanians or by stray *gringo* bullets. I'll bet a limb that no *gringo* shot a Panamanian on purpose"; see Méndez, *Panamá, 9 de enero de 1964,* p. 246.

70. Moreno to Solís, Washington, 7 February 1964, Sucesos del 9 y 10 de enero, 1964, vol. 2, PAMINREX.

71. "Onda Popular" in "Riot Incidents as Reported by Radio and TV Broadcasts from the Republic of Panama, January 9–10, 1964," box 15, Declassified General Correspondence, 1945–1979, Internal Security Office, RG 185, NARA.

72. "Views of a Former Panamanian Newspaperman," 17 April 1964, folder POL PAN-US 4/14/64, box 2564, Central Files 1964–1966, RG 59, NARA; Harry McPherson interview by Jorden, 28 March 1964, Jorden Papers, LBJL; Emilio Gastelú interview by author. For visual evidence of APCs, see *Riot in Panama,* motion picture, 35 mm, NWDNM(m)-111-LC-47562, RG 111, NARA.

73. SOUTHCOM to State, folder Political Affairs & Rel. PAN-US 1/12/64, box 2561, Central Files 1964–1966, RG 59, NARA; "Background and Chronology"; memorandum of a meeting with the OAS, 4:30 p.m., 11 January 1964, Panama City, *Crises in Panama and the Dominican Republic: National Security File and NSC Histories, 1963–1969* (Frederick, Md.: UPA, 1982), 4: 088. Panamanian diplomats privately understood that the Bridge of the Americas, blocked by U.S. forces, was not under Panamanian jurisdiction; see "Reunión de la tarde," 12 January 1964, folder Miscellaneous, box 4, lot 67D467, Records Relating to Panama, 1959–1965, Office of Central American and Panamanian Affairs, RG 59, NARA.

74. Vallarino to OAS investigators, 14 February 1964, Serie 9 de enero 1964, Expedientes No. 9 Sucesos del 9 de Enero 1964, PAMINREX.

75. Affidavit by Daniel Morales, 24 January 1964, Serie 9 de enero 1964, Expedientes No. 7 Fiscalia Auxiliar 1964, PAMINREX; U.S. embassy in Panama to State, 9 January 1964, JCS to State, 10 January 1964, and USCINCSO to State, 10 January 1964, all in folder POL—Political Activities & Rel. PAN-US 1/1/64, box 2561, Central Files 1964–1966, RG 59, NARA; U.S. embassy in Panama "CRITIC" to State, 10 January 1964, *Crises* 4: 063; "Background and Chronology"; "Women Tell of Panama Escape," *Miami Herald,* 21 January 1964.

76. U.S. presentation to the OAS/OC, 12 February 1964, Panama Canal Company and the Canal Zone Government Vol. II, Administrative Histories, LBJL; USCINCSO to JCS, 11 January 1964, folder POL—Political Affairs & Rel. PAN-US 1/1/64, and Mann to Rusk, 12 January 1964, folder Political Affairs & Rel. PAN-US 1/12/64, both in box 2561, Central Files 1964–1966, RG 59, NARA; JCS situation report, 11 January 1964, *Crises* 4: 065; Dubois, *Danger over Panama,* p. 291.

77. NSC meeting notes, folder 407th Meeting of NSC May 21 1959, NSC Series, Eisenhower Papers as President, 1953–1961, DDEL.

78. Cabot in Schlesinger, *A Thousand Days: John F. Kennedy in the White House* (Boston: Houghton Mifflin, 1965), p. 179. See also USIA, "Awareness of the Alliance for Progress," 1962, folder S-46–62, box 23, 1962, Special Reports, 1953–1963, Office of Research, RG 306, NARA; and USIA, "The Economic and Political Climate of Opinion in Latin America and Attitudes toward the Alliance for Progress," 30 April 1964, folder R-50–64, box 2, Office of Research "R" Reports, RG 306, NARA.

79. "A Review of USIA Research," 4 March 1963, folder USIA Review of US Research 3/4/63, box 91, Departments & Agencies, President's Office Files, Kennedy Papers, JFKL. See also USIA, "The Role and Trend of Public Opinion in Latin America: 1961," folder P-4 No.3 1959–1962 Area Background—ARA, box 205, Country Files 1955–1964, Planning and Development Staff, Bureau of Cultural Affairs, RG 59, NARA.

80. Bryant Wedge, "Nationality and Social Perception," folder 1968, box 8, 1963, Multi Area (World) Project Files, 1953–1963, Office of Research, RG 306, NARA; president of Colombia cited in Elizabeth Cobbs Hoffman, *All You Need Is Love: The Peace Corps and the Spirit of the 1960s* (Cambridge, Mass.: Harvard University Press, 1998), p. 26.

81. LaFeber, "Thomas C. Mann and the Devolution of Latin American Policy: From the Good Neighbor to Military Intervention," in Thomas McCormick and Walter LaFeber, eds., *Behind the Throne: Servants of Power to Imperial Presidents, 1898–1968* (Madison: University of Wisconsin Press, 1993), pp. 166–203. See also Schlesinger, interview; Martin interview. The announcement of the "Mann Doctrine" was in Tad Szulc's "U.S. May Abandon Effort to Deter Latin Dictators," *New York Times,* 19 March 1964, p. 1. Rabe, *Most Dangerous Area,* pp. 27, 177, 178.

82. Mann to Vaughn, 12 February 1965, folder Information Activities (GEN), box 5, lot 67D467, Records Relating to Panama, 1959–1965, Office of Central America and Panamanian Affairs, RG 59, NARA; Mann interview by Burg; Mann to Douglas Dillon, 24 November 1959, folder Cuba 1959 Aug.–Dec., box 1, Bonsal Papers, Manuscript Division, LCong.

83. Rowan to Rusk and Johnson, 31 December 1964, folder FG 296 U.S. In-

formation Agency (1964–1966), box 33, Subject Files, Confidential File, LBJL.

84. Recording of telephone conversation between Johnson and Mann, 19 February 1964, tape WH6402.18, LBJL.

85. Robert Dallek, *Flawed Giant: Lyndon Johnson and His Times, 1961–1973* (New York: Oxford University Press, 1998), p. 91; recording of telephone conversation between Johnson and Russell, 10 January 1964, tape WH6401.11, LBJL.

86. Miguel Moreno interview by author.

87. Ramón Pereira interview by author; "Panama: A Communications Fact Book," 27 September 1960, folder R-58-60, box 3, Office of Research "R" Reports, 1960–1963, 1960, RG 306, NARA; Scott, "Political Orientations," p. 82; Thomas Crystal, "Panama, the United States, and the Canal, 1954–64" (Ph.D. diss., Stanford University, 1968), pp. 61.05–61.1.

88. José Bazán in Martin to Mann, 22 January 1964, folder Political Affairs & Rel. PAN-US 1/22/64, box 2562, Central Files 1964–1966, RG 59, NARA. See also Robert Berrellez in Fleming to Sheffey, 28 January 1964, folder Political Affairs & Rel. PAN-US 1/25/64, box 2562, Central Files, 1964–1966, RG 59, NARA; Humberto Ricord interview by author; USIA-Davíd to USIA in Washington, 12 January 1964[?], folder POL Riots and Related Developments, box 4, lot 67D467, Records Relating to Panama, 1959–1965, Office of Central American and Panamanian Affairs, RG 59, NARA; Mann to Rusk and McNamara, folder Political Affairs & Rel. PAN-US 1/12/64, box 2561, Central Files 1964–1966, RG 59, NARA; Gastelú interview.

89. Cottrell to Mann, 24 February 1964, folder POL PAN-US 2/22/64, box 2563, Central Files 1964–1966, RG 59, NARA. See also Fleming conversation with Carlos Eleta and Joaquín Vallarino, 26 February 1964, folder C/REP 6/4 Public Incidents FLAG January 9, 1964, box 14, Declassified General Correspondence, 1945–1979, Internal Security Office, RG 185, NARA.

90. Manuel Solís Palma interview by author; Daira Arias Chiari interview by author; *Panama Free Zone* (Colón Free Zone), February and March 1964. Solís Palma confirmed that Bazán opposed the break in relations.

91. Pressure from the business community came early: CIA 01582, 19 January 1964, folder Panama Riots Vol. II Part D 1/64–2/64, box 64, Latin America, Country file, National Security File, LBJL; Fleming to Ailes, 19 January 1964, folder C/DEF 3-1/a Situation Reports—Panama January 9, 1964 to February 1964 volume 1 (a), box 5, Declassified General Correspondence, Internal Security Office, RG 185, NARA; Cottrell to Mann, and Bundy to Johnson, 5 March 1964, *Crises* 1: 442–443.

92. Federico Britton interview by author; Adolfo Ahumada interview by

author; Martin to Mann, 17 January 1964, folder Panama—Political Affairs & Rel. PAN-US 1/15/64, box 2562, Central Files 1964–1966, RG 59, NARA; Fleming to Colonel John Sheffey, 27 January 1964, folder Political Affairs & Rel. PAN-US 1/25/64, box 2562, Central Files 1964–1966, RG 59, NARA.

93. Britton interview; USCINCSO to State, 10 February 1964, folder POL PAN-US 2/3/64, box 2563, Central Files 1964–1966, RG 59, NARA. On Youth Congress, USCINCSO to State, 22 March 1964 and 23 March 1964, both folder POL 13-3 PAN 1/1/66, box 2559, Central Files 1964–1966, RG 59, NARA; and "Violencia y caos en el Congreso de Juventud," *Crítica*, 23 March 1964.

94. Bundy to Johnson, 12 January 1964, folder Panama—Riots Vol. II Part B 1/64–2/64, box 64, Latin America, Country File, National Security File, LBJL; "Analysis of Panama Canal Letters," 23 January 1964, folder Panama, box 5, Records of the Assistant Secretary for Public Affairs, 1961–1965, RG 59, NARA; "'Firm' Policy on Panama Favored by Americans," *Washington Post,* 12 February 1964; George Horace Gallup, *The Gallup Poll, 1935–1971* (New York: Random House, 1972), p. 1864; Mann's comment in meeting with the OAS, 4:30 p.m., 11 January 1964, Panama City, *Crises* 4: 090.

95. Ruark, "Now Is Time for U.S. to Growl a Bit," *Miami Herald,* 27 January 1964, p. 14-AW; "Panama Emotionalism," *Herald* (Healdon, Okla.), 30 January 1964; Sulzberger, "Pitfalls of Paradox in Panama," *New York Times,* 22 January 1964, p. 36; idem, "The Cost of Backyard Negligence," *New York Times,* 13 January 1964, p. 34; Niebuhr, "The Panama Crisis," *New Republic,* 1 February 1964, pp. 5–6.

96. "A Nation That Hates Gringos," *San Francisco Chronicle,* 13 January 1964, p. 1; Martin, "Why Do They *Hate* Us?"; Trevor Armbrister, "Panama: Why They Hate Us," *Saturday Evening Post,* 7 March 1964.

97. McCormack, "Panama from Both Sides of the Fence," *U.S. Lady,* April 1964, p. 40; Mrs. Loring (Louise) White, cited in "On-the-Spot Report from Panama," *Herald* (Ansley, Nebr.), 23 January 1964.

98. Donald Wilson to Bundy, "Foreign Reaction to the Panama Situation," 13 January 1964, *Crises* 1: 206.

99. Recording of telephone conversation between Johnson and Adlai Stevenson, 26 February 1964, tape WH6402.22, LBJL; Senate Committee on Foreign Relations, *Report of Proceedings: Briefing by Secretary of State Dean Rusk on the World Situation* Washington, D.C.: 16 January 1964, 5: 45, 49; recording of telephone conversation between Johnson and Spessard Holland, 25 March 1964, tape WH6403.16, LBJL.

100. Recordings of telephone conversations between Johnson and Russell, 10

and 22 January 1964, tapes WH6401.10 and WH6401.19, LBJL; Donald Wilson to Bundy, "Foreign Reaction to the Panama Situation," 13 January 1964, *Crises* 1: 206–211. U.N. Ambassador Adlai Stevenson reported that Latin Americans were "solidly behind Panama" but "fearful their views will have no effect on U.S." (22 January 1964, *Crises* 4: 158–159).

101. For examples, see CIA 97562, 13 January 1964, folder Panama—Riots Vol. II Part D 1/64–2/64, box 64, and 38298, 13 March 1964, folder Panama Vol. III Cables 3/64, box 65, both in Latin America, Country Files, National Security File, LBJL; Denney to Rusk, 31 January 1964, folder P10g9 Country Background—Panama, box 209, Country Files 1955–1964, Planning and Development Staff, Bureau of Cultural Affairs, RG 59, NARA; and "Panama," 27 March 1963, *CIA Research Reports: Latin America, 1946–1976* (Frederick, Md.: UPA, 1982), 1: 0193.

102. Stevenson to State, 7 April 1964, folder Political Affairs & Relations PAN-US 4/1/64, box 2564, Central Files 1964–1966, RG 59, NARA; State report, written probably in early April 1964, folder Speeches PR-12, box 6, lot 67D467, ARA—Office of Central American and Panamanian Affairs, Records Relating to Panama, 1959–1965, RG 59, NARA.

103. Mann to Rusk, 11 January 1964, folder Panama—Riots Vol. II Part A 1/64–2/64, box 63, Latin America, Country File, National Security File, LBJL; Mann cited in Lyndon Johnson, *The Vantage Point* (New York: Popular Library, 1971), p. 183; Mann interview by Jorden, 11 October 1979, Jorden Papers, LBJL. See also Mann interview by Frantz.

104. Mann to Rusk, 11 January 1964, folder POL—Political Affairs & Rel. PAN-US 1/1/64, box 2561, Central Files 1964–1966, RG 59, NARA, and Rusk to Mann, 11 January 1964, folder Panama—Riots Vol. II Part A 1/64–2/64, box 63, Latin America, Country File, National Security File, LBJL.

105. Solís Palma interview.

106. All citations from memorandum of conference with the president, 13 January 1964, Cabinet Room, folder Miscellaneous Meetings Vol. 1, box 18, Bundy Papers, National Security File, LBJL. CIA warnings of coup attempts include 97638, 13 January 1964, and a mostly blacked-out report sent to Bundy, 13 January 1964, both in folder Panama—Riots Vol. II Part D 1/64–2/64, box 64, Latin America, Country File, National Security File, LBJL.

107. Memorandum of conference with the president, 13 January 1964; Senate Committee on Foreign Relations, *Report of Proceedings: Briefing by Secretary of State Dean Rusk on the World Situation* Washington, D.C., 16 January 1964, 5: 22.

108. Recording of telephone conversation between Mann and Johnson, 10 March 1964, tape WH6403.07, LBJL.

109. Recording of telephone conversation between Bundy and Johnson, 24 March 1964, tape WH6403.15, LBJL.

110. Recording of telephone conversation between Mann and Johnson, 27 January 1964, tape WH6401.23, LBJL; Mann to Johnson, 27 January 1964, folder Panama—Riots Vol. II Part F 1/64–2/64, box 65, Latin America, Country File, National Security File, LBJL; IAPC communiqué in Martin to Mann, 15 January 1964, folder POL—Political Affairs & Rel., box 2562, Central Files 1964–1966, RG 59, NARA; "Statement of the President on Panama and Related Subjects," 23 January 1964, *Crises* 1: 107–108.

111. Mann teleconference with Ball and Dungan, 25 January 1964, folder Panama [12/17/63–7/7/66], box 5, Ball Papers, LBJL; Mann to Martin, 17 January 1964, folder Panama—Riots Vol. II Part A 1/64–2/64, box 63, Latin America, Country File, National Security File, LBJL.

112. Tad Szulc, "Panama Demands O.A.S. Protection Lest U.S. Attack," *New York Times*, 1 February 1964.

113. Moreno interview.

114. Philip Geyelin, *Lyndon B. Johnson and the World* (New York: Praeger, 1966), pp. 106–110; Mann to Rusk, 11 March 1964, *Crises* 1: 433; recording of telephone conversation between Bundy and Johnson, 12 March 1964, tape WH6403.09, LBJL.

115. Transcript of telephone conversation between Chiari and Johnson, 10 January, folder Panama 1964, box 2, Records of the Assistant Secretary for Public Affairs, 1961–1965, RG 59, NARA.

116. "Joint Declaration," 3 April 1964, including Johnson statement of 21 March and Chiari response of 24 March, folder Panama Vol. IV Memos & Misc. 4/64–5/64, box 66, Latin America, Country File, National Security File, LBJL.

117. Hermann y Carrasco, *El Día*, 23 March 1964.

118. Moreno interview.

119. Chiari cited by Solís Palma, interview. On Moreno-Bunker meetings, see memorandum of conversation, 23 March 1964, *Crises* 4: 290; Bundy to Johnson, 1 April 1964, folder Panama vol. IV Memos & Misc. 4/64–5/64, box 66, Latin America, Country File, National Security File, LBJL; and Ellsworth Bunker interview by Jorden, 26 March 1979, Jorden Papers, LBJL; Johnson telephone conversation with Chiari, 3 April 1964, tape WH6404.02, LBJL; NSC meeting with Congressional leaders, 3 April 1964, folder NSC Meetings, Vol. 1 Tab 7, 4/3/64 Various Topics (Panama, etc.), box 1, NSC Meetings File, National Security File, LBJL.

120. U.S. embassy in Panama City to State, 8 January 1964, folder POL 2 General Report & Statistics PAN 1/1/64, box 2557, Central Files 1964–1966, RG 59, NARA; embassy to State, 14 October 1963, folder POL 12 Political

Parties PAN, box 4007, Central Files 1963, RG 59, NARA; Britton interview.

121. Martin to Mann, 30 January 1964, folder S/REP 6/4 Flag Incident 1/9/64 Panama-US, box 14, Declassified General Correspondence, 1945–1979, Internal Security Office, RG 185, NARA.

122. Martin to Mann, 21 January 1964, folder C/REP 6-4 Public Incidents FLAG January 9, 1964, box 14, Declassified General Correspondence, 1945–1979, Internal Security Office, RG 185, NARA; memorandum of conversation, 22 January 1964, folder Political Affairs & Relations PAN-US 1/14/64, box 2562, Central Files 1964–1966, RG 59, NARA.

123. *La Prensa,* January–May 1964.

124. "Farland busca apoyo del State Department para Arnulfo Arias," *El Día,* 11 March 1964; *Gráfico,* 16 May 1964; Panama consulate to State, 17 March 1964, folder POL 2 General Reports & Statistics, box 2557, Central Files 1964–1966, RG 59, NARA; Vaughn to Rusk, 9 May 1964, folder SOC—Social Conditions PAN 1/1/64, box 3233, Central Files 1964–1966, RG 59, NARA. The *gringa* was the daughter of the Commander of the Southern Forces, General O'Meara. Both Arias and Canal Zone authorities rushed to deny the rumor, which Vaughn called "one of [the] more ludicrous of last-ditch Robles efforts [to] discredit Arnulfo."

125. Vaughn to Rusk, 5 May 1964, folder POL 14 Elections PAN 1/1/64, box 2559, Central Files 1964–1966, RG 59, NARA.

126. Vaughn to Rusk, 13 May 1964, folder POL 14 Elections PAN 1/1/64, box 2559, Central Files 1964–1966, RG 59, NARA; U.S. embassy in Panama City to State, 17 September 1964, folder POL 15–1 PAN 1/1/64, box 2560, Central Files 1964–1966, RG 59, NARA. See also Mann to Rusk, 13 May 1964, folder Latin America Vol. 1 11/63–6/64, box 1, Latin America, Country File, National Security File, LBJL. Southern Command reported that after first returns had Arias winning, booths closed early in the evening and Electoral Tribunal members left drunk; the morning after, Government Coalition members had replaced them and were now giving Robles the lead. Robles won by just over 10,000 votes, while about 25,000 votes were missing. See memorandum to State, 12 May 1964, *Crises* 2: 005. More evidence of fraud comes from the archives of the Dominican Republic. Ambassador to Panama Ciro Amaury Dargam Cruz wrote to Dominican President Donald Reid Cabral that fraud was planned and extensive. According to him, Chiari and Robles supporters raided Arias headquarters, censured his radio station, and declared he had lost in his stronghold of Chiriquí. "I was informed that Dr. Arnulfo Arias had won the elections, but that the Government was funneling all its resources into committing fraud in the interior and swinging the election to Robles." Amaury to Reid, 14 May

1964, folder Panama, box 30101-3 Países Alemania—Puerto Rico 1964–66, Fondo Documental de la Presidencia, AGNDR.

127. Fernando Eleta interview by author; for a similar statement, see McPherson, *A Political Education* (Boston: Little, Brown, 1972), p. 223.

128. Editorial, "Rebeldía desorientada," *La Prensa*, 7 July 1964; Panamanian Desk Officer to Mann, 14 August 1964, folder E7 Visits David Samudio 1964, box 4, lot 67D467, Records Relating to Panama, 1959–1965, Office of Central American and Panamanian Affairs, RG 59, NARA; "Reformas sociales—nuevo tratado—gobierno de unión nacional—hará el gobierno de Marco A. Robles," *El Día*, 29 August 1964.

129. W. J. McNeil to Mann, 7 July 1964, folder POL 15–1 PAN 1/1/64, box 2560, Central Files 1964–1966, RG 59, NARA.

130. Eleta interview; for Eleta's full version, see República de Panamá, Ministerio de Relaciones Exteriores, *Acalaración para la historia: Dirigida a todos los panameños a través de una cadena nacional de radio y televisión el día 25 de noviembre 1964,* (Panama City: Dirección de Relaciones Públicas, 1964); Jorge Illueca (Eleta's main opponent) interview by author; Robles' new negotiating team was made up of Ricardo Arias, Roberto Alemán, and Diógenes de la Rosa.

131. Smith, 10 December 1964, folder POL PAN-US 9/3/64, box 2565, Central Files 1964–1966, RG 59, NARA; Bundy to Johnson, 30 November 1964, folder Panama Vol. VI, box 67, Country File, National Security File, LBJL.

132. Recording of telephone conversation between Johnson and Mann, 18 November 1964, tape WH6411.23, LJBL; John Major argues that negotiator Robert Anderson was the leader in proposing a 3-in-1 treaty in December; see Major, *Prize Possession,* p. 338. But unless someone eliminated all references to Anderson in the records, they show Mann making the key decision to accept a new treaty for the old canal. Mann also convinced Secretary of the Army Stephen Ailes; see Bundy to Johnson, 30 November 1964, folder Panama Vol. VI, box 67, Country File, National Security File, LBJL. See also "Vance's List," 17 December 1964; "Steve Ailes' list," 18 December [1964?]; "Tom Mann's list," 18 December 1964; and Bundy to Johnson [i.e. Bundy's list], 18 December 1964, all in folder McGeorge Bundy 10/1–12/31/64 Vol. 7 [1 of 2], box 2, Memos to the President, National Security File, LBJL; Eisenhower to Milton Eisenhower, 30 March 1964, folder Milton S. Eisenhower Papers, Correspondence 1964, box 15, Milton Eisenhower Papers, 1938–1973, DDEL; Robert Anderson interview by Jorden, 14 May 1979, Jorden Papers, LBJL.

133. "President's Statement on Panama Canal," 18 December 1964, *Crises* 2: 262–264.

134. Recording of telephone conversation between Johnson and Mann, 18 November 1964, tape WH6411.23, LBJL.
135. Emphases added; "President's Statement on Panama Canal," 18 December 1964, *Crises* 2: 262.
136. Solís to Chiari, 31 July 1964, Diógenes de la Rosa Papers, *Correspondencia sobre las negociaciones,* Expediente No. 1, junio a septiembre de 1964, Biblioteca Nacional, Panama City; minutes of the CNRE, 27 November 1964, Actas del Consejo Nacional de Relaciones Exteriores, 2 de nov. al 28 de dic. 1964, PAMINREX; *Memoria que el Ministro de Relaciones Exteriores presenta a la Honorable Asamblea Nacional en sus sesiones ordinarias de 1965* (Panama City: 1965), p. 10; Solís to Illueca, 26 June 1964, in Diógenes de la Rosa Papers, *Correspondencia sobre las negociaciones,* Expediente No. 1, junio a septiembre de 1964, Biblioteca Nacional, Panama City.
137. Recording of telephone conversation between Johnson and Mann, 26 April 1965, tape WH6504.05, LBJL; Panamanian quotations from Actas del Consejo Nacional de Relaciones Exteriores, PAMINREX. See also Eloy Benedetti to Solís, Washington, D.C., 29 July 1964; and Solís to Illueca, Panama City, 7 September 1964, both in Diógenes de la Rosa Papers, *Correspondencia sobre las negociaciones,* Expediente No. 1, junio a septiembre de 1964, Biblioteca Nacional, Panama City.
138. Geyelin, *Johnson and the World,* pp. 274, 101.

4. Dominican Republic, 1965

1. Piero Gleijeses, *The Dominican Crisis: The 1965 Constitutionalist Revolt and American Intervention,* trans. Lawrence Lipson (Baltimore, Md.: Johns Hopkins University Press, 1978), p. 1; Selden Rodman, *Quisqueya: A History of the Dominican Republic* (Seattle: University of Washington Press, 1964), pp. 10–22; Frank Moya Pons, *The Dominican Republic: A National History* (New Rochelle, N.Y.: Hispaniola Books, 1995), pp. 43–46, 63. See also Mu-Kien Adriana Sang, *Historia dominicana: Ayer y hoy* (Santo Domingo: SUSAETA Ediciones Dominicanas, 1999).
2. See Manuel Arturo Peña Battle, *Historia de la cuestión fronteriza dominicana-haitiana,* vol. 1, 2nd ed. (Santo Domingo: Sociedad Dominicana de Bibliófilos, 1988; orig. pub. 1946); and idem, *La Isla de la Tortuga,* 3rd ed. (Santo Domingo: Editora Taller, 1988; orig. pub. 1951).
3. Cited in Sumner Welles, *Naboth's Vineyard: The Dominican Republic, 1844–1924,* 2 vols. (New York: Payson and Clarke, 1928), p. 103.
4. The Haitian occupation had its moments of brutality but was, in a larger sense, an effort by Haitian revolutionaries like Toussaint L'Ouverture to

bring land redistribution and indigenous development to the rest of the island. See Gleijeses, *Dominican Crisis,* p. 6; and Moya Pons, *The Dominican Republic,* pp. 106–107, 108, 139.

5. Elaine Marie Thelmo, "The Processes and Structures in the Development of Nationalism: A Case Study of the Dominican Republic" (Ph.D. diss., American University, 1969), p. 197; James Ferguson, *The Dominican Republic: Beyond the Lighthouse* (London: Latin American Bureau, 1992), p. 15. See also Manuel Arturo Peña Battle, *Política de Trujillo* (Ciudad Trujillo: Impresora Dominicana, 1954); Roberto Cassá, *Los doce años: Contrarrevolución y desarrollismo,* vol. 1 (Santo Domingo: Búho, 1991), p. 405; Pedro San Miguel, *La isla imaginada: Historia, identidad y utopía en la Española* (San Juan–Santo Domingo: Isla Negra / La Trinitaria, 1997), p. 133; Manuel Nuñez, *El ocaso de la nación dominicana* (Santo Domingo: Alfa y Omega, 1990), pp. 37, 40; and Mons. Hugo Polanco Brito, *Síntesis de la historia de la Iglesia en Santo Domingo* (Santo Domingo: Amigo del Hogar, 1995), p. 55.

6. George Pope Atkins and Larman Wilson, *The Dominican Republic and the United States: From Imperialism to Transnationalism* (Athens: University of Georgia Press, 1998), pp. 20, 32.

7. James Clark, *The Church and the Crisis in the Dominican Republic* (Westminster, Md.: Newman Press, 1967), p. 15.

8. Tomás Morel museum, Santiago, Dominican Republic.

9. Calder, *The Impact of Intervention: The Dominican Republic during the U.S. Occupation of 1916–1924* (Austin: University of Texas Press, 1984), pp. 13, 8, 9, 3.

10. Calder, *Impact,* pp. 119, 121–122; Atkins and Wilson, *The Dominican Republic,* p. 53; Andrés Mateo, *Mito y cultura en la era de Trujillo* (Santo Domingo: Librería la Trinitaria e Instituto del Libro, 1993), p. 59.

11. Pendleton cited in Captain Stephen Fuller and Graham Cosmas, *Marines in the Dominican Republic, 1916–1924* (Washington, D.C.: History and Museums Division, U.S. Marine Corps, 1974), p. 25; Russell quoted in Calder, *Impact,* p. 20.

12. Eric Paul Roorda, *The Dictator Next Door: The Good Neighbor Policy and the Trujillo Regime in the Dominican Republic, 1930–1945* (Durham, N.C.: Duke University Press, 1998), p. 101. See also G. Pope Atkins, "The United States and the Dominican Republic during the Era of Trujillo" (Ph.D. diss., American University, 1966), p. 157.

13. Trujillo letter to Ramfis, 3 May 1958, in Bernardo Vega, *Los Trujillos se escriben* (Santo Domingo: Fundación Cultural Dominicana, 1987), p. 92; on propaganda, Bernardo Vega, *Kennedy y los Trujillo* (Santo Domingo: Fundación Cultural Dominicana, 1991), p. 17, and Mateo, *Mito,* p. 94; on

bribes, Arturo Espaillat, *Trujillo: El último de los cesares* (n.p., n.d.; translation Chicago: Regnery, 1963), p. 90; Roorda, *Dictator,* p. 114.

14. Jerome Slater, "The United States, the Organization of American States, and the Dominican Republic, 1961–1963," *International Organization* 18 (March 1964): 268–291; idem, "The Limits of Legitimization in International Organizations: The Organization of American States and the Dominican Crisis," *International Organization* 23 (December 1969): 48–72; Atkins, "The United States," pp. 255, 258; Víctor Grimaldi, *Los Estados Unidos en el derrocamiento de Trujillo* (Santo Domingo: n.p., 1985), pp. 42, 50; and Stephen Rabe, "The Caribbean Triangle: Betancourt, Castro, and Trujillo and U.S. Foreign Policy, 1958–1963," *Diplomatic History* 20 (Winter 1996): 55–78.

15. Robert Crassweller, *Trujillo: The Life and Times of a Caribbean Dictator* (New York: MacMillan, 1966), p. 332, see also pp. 424–425 (Crassweller is the journalist cited); "Current Policy toward the Dominican Republic," probably December 1959, folder 1959 Dominican Republic, box 12, lot 61D279, Subject Files 1957–1959, Records of the Assistant Secretary of State for Inter-American Affairs Roy R. Rubottom, RG 59, NARA; Martin Diary, 18 May 1962, folder Ambassador's Journal (Memorandum for the files) Jan.–Dec. 1962, box 44, Martin Papers, Manuscripts Division, LCong; Atkins, "The United States," p. 273; Roberto Cassá interview by author, 10 February 1998.

16. Bernardo Vega, *Los Estados Unidos y Trujillo: Los días finales, 1960–1961* (Santo Domingo: Fundación Cultural Dominicana, 1999), pp. 243, 244, quotation from press on p. 391; Trujillo cited in Crassweller, *Trujillo,* p. 422.

17. Mario Álvarez Dugan, director of Radio Caribe, in *El Caribe,* 16 March 1961, p. 1; William Wipfler, *Poder, influencia e impotencia: La Iglesia como factor socio-político en República Dominicana,* trans. Samuel James (Santo Domingo: Editora Santo Domingo, 1980), pp. 125, 145.

18. Richard Owen to "Dick" [Richard Roy Rubottom?], 11 April 1961, folder Church (Roman Catholic) 1961 Dominican Republic, box 3, Records Relating to the Dominican Republic, 1958–1966, Office of Caribbean and Mexican Affairs, RG 59, NARA; Vega, *Kennedy,* pp. 8, 9.

19. Gregorio Selser, ed., *¡Aqui, Santo Domingo! La tercera guerra sucia* (Buenos Aires: Editora Palestra, 1966), p. 288; Gleijeses, *Dominican Crisis,* pp. 313, 321; George Pope Atkins, *Arms and Politics in the Dominican Republic* (Boulder, Colo.: Westview Press, 1981), p. 25; Carlos María Gutiérrez, *El experimento dominicano* (Mexico City: Editorial Diógenes, 1974), p. 39; CIA, 27 March 1963, *CIA Research Reports: Latin America, 1946–1976* (Frederick, Md.: UPA, 1982), 1: 160.

20. Cited in John Gerassi, *The Great Fear: The Reconquest of Latin America by Latin Americans* (New York: Macmillan, 1963), p. 181.

21. Guzmán interview by author; Tolentino Dipp interview by author; Cordero Michel interview by author.

22. Ramón Marrero Aristy, *Over* (Santo Domingo: Taller, 1994; orig. pub. 1940), quotation p. 93; Marcio Veloz Maggiolo interview by author; Cassá, *Movimiento obrero y lucha socialista en la República Dominicana: Desde los orígenes hasta 1960* (Santo Domingo: Fundación Cultural Dominicana, 1990), p. 247 (emphasis added).

23. Leandro Guzmán, *1J4, de espigas y de fuegos—Aportes para la memoria necesaria: Testimonios de un militante* (Santo Domingo: Editora de Colores, 1998), p. 207.

24. Tony Raful, *Movimiento 14 de Junio: Historia y documentos* (Santo Domingo: Editora Alfa y Omega, 1983), pp. 145, 190; *Unión Cívica*, 23 February, 1, ARC.

25. Cited in Slater, "The United States," p. 283.

26. "Martin Report on the Dominican Republic," p. 52, 3 October 1961, folder Dominican Republic Martin Report, box 115A, Countries, President's Office Files, Kennedy Papers, JFKL; *El Caribe*, 9 March 1962, 13 April 1962; Martin, *Overtaken by Events: The Dominican Crisis, from the Fall of Trujillo to the Civil War* (Garden City, N.Y.: Doubleday, 1966), pp. 3, 4.

27. Martin, *Overtaken by Events*, p. 98.

28. Richard Pells, *Not Like Us* (New York: Basic Books, 1997), pp. 88, 89; John Henderson, *The United States Information Agency* (New York: Praeger, 1969), p. 66; Kennedy to Murrow, 25 January 1963, folder United States Information Agency Vol. 3 [2 of 2], box 73, Agency File, National Security File, LBJL; Thomas Sorensen to Kennedy, 16 April 1962, folder USIA 1/62–6/62, box 91, Departments & Agencies, President's Office Files, Kennedy Papers, JFKL.

29. Mark Haefele, "John F. Kennedy, USIA, and World Public Opinion," *Diplomatic History* 25 (Winter 2001): 63–84; Thomas Sorensen, *The Word War: The Story of American Propaganda* (New York: Harper and Row, 1968).

30. Unsigned report (perhaps by Schlesinger), "The Intellectual in the Latin American Cultural Program," 24 May 1962, folder Alianza Para el Progreso (Political—Ideological Force), box 15, Office Files of the Deputy Assistant Secretary for Inter-American Affairs, lot 64D369, RG 59, NARA; John Johnson, "The United States and the Latin American Left Wings," *Yale Review* 56 (March 1967): 326.

31. D. H. Radler, *El Gringo: The Yankee Image in Latin America* (Philadelphia, Pa.: Chilton, 1962), p. 88; Schlesinger to Kennedy, 6 February 1961, folder

Schlesinger, Arthur M. 11/60–2/61, box 65, Staff Memos, President's Office Files, Kennedy Papers, JFKL.

32. "The Intellectual in the Latin American Cultural Program," NARA.

33. Thomas Hughes to Rusk, 23 October 1963, "Anti-US Student Sentiment in Latin America," folder P-4 No. 5 Area Background—ARA '63, box 205, Country Files 1955–1964, Planning and Development Staff, Bureau of Cultural Affairs, RG 59, NARA. Johnson, "The United States," p. 328.

34. "Interim Report of Subcommittee on Policy Review of Interagency Youth Committee," 22 January 1964, folder P-4 Area Background—ARA—1964, box 205, Country Files 1955–1964, Planning and Development Staff, Bureau of Cultural Affairs, RG 59, NARA.

35. Lloyd Free, Institute for International Social Research, "Attitudes, Hopes and Fears of the Dominican People," 25 June 1962, folder 1 Dominican People Nov.–Dec. 1962 Media Habits + Attitudes, box 24, Country Project Files, 1951–1964, Office of Research, RG 306, NARA; Murrow to Kennedy, 14 May 1962, folder USIA 1/62–6/62, box 91, Departments & Agencies, President's Office Files, Kennedy Papers, JFKL.

36. "Public Opinion Study Dominican Republic," folder DR 6202 Dominican Republic Nov.–Dec. 1962 Media Habits and Attitudes, box 24, Country Project Files, 1951–1964, Office of Research, RG 306, NARA; see also "Aspirations and Political Attitudes in the Dominican Republic," April 1963, folder R-70-63, box 14, Office of Research "R" Reports, 1900–1963, RG 306, NARA.

37. USIS Santo Domingo to USIA Washington, 12 May 1964, folder Santo Domingo—Country Background, box 211, Country Files 1955–1964, Planning and Development Staff, Bureau of Cultural Affairs, RG 59, NARA.

38. Martin Diary, 23 August 1962, folder Overtaken by Events Notebooks, Ambassador's Notebooks, 1962–1963, book R51, box 272, Martin Papers, Manuscripts Division, LCong; Martin, *Overtaken by Events,* pp. 97, 143; Tolentino doubted that riots were financed (interview with author); Martin to Edwin Martin, 20 June 1962, folder Dominican Republic Cables 3/62–6/62, box 67, Countries, National Security File, Kennedy Papers, JFKL.

39. Martin Diary, 27 January 1963, folder Ambassador's Journal (Memorandum for the files) Jan.–Aug. 1963, box 44, Martin Papers, Manuscripts Division, LCong; "Martin Report on the Dominican Republic," p. 89, 3 October 1961, folder Dominican Republic Martin Report, box 115A, Countries, President's Office Files, Kennedy Papers, JFKL.

40. Recording of Kennedy meeting with advisors, 4 October 1963, tape 114/A50, JFKL; Gleijeses, *Dominican Crisis,* p. 98.

41. Some documents are marked "*Not* for JBM," e.g., box 6, lot 69D228, Records Relating to the DR, 1958–1966, Office of Caribbean and Mexican Affairs, RG 59, NARA; Martin Diary, 29 November 1962, folder Ambassador's Journal (Memorandum for the files) Jan.–Dec. 1962, box 44, Martin Papers, Manuscripts Division, LCong; Martin, *Overtaken by Events,* pp. 548, 565, 630.

42. U.S. embassy in Santo Domingo to State, 16 October 1963, folder POL 15 Government Dom Rep 2/1/63, box 3889, Central Files 1963, RG 59, NARA.

43. Belisario Peguero Guerrero to minister of Interior and Police, 22 July 1965, legajo 5543, Fondo documental del Secretario de Estado de Interior y Policía, AGNRD; U.S. consulate in Santiago to State, 19 March 1963, folder POL 23 Internal Security Dom Rep 2/1/63, box 3890, Central Files 1963, RG 59, NARA.

44. Avedis Arthur Derounian [Deroudian?] report, September 1963, folder Background Material—Not for JBM 1963, box 6, lot 69D228, Records Relating to the DR, 1958–1966, Office of Caribbean and Mexican Affairs, RG 59, NARA.

45. Draper, *The Dominican Revolt: A Case Study in American Policy* (New York: Commentary, 1968), p. 1.

46. See "CRITIC ONE" and "CRITIC TWO" to State, 24 April 1965, *Crises in Panama and the Dominican Republic: National Security File and NSC Histories, 1963–1969* (Frederick, Md.: UPA, 1982), 5: 001–003.

47. Tad Szulc, *Dominican Diary* (New York: Dell, 1965); J. I. Quello and Narciso Isa Conde, "Revolutionary Struggle in the Dominican Republic and Its Lessons," *World Marxist Review* (Toronto) 8 (December 1965): 97.

48. State teleconference with embassy officials, 27 April 1965, folder POL 23-9 Dom Rep 1966, box 2134, Central Files, RG 59, NARA; U.S. embassy in Santo Domingo to State, 25 April 1965, folder POL 23-9 Dom Rep 4/16/65, box 2125, Central Files, RG 59, NARA.

49. U.S. embassy in Santo Domingo 1043 to State, 25 April 1965, folder POL 23-9 Dom Rep 4/16/65, box 2125, Central Files, RG 59, NARA; U.S. embassy in Santo Domingo 1047 to State, 25 April 1965, *Crises* 5: 017; U.S. embassy in Santo Domingo 1051 to State, 25 April 1965, folder POL 23-9 Dom Rep 4/16/65, box 2125, Central Files, RG 59, NARA; U.S. embassy in Santo Domingo 1066 to State, 26 April 1965, folder POL 23-9 Dom Rep 4/16/65, box 2125, Central Files, RG 59, NARA.

50. Galvá interview by author; see also Thomas Halper, "Appearance and Reality in Five American Foreign Policy Crises" (Ph.D. diss., Vanderbilt University, 1970), p. 144; and Abraham Lowenthal, *The Dominican Interven-*

tion (Baltimore, Md.: Johns Hopkins University Press, 1995; orig. pub. 1972), p. 143; Miguel Ángel Hernando Ramírez interview by author.

51. Bosch cited in Dan Kurzman, *Santo Domingo: Revolt of the Damned* (New York: Putnam's, 1965), p. 144.

52. Clark, *The Church,* p. 119; Gleijeses, *Dominican Crisis,* p. 245.

53. For a portrait of Bennett, see Peter Felten, "The 1965–1966 United States Intervention in the Dominican Republic" (Ph.D. diss., University of Texas at Austin, May 1995), pp. 16, 59, see also 108; Gleijeses, *Dominican Crisis,* p. 245.

54. Rusk to U.S. embassy in Santo Domingo, 27 April 1965, *Crises,* 5: 357; Bennett to State, 28 April 1965, folder POL 23-9 Dom Rep 4/16/65, box 2125, Central Files, RG 59, NARA.

55. *Top-Secret Hearings by the U.S. Senate Committee on Foreign Relations, 1959–1966* (Frederick, Md.: UPA, 1981), 6: 528, 535, 539. Jerome Slater agreed with Theodore Draper that Bennett's behavior on 27 April "was not an emotional blunder, but was entirely consistent with U.S. policy"; see Slater, *Intervention and Negotiation: The United States and the Dominican Revolution* (New York: Harper and Row, 1970), p. 29.

56. Jottin Cury interview by author.

57. Luis Homero Lajara Burgos, *¿Por qué se produjo la revolución del 24 de abril del año 1965?* (n.p., n.d.), pp. 107, 106, 108; a similar account is Fidelio Despradel, *Historia gráfica de la guerra de abril* (Santo Domingo: Nuevo Rumbo, 1992; orig. pub. 1975), p. 114; Claudio Caamaño interview by author; Quello and Isa Conde, "Revolutionary Struggle," p. 98.

58. Caamaño interview; John Bartlow Martin compared Caamaño to Castro, in 1256 to State, folder POL 23-9 Dom Rep 5/2/65 Rebellion Coups, box 2126, Central Files, RG 59, NARA, and in *Overtaken by Events,* p. 676; Hamlet Hermann interview by author.

59. Lajara Burgos, *¿Por qué?* p. 116.

60. Hermann interview; Hermann, *Francis Caamaño* (Santo Domingo: Alfa y Omega, 1983); "Juan Bosch—Bitter as He Calls It Quits," *Life,* 14 May 1965, p. 38C.

61. Caamaño telephone interview with Puerto Rican radio, translated, 28 April 1965, folder Dominican Republic Vol. III Memos & Miscellaneous to 5/7/65, box 39, Latin America, Country File, National Security File, LBJL; Caamaño interview.

62. Fidelio Despradel, *A Francis y a los demás . . . a 10 años de su caída* (n.p., n.d.), p. 13; Quello and Isa Conde, "Revolutionary Struggle," p. 98.

63. Bennett and Connett teleconference with U.S. embassy in Santo Domingo, 29 April 1965, folder POL 23-9 Dom Rep, box 2126, Central Files, RG 59,

NARA; John Bartlow Martin interview; Lowenthal, *Intervention,* pp. 88, 109; Slater, *Intervention and Negotiation,* p. 28.

64. Bourke Hickenlooper interview; Bennett briefing to journalists in Draper, *Revolt,* p. 91; "LBJ Statement on Dominican Republic," motion picture, 16 mm, USIA, 2 May 1965, NWDNM(m)-306.3293, RG 306, NARA. On images of savagery see LeeAnna Keith, "The Imperial Mind and U.S. Intervention in the Dominican Republic, 1961–1966" (Ph.D. diss., University of Connecticut, 1999), pp. 185–188.

65. State to American Republics posts, 28 April 1965, folder Dominican Republic Vol. I Cables 6/64–4/65, box 38, Latin America, Country File, National Security File, LBJL.

66. CIA 53329, 27 April 1965, *CIA Research Reports,* 4: 318–319; Draper, *Revolt,* p. 106; USIA, "Personal Accounts of the Chaos during the Dominican Revolution and Some Impressions about Communist Involvement," 28 May 1965, folder M-208–65, box 6, Office of Research Memorandums, 1963–1982, RG 306, NARA. The Socialist *El Popular* called Bonilla Aybar "the paid spokesman of native reactionaries and of Yankee imperialism in our country" (8 August 1963, p. 2, ARC).

67. Businessman David Sofaer cited in Kurzman, *Damned,* pp. 147–148; Halper, "Appearance and Reality," p. 115.

68. Hernando Ramírez interview; U.S. embassy in Santo Domingo 1095 to State, 26 April 1965, folder POL 23-9 Dom Rep 4/16/65, box 2125, Central Files, RG 59, NARA; USIA, "Personal Accounts."

69. Bennett testimony, 16 July 1965, *Top-Secret Hearings,* 6: 516–518.

70. Recording of telephone conversation between Rusk and Johnson, 29 April 1965, WH6504.07, LBJL; *Public Papers of the Presidents of the United States: Lyndon Johnson,* 1965, part I (Washington, D.C.: GPO, 1966), pp. 469–474.

71. Cited in Thomas Hughes to Rusk, 30 April 1965, folder Dominican Republic Vol. II Memos & Miscellaneous, box 38, Latin America, Country File, National Security File, LBJL.

72. Foreign Broadcast Information Service, "Foreign Radio and Press Reaction to U.S. Involvement in the Dominican Revolt," 4 May 1965, folder ND 19/CO62 1/1/65–5/5/65, box 201, National Defense, Subject File, White House Central Files, LBJL; General Bruce Palmer, Jr., *Intervention in the Caribbean: The Dominican Crisis of 1965* (Lexington: University Press of Kentucky, 1989), p. 72; "Patterns of Latin American Views on the Dominican Crisis: The First Month," 17 June 1965, book V: Documents for Hearings—Secret, box 1, Records Relating to the Dominican Crisis, 1965–1966, Subject Files, Under Secretary for Economic Affairs, RG 59, NARA; "How the World Views the U.S.," *Newsweek,* 21 June 1965, p. 39; Gregorio

Ortega, *Santo Domingo, 1965* (Havana: Ediciones Venceremos, 1965), pp. 77–80, 104, 115–118.

73. Johnson speech, 2 May, *Public Papers of the Presidents: Lyndon Johnson, 1965,* part I, pp. 469–474. Most authors recognize that the Johnson government made serious miscalculations about communism. Journalistic narratives include Szulc, *Diary;* Kurzman, *Damned;* and Marcel Niedergang, *La révolution de Saint-Domingue* (Rennes: Librairie Plon, 1966). Deeper analyses include the Draper-Slater exchange: Draper, *Revolt;* Slater, *Intervention and Negotiation;* and Draper, "The Dominican Intervention Reconsidered," *Political Science Quarterly* 86 (March 1971): 1–36. See also Lowenthal, *Intervention;* Gleijeses, *Dominican Crisis;* and Michael Kryzanek, "The Dominican Intervention Revisited: An Attitudinal and Operational Analysis," in John Martz, ed., *United States Policy in Latin America: A Quarter Century of Crisis and Challenge, 1961–1986* (Lincoln: University of Nebraska Press, 1988), pp. 135–156. Admitting shortcomings from inside the U.S. government are Arthur Schlesinger, Jr., interview by Frantz; Cyrus Vance interview; and Ray Cline, *Secrets, Spies and Scholars* (Washington, D.C.: Aeropolis Books, 1976), p. 212. Dominicans on the left have admitted that there was a lack of preparation and of control in late April: Quello and Isa Conde, "Revolutionary Struggle," pp. 98, 99. Others disagree. Slater indicates that communists were in a position to take over the chaotic military movement *on 28 April,* in *Intervention and Negotiation,* pp. 37–42. Several Dominicans have admitted that communists were close to taking over on 28 April and that only the U.S. intervention prevented them from doing so. See, for instance, Bryant Wedge to Bennett, 16 December 1965, folder Correspondence with Ambassadors, box 16, Files of McGeorge Bundy, National Security File, LBJL.

74. Kurzman, *Damned,* p. 24; recording of telephone conversation between McNamara, Fortas, and Johnson, 30 April 1965, 10:50 a.m., WH6504.08, LBJL; Selser, ed., *¡Aqui, Santo Domingo!*

75. CIA report 28, 6 May 1965, *CIA Research Reports,* 4: 445–446.

76. Mann to U.S. embassy in Santo Domingo, folder POL 23-9 Dom Rep 5/2/65 Rebellion Coups, box 2126, Central Files, RG 59, NARA; Bennett 1272 to State, folder POL 23-9 Dom Rep 5/2/65 Rebellion Coups, box 2126, Central Files, RG 59, NARA.

77. Szulc citing himself from *New York Times,* 15 May 1965, in *Diary,* pp. 210–211. Calder noted this dilemma in *Impact,* p. xxii.

78. Caamaño cited in *La Nación,* 7 May 1965, p. 4; Peña Gómez in *La Nación,* 15 May 1965, p. 3.

79. *Caamaño frente a la OEA* (Santo Domingo: Editorial Universitaria, 1985), p. 62.

80. *El 1J4,* 15 May 1965, p. 2.
81. Quotation is from "Dominican Puzzle," *U.S. News and World Report,* 24 May 1965, p. 39; Richard Mayhew Brown, "United States Propaganda Performance in Crisis, 1960–1965" (Ph.D. diss., University of North Carolina at Chapel Hill, 1970), p. 213.
82. *La Nación,* 13 May 1965, pp. 4, 2; 20 May 1965, p. 4; 2 June 1965, p. 4; 4 June 1965, p. 3; photos in 9 July 1965, p. 3, and 10 July 1965, p. 1; Bosch cited in Drew Pearson, "Washington Merry-Go-Round," *New York Post,* 17 June 1965, p. 31.
83. Radio Constitución cited in 1398 to State, 6 May 1965, folder 23–9 Dom Rep 5/6/65 Rebellion Coups, box 2127, Central Files, RG 59, LBJL.
84. Brown, "United States Propaganda," p. 213.
85. Cury interview.
86. Rebel spokesman cited in Clark, *Church,* pp. 179–180; Constitutionalist memorandum, August 1965, AHT.
87. Constitutionalist broadcast, 5 July 1965, AHT; *La Nación,* 28 May 1965, p. 2.
88. Alberto Baeza Flores, "Los poetas de 1965," *Eme eme* 9 (May 1983): 76. The most comprehensive portraits of life in the Colonial Zone are José Moreno, *El pueblo en armas: Revolución en Santo Domingo* (Madrid: Editorial Tecnos, 1973); and Margarita Cordero, *Mujeres de abril* (Santo Domingo: Ediciones Populares Feministas, 1985).
89. Despradel, *Historia gráfica,* p. 27. On the Peace Corps in Santo Domingo, Frank Mankiewicz interview; Kurzman, *Damned,* p. 27; and Elizabeth Cobbs Hoffman, *All You Need Is Love: The Peace Corps and the Spirit of the 1960s* (Cambridge, Mass.: Harvard University Press, 1998), pp. 69–70.
90. Brown, "United States Propaganda," p. 191; Rafael Chaljub Mejía interview by author.
91. Rafael Chaljub Mejía, *Cuesta arriba: Memorias* (Santo Domingo: Editora Taller, 1997), p. 19; the PSP made the decision on 8 August 1965, *El Popular,* 16 August 1965, p. 11, ARC; Roberto Cassá interview by author, 27 January 1998.
92. Johnson cited in Cline, *Secrets,* p. 213, and in Philip Geyelin, *Lyndon B. Johnson and the World* (New York: Praeger, 1966), p. 238.
93. Recording of telephone conversation between Bundy and Johnson, 1 May 1965, WH6505.01, LBJL; *La Nación,* 10 May 1965, p. 3.
94. Goodwin to Johnson, 29 April 1965, folder [Valenti File Re: Dominican Republic], box 8, Name File, National Security File, LBJL.
95. Recording of telephone conversation between Johnson, Fortas, and McNamara, 23 May 1965, WH6505.29, LBJL.
96. Johnson cited on 2 May 1965, in Charles Roberts, *LBJ's Inner Circle* (New York: Delacorte, 1965), p. 205.

97. Record of Johnson's meeting with congressional leadership, 28 April 1965, folder Dominican Republic Dominican Crisis Chronology 8/67, box 52, Latin America, Country File, National Security File, LBJL.

98. Cited in Kryzanek, "Dominican Intervention Revisited," p. 140.

99. Felten, "The 1965–1966 United States Intervention," pp. 178, 230; George Horace Gallup, *The Gallup Poll, 1935–1971* (New York: Random House, 1972), May poll on pp. 1942–1943, November poll on p. 1976; Peter Richardson, "A Note on the Origins of Anti-Castro Sentiment: The Press Treatment of Cuba's War Crimes Trials," *Jahrbuch für Geschichte von Staat Wirtschaft und Gesellschaft Lateinamerikas* 19 (1982): 394; Atkins and Wilson, *The Dominican Republic,* p. 137.

100. "Presentation of Our Action in the Dominican Republic," 5 May 1965, folder Dominican Republic, box 4, Records of the Assistant Secretary for Public Affairs, 1961–1965, RG 59, NARA.

101. Andrew Goodpaster, 30 April 1965, folder Goodpaster Briefings, 3 (February 16, 1965–August 3, 1965), box 1, Augusta–Walter Reed Series, Eisenhower Post-Presidential Papers, 1961–1969, DDEL.

102. Mann meeting with Loyalist officers, 15 May 1965, folder Miscellaneous memoranda, letters, etc. DR May 15–31, 1965, box 1, Records Relating to the Dominican Crisis, 1965–1966, Subject Files, Under Secretary for Economic Affairs, RG 59, NARA. Rebels have preferred to reason that the Johnson government did not allow the rightist troops to destroy them mainly because the rebels had mined the banks of the Colonial Zone: Narciso Isa Conde interview by author; and Mario Sánchez interview by author.

103. Palmer, *Intervention in the Caribbean,* p. 51; Kurzman, *Damned,* p. 248; Slater, *Intervention and Negotiation,* pp. 55, 56; McNamara to Cyrus Vance, 20 May 1965, folder POL 23-9 Dom Rep 5/19/65 Rebellion Coups, box 2130, Central Files, RG 59, NARA; Kryzanek, "Dominican Intervention Revisited," p. 141.

104. CIA, 4 May 1965, folder Dominican Republic Vol. II Cables 5/65, box 38, Latin America, Country File, National Security File, LBJL. See also CIA cables 61405, 7 May 1965, and 62659, 9 May 1965, folder Dominican Republic Vol. III Cables 5/65, box 38, Latin America, Country File, National Security File, LBJL; Chaljub Mejía, *Cuesta arriba.*

105. Palmer, *Intervention in the Caribbean,* p. 56.

106. There is disagreement over whether Caamaño paid commando members. Some say he did: Mirna Santos, "Abril de 1965," *Hoy,* 30 April 1998, p. 11E; "Marvin" to Johnson, 11 June 1965, folder June 1965 (Notes, instructions, doodles) [2 of 3], box 8, Handwriting File, LBJL. Others say he did not: Gustavo Díaz interview by author; Despradel, *Historia gráfica,* pp. 184–185; Despradel interview by author; Cordero interview.

107. Fafa Taveras, *Abril, la liberación efímera* (Santo Domingo: Ediciones Bloque Socialista, 1990), p. 31; Cassá interview by author, 2 February 1998. On commandos, see Moreno, *El pueblo en armas.*

108. Cury interview.

109. White House Situation Room to Jack Valenti and Johnson, 30 May 1965, folder Dominican Republic 4/65–7/65 White House Cables [1 of 2], box 50, Latin America, Country File, National Security File, LBJL.

110. 5 July 1965 meeting, *Caamaño frente a la OEA* (Santo Domingo: Editorial Universitaria, 1985), p. 65.

111. Bosch cited in Bosch, "A Tale of Two Nations," *New Leader,* 21 June 1965, p. 6; trooper cited in Ivan Musicant, *The Banana Wars* (New York: MacMillan, 1990), p. 368; Charles Moskos, Jr., "Grace under Pressure: The U.S. Soldier in the Dominican Republic," *Army,* September 1966, pp. 41–44; Paul Berger, "Rebels Fire First . . . ," *Leatherneck,* July 1965, pp. 32–35; idem, "Embassy Beachhead," *Leatherneck,* August 1965, pp. 68–69; Lawrence Yates, *Power Pack: U.S. Intervention in the Dominican Republic, 1965–1966* (Fort Leavenworth, Kans.: Combat Studies Institute, 1988), p. 140; George Lister to Vaughn, 3 June 1965, folder RUYLE Chronology—DR, box 1, Records Relating to the Dominican Crisis, 1965–1966, Subject Files, Under Secretary for Economic Affairs, RG 59, NARA; Szulc, *Diary,* p. 200.

112. Mann to Bunker, 11 June 1965, folder POL 14 Elections Dom Rep 1/1/64, box 2120, Central Files, RG 59, NARA.

113. Johnson cited in Cline, *Secrets,* p. 213; Joseph Califano interview by Gillette, 27 January 1988, folder Dominican Republic Oral History, box 50, Califano Papers, LBJL.

114. Recording of telephone conversation between Johnson and Mann, 26 April 1965, WH6504.05, LBJL.

115. Bundy in meeting with Johnson, 8 May 1965, folder Dominican Republic Vol. 6, box 40, Country File, National Security File, LBJL (650 Brazilians, 250 Hondurans, 75 Nicaraguans, and 20 Costa Ricans joined the U.S. troops). First Bundy quotation in Bundy to Johnson, 1 May 1965, folder McGeorge Bundy 4/15–5/31/65 Vol. 10 [2 of 3], box 3, Memos to the President, National Security File, LBJL; on OAS reluctance, see V. Shiv Kumar, *U.S. Interventionism in Latin America* (New York: Advent Books, 1987), p. 31.

116. Kurzman quotations in *Damned,* p. 24; Thomas Hughes to Rusk, 30 April 1965, folder Dominican Republic Vol. II Memos & Miscellaneous, box 38, Latin America, Country File, National Security File, LBJL; "Some Reactions from Latin American Leaders," 11 May 1965, folder Dominican Republic—Histories and Chronologies, box 4, Files of Gordon Chase,

National Security File, LBJL; Pearson, "Washington Merry-Go-Round"; U.S. embassy in Santo Domingo to State, 22 May 1965, folder POL 23-9 Dom Rep 5/21/65 Rebellion Coups, box 2130, Central Files, RG 59, NARA.

117. Meeting with Johnson, 8 May 1965, folder Dominican Republic Vol. 6, box 40, Country File, National Security File, LBJL.

118. George Lister to Vaughn, 3 June 1965, folder RUYLE Chronology—DR, box 1, Records Relating to the Dominican Crisis, 1965–1966, Subject Files, Under Secretary for Economic Affairs, RG 59, NARA.

119. White House meeting, 3 May 1965, folder Meeting on the Dominican Republic—Planning Group, box 2, Files of Gordon Chase, National Security File, LBJL. See also Rowan to Johnson, 4 May 1965, folder United States Information Agency Vol. 4 4/14/65 [2 of 2], box 74, Agency File, National Security File, LBJL; and Rusk testimony, 21 May 1965, *Top-Secret Hearings*, 6: 131.

120. Bennett testimony, 16 July 1965, *Top-Secret Hearings*, 6: 568.

121. Recording of telephone conversation between Johnson and Martin, 2 May 1965, WH6505.02, LBJL. Martin's mission, according to one telegram, was to "assist the ambassador in developing tactics to divide the rebels and isolate the extremists"; reproduced in Víctor Grimaldi, *El diario secreto de la intervención norteamericana de 1965*, 2nd ed. (Santo Domingo: n.p., 1989), p. 72.

122. Recording of telephone conversation between Martin and Johnson, 3 May 1965, WH6505.03, LBJL.

123. Martin to State, 6 May 1965, folder Dominican Republic Vol. III Cables 5/65, box 38, Latin America, Country File, National Security File, LBJL.

124. On Caamaño's refusal, see Felten, "The 1965–1966 United States Intervention," p. 241. On Imbert's acceptance, see Szulc, *Diary*, p. 200; Martin, "To Bring Together Two Sides," *Life*, 28 May 1965.

125. Mann to Bunker, 11 June 1965, folder POL 14 Elections Dom Rep 1/1/64, box 2120, Central Files, RG 59, NARA; situation report to the president, 9 June 1965, folder POL 23-9 Dom Rep 6/5/65, box 2131, Central Files, RG 59, NARA.

126. Transcript of telephone conversation between Mann and George Ball, 18 June 1965, folder Dominican Republic [4/28/65–6/26/65], box 3, Ball Papers, LBJL; Audrey Bracey, *Resolution of the Dominican Crisis, 1965* (Washington, D.C.: Institute for the Study of Diplomacy, Georgetown University, 1980), p. 3.

127. Cited in Danilo Brugal Alfau, *Tragedia en Santo Domingo: Documentos para la historia* (Santo Domingo: Editora del Caribe, 1966), p. 205; Bundy meeting with aides, 4 September 1965, folder Dominican Republic Vol. X

Memos & Miscellaneous 8/65–9/65 [1 of 2], box 43, Latin America, Country File, National Security File, LBJL.

128. Martin to State, 10 May 1965, folder Dominican Republic Volume 3 Cables 5/65, box 38, Country File, National Security File, LBJL.

129. Emphasis in original; cited in Valenti meeting notes, 30 April 1965, folder Meeting Notes (Handwritten) 4/30–5/15/65, box 13, Office of the President File, LBJL.

130. Berle to Johnson, 3 June 1965, folder ND 19/CO 62 6/3/65–6/10/65, box 202, National Defense, Subject File, White House Central Files, LBJL; Rowan to Johnson, 1 May 1965, folder Dominican Republic Vol. III Memos & Miscellaneous to 5/7/65, box 39, Latin America, Country File, National Security File, LBJL.

131. David Atlee Phillips, *The Night Watch* (New York: Atheneum, 1977), pp. 146–147; Yates, *Power Pack,* p. 103.

132. Mann's "List of Assignments," 1 May 1965, folder Mann Telcon Bundy Chron, box 1, Records Relating to the Dominican Crisis, 1965–1966, Under Secretary for Economic Affairs Subject Files, RG 59, NARA; Keith, "The Imperial Mind," pp. 234–235, 243.

133. Rowan to Johnson, 2 May 1965, folder Dominican Republic Vol. III Memos & Misc. to 5/7/65, box 39, Latin America, Country File, National Security File, LBJL; "Military Operations in the Dominican Republic," n.d., in book V of "Documents for Hearings," box 1, Records Relating to the Dominican Republic Crisis, 1965–1966, Subject Files, Under Secretary for Economic Affairs, NARA. On jamming efforts, see Rowan to Johnson, 5 May and 29 May 1965, both in folder Dominican Republic USIA Psychological Situation Reports 5/65, box 49, Latin America, Country File, National Security File, LBJL; Gordon Chase to Bundy, 6 May 1965, folder Dominican Republic Vol. III Memos & Miscellaneous to 5/7/65, box 39, Latin America, Country File, National Security File, LBJL; and situation report to the president, 10 May 1965, *Crises* 8: 035.

134. Bennett to State, folder POL 23-9 Dom Rep 5/25/65 Rebellion Coups, box 2130, Central Files, RG 59, NARA; Brown, "United States Propaganda," p. 243.

135. Herbert Garrettson Schoonmaker, *Military Crisis Management: U.S. Intervention in the Caribbean* (Westport, Conn.: Greenwood Press, 1990), p. 103; Slater, *Intervention and Negotiation,* pp. 112–113.

136. Franklin Franco interview by author; this was Bosch's assessment of the U.S. force, in U.S. embassy in Santo Domingo 314 to State, 2 August 1965, folder POL 23-9 Dom Rep 8/1/65 Rebellion Coups, box 2133, Central Files, RG 59, NARA; Moskos, "Grace under Pressure," p. 42.

137. Bonaparte Gautreaux Pineyro interview by author.

138. Chaljub Mejía interview; Palmer, *Intervention in the Caribbean,* p. 123.
139. *Patria,* 16 June 1965, p. 2; Franco interview.
140. Juan Miguel De Mora, *Misión de prensa en Santo Domingo,* 2nd ed. (Mexico City: El Día, 1965), pp. 71–74; Kurzman, *Damned,* p. 293; Bonaparte Gautreaux Pineyro, *El tiempo de la tormenta: Bosch, Caamaño y el PRD,* 2nd ed. (Santo Domingo: Editora de Colores, 1994), p. 57.
141. *Patria,* 29 May 1965, p. 3 (italics denote English in original); U.S. embassy in Santo Domingo to State, 24 August 1965, folder POL 23-9 Dom Rep 8/20/65 Rebellion Coups, Box 2133, Central Files, RG 59, NARA; see also Ramón Ferreras, *Guerra Patria: Santo Domingo, 28 de abril 1965–1ro. de octubre 1966,* 2nd ed. (Santo Domingo: Editorial del Nordeste, 1985).
142. Veloz interview; Gautreaux interview.
143. Rafael Chaljub Mejía, *La guerrilla del decoro: Memorias,* 2nd ed. (Santo Domingo: Taller, 1995); Cassá interview, 27 January 1998; Martin to State, 4 May 1965, folder POL 23-9 Dom Rep 5/4/65 Rebellion Coups, box 2127, Central Files, RG 59, NARA; "Sobre el mitín del 12 de julio," Constitutionalist broadcast, July 1965, AHT; U.S. embassy in Santo Domingo to State, 12 July 1965, folder POL 23-8 Dom Rep Demonstrations Riots Protests 6/1/65, box 2124, Central Files, RG 59, NARA.
144. Valenti to Johnson, 30 April 1965, folder Dominican Republic Vol. II Memos & Miscellaneous 1/64–4/65, box 38, Latin America, Country File, National Security File, LBJL; Sánchez interview; "The Grim Price of Power," *Look,* 15 June 1965, p. 40; Kurzman, *Damned,* p. 245.
145. Cobbs Hoffman, *All You Need Is Love,* pp. 202–203; Clark, *Church,* p. 103; Palmer, *Intervention in the Caribbean,* p. 48.
146. "The Grim Price of Power," p. 40; Quello and Isa Conde, "Revolutionary Struggle," p. 99; Radio Santo Domingo cited in U.S. embassy in Santo Domingo to State, 9 June 1965, folder POL 23-9 Dom Rep 6/5/65, box 2131, Central Files, RG 59, NARA.
147. Kurzman, *Damned,* p. 245.
148. USIA, "Negative Stereotypes about the United States Held by Latin American University Students," June 1965, folder R-80-65, box 8; and "Material for Countering Negative Stereotypes about the U.S. Held by Latin American Students," September 1966, folder R-118-66, box 13, both in Office of Research "R" Reports, 1964–1974, RG 306, NARA.
149. Wedge to Bennett, 16 December 1965, folder Correspondence with Ambassadors, box 16, Files of McGeorge Bundy, National Security File, LBJL; Wedge, "The Case Study of Student Political Violence," *World Politics* 21 (January 1969): 188, 202, 203. Bennett was so impressed with Wedge's findings that he sent them to Bundy, 8 January 1966, folder Correspondence with Ambassadors, box 16, Files of McGeorge Bundy, National Se-

curity File, LBJL, and to Rusk, 11 January 1966, folder POL 13 Dom Rep Non-Party Blocs 1/1/64, box 2119, Central Files, RG 59, NARA.

150. Quotation from U.S. embassy in Santo Domingo to State, 30 November 1965, folder POL 23-9 Dom Rep 11/1/65, box 2134, Central Files, RG 59, NARA. See also U.S. embassy in Santo Domingo to State, 2 September 1965, folder POL 13 Dom Rep Non-Party Blocs 1/1/64, box 2119, Central Files, RG 59, NARA; and L. C. Kilday, "Political Groups of Dominican Youth," 8 May 1966, folder POL 13 Dom Rep Non-Party Blocs 1/1/64, box 2119, Central Files, RG 59, NARA.

151. U.S. embassy in Santo Domingo to State, 11 August and 28 September 1966, folder Education & Culture Dom Rep 1/1/64, box 361, Central Files 1964–1966, RG 59, NARA.

152. "Los estudiantes y la reforma de la educación," ¡Ahora! 14 December 1970, pp. 49–52; 21 December 1971[?], pp. 26–28; and 28 December 1971[?], pp. 26–27; Tolentino interview.

153. CIA, 27 April 1965, folder Dominican Republic Vol. II Memos & Miscellaneous 1/64–4/65, box 38, Latin America, Country File, National Security File, LBJL; situation report for the president, 18 May 1965, folder POL 23-9 Dom Rep 5/17/65 Rebellion Coups, box 2129, Central Files, RG 59, NARA.

154. Caamaño, 25 March 1966, cited in Hermann, *Francis Caamaño,* p. 351; Bunker cited in *Caamaño frente a la OEA,* p. 254; Mann testimony, 14 July 1965, folder Senate Committee Hearings Mann-Vance July 14–15 DR, box 1, Records Relating to the Dominican Republic Crisis, 1965–1966, Subject Files, Under Secretary for Economic Affairs, RG 59, NARA.

155. U.S. embassy in Santo Domingo to State, 25 September 1965, folder POL 23-9 Dom Rep 9/15/65 Rebellion Coups, box 2134, Central Files, RG 59, NARA; Slater, *Intervention and Negotiation,* p. 143; U.S. embassy in Santo Domingo to State, 25 September 1965, folder POL 23-9 Dom Rep Demonstrations Riots Protests 6/1/65, box 2124, Central Files, RG 59, NARA. Situation report, 30 September 1965, folder POL 23-9 Dom Rep 9/15/65 Rebellion Coups, box 2134, Central Files, RG 59, NARA; *El Popular,* 9 October 1965, p. 3, ARC.

156. W. G. Bowdler to Bundy, 19 October 1965, folder Dominican Republic Vol. XII Memos & Miscellaneous 10/65–11/65, box 45, Latin America, Country File, National Security File, LBJL.

157. Unsigned memorandum for State, 26 April 1966, folder Dominican Republic Elections, 1966, box 10, Intelligence File, National Security File, LBJL; Valenti to Johnson with information from J. Edgar Hoover, 11 April 1966, folder Dominican Republic Vol. XIV Memos & Misc. 1/66–4/66 [1 of 2], box 46, Latin America, Country Files, National Security File, LBJL.

158. "Elections in the DR," 14 March 1966, folder Dominican Republic Vol. XIV Memos & Misc. 1/66–4/66 [1 of 2], box 46, Latin America, Country Files, National Security File, LBJL.

159. Moskos, "Grace under Pressure," p. 42; Eugenio Chang-Rodriguez, ed., *The Lingering Crisis: A Case Study of the Dominican Republic* (New York: Las Americas, 1969); Slater, *Intervention and Negotiation,* pp. 164, 174; Rostow to Johnson, 10 May 1966, folder Dominican Republic Elections, 1966, box 10, Intelligence File, National Security File, LBJL; Edward Herman and Frank Brodhead, *Demonstration Elections: U.S.-Staged Elections in the Dominican Republic, Vietnam, and El Salvador* (Boston: South End Press, 1984).

160. Califano interview.

161. Wiarda, "From Fragmentation to Disintegration: The Social and Political Effect of the Dominican Revolution," in Chang-Rodriguez, *Lingering Crisis,* p. 30; Balaguer received $118 million in AID support (Kryzanek, "Dominican Intervention Revisited," p. 145); Cassá, *Los doce años;* Isis Duarte and José Pérez, "Consideraciones en torno a la política represiva y asistencial del estado dominicano, 1966–1978," *Realidad contemporánea* 10–11 (year 2): 61–77; Atkins, *Arms and Politics;* Richard Pearson, "Joaquin Balaguer Dies at 95," *Washington Post,* 15 July 2002, p. B4.

162. Ball, *The Past Has Another Pattern: Memoirs* (New York: W. W. Norton, 1982), p. 325; Goodwin, *Remembering America* (Boston: Little, Brown, 1988), p. 406.

163. Bundy meeting with aides, 4 September 1965, folder Dominican Republic Vol. X Memos & Miscellaneous 8/65–9/65 [1 of 2], box 43, Latin America, Country File, National Security File, LBJL; Center for Strategic Studies, *Dominican Action, 1965: Intervention or Cooperation?* (Washington, D.C.: Center for Strategic Studies, July 1966), pp. viii–ix. See also John Carey, ed., *The Dominican Republic Crisis, 1965: Background Paper and Proceedings of the Ninth Hammarskjöld Forum* (Dobbs Ferry, N.Y.: Oceana, 1967), p. 8.

164. Mann, Annual Meeting of the Inter-American Press Association, 12 October 1965, folder Dominican Republic Vol. XI Memos & Misc. 9/65–10/65 [1 of 2], box 44, Latin America, Country File, National Security File, LBJL.

Epilogue

1. "South Korea: When Friends Irritate," *The Economist,* 20–26 May 2000, p. 54.

2. Cited in Richard West, "Why Latin Americans Say, 'Go Home, Yanqui,'" *New York Times Magazine,* 29 May 1966, p. 8; Morgan, *Among the Anti-Americans* (New York: Holt, Rinehart and Winston, 1967), p. 4.

3. Martin, *Overtaken by Events: The Dominican Crisis, from the Fall of Trujillo to the Civil War* (Garden City, N.Y.: Doubleday, 1966), p. 736.

4. Emphasis added; Frachon, "L'Amérique mal-aimée," *Le Monde*, 24 November 2001; see also Jean Birnbaum, "Enquête sur une détestation française," in the same issue.

5. Ambassador cited in Daniel Ellwood, "French Anti-Americanism and McDonald's," *History Today* (February 2001): 34. Overviews of French anti-Americanism include the 24 November 2001 issue of *Le Monde*; and Sophie Meunier, "The French Exception," *Foreign Affairs* 79 (July–August 2000): 104–116. Lengthier studies are David Strauss, *Menace in the West: The Rise of French Anti-Americanism in Modern Times* (Westport, Conn.: Greenwood Press, 1978); Leo Winston Hindsley, "In Search of an Ally: French Attitudes toward America, 1919–1929" (Ph.D. diss., Michigan State University, 1980); Georges Suffert, *Les nouveaux cow-boys: Essai sur l'anti-américanisme primaire* (Paris: Olivier Orban, 1984); Denis Lacorne, Jacques Rupnik, and Marie-France Toinet, eds., *The Rise and Fall of Anti-Americanism: A Century of French Perception,* trans. Gerry Turner (New York: St. Martin's Press, 1990), originally published as *L'Amérique dans les têtes: Un siècle de fascinations et d'aversions* (Paris: Hachette, 1986); Helene Laurendeau-Johnson, "French News Magazines on America, 1974–1984: Influences of Political Ideology on Media Content" (Ph.D. diss., New York University, 1994); Richard Kuisel, *Seducing the French: The Dilemma of Americanization* (Berkeley: University of California Press, 1993); and Seth David Armus, "Primacy of the Spiritual: French Resistance to America and the Formation of French Identity" (Ph.D. diss., SUNY—Stony Brook, 1998).

6. Peter MacKinnon, "Confessions of an Anti-American," *Reason,* August 1985, p. 37.

7. Crespi, "The Extent of Anti-Americanism Abroad in the Wake of Iranian Developments," folder S-11-79, box 19, Research Reports 1964–1982, Office of Research, RG 306, NARA; see also USIA draft, "Anti-Americanism: A Cruel New World for the US?" 5 December 1979, folder S-19-79, box 20, Special Reports 1964–1982, same location.

8. Robert Snyder, "Explaining the Iranian Revolution's Hostility toward the United States," *Journal of South Asian and Middle Eastern Studies* 17 (Spring 1994): 19–31; Gi-Wook Shin, "South Korean Anti-Americanism: A Comparative Perspective," *Asian Survey* 36 (August 1996): 787–803; Diane Hoffman, "Culture, Self, and 'URI': Anti-Americanism in Contemporary South Korea," *Journal of Northeast Asian Studies* 12 (Summer 1993): 3–20; Eric Shiraev and Vladislav Zubok, *Anti-Americanism in Russia: From Stalin to Putin* (New York: Palgrave, 2000).

9. Graffiti reported in David Atlee Phillips, *The Night Watch* (New York: Atheneum, 1977), p. 167; and West, "Why Latin Americans," p. 8.

10. John Johnson, "The United States and the Latin American Left Wings," *Yale Review* 56 (March 1967): 333.

11. Frachon, "L'Amérique mal-aimée"; Pew Research Center for the People and the Press (Washington, D.C.), "The Pew Global Attitudes Project," 19 December 2001, available, along with other polls, at www.people-press.org; Alexander Stille, "'Nous sommes tous américains,'" *Correspondence* (Council on Foreign Relations), Spring 2002, p. 7.

12. Stephen Haseler, *Anti-Americanism: Steps on a Dangerous Path* (London: Institute for European Defence and Strategic Studies, 1986), p. 8; James Wallace, "What's Wrong in Latin America: Story Back of Hemisphere's Problems," *U.S. News and World Report,* 24 May 1965, p. 40; see also "How the World Views the U.S.," *Newsweek,* 21 June 1965, p. 39.

13. Luis Carlos Prestes cited in Castañeda, *Utopia Unarmed: The Latin American Left after the Cold War* (New York: Knopf, 1993), p. 286. Historians have also responded to dependency theory by arguing that internal factors long prepared underdevelopment before the arrival of the United States as a major investor. See for instance Stephen Haber, ed., *How Latin America Fell Behind: Essays on the Economic Histories of Brazil and Mexico, 1800–1914* (Stanford, Calif.: Stanford University Press, 1997). On new economic history in Latin America, see John Coatsworth and Alan Taylor, eds., *Latin America and the World Economy since 1800* (Cambridge, Mass.: Harvard University, David Rockefeller Center for Latin American Studies, 1998), pp. 3–10.

14. Thomas Perry Thornton, "Preface," *Annals of the American Academy of Political and Social Science* 497 (May 1988): 13.

15. Ellwood, "French Anti-Americanism and McDonald's," p. 34; Frachon, "L'Amérique mal-aimée"; "'L'antiaméricanisme n'est pas un sentiment populaire,'" *Le Monde,* 24 November 2001.

16. The issue of anti-Americanism adds an argument for continuity to the debate over the nature of change in U.S. policy toward Latin American in the 1950s and 1960s. Most recently, scholars have emphasized similarities. See Stephen Rabe, "The Johnson (Eisenhower?) Doctrine for Latin America," *Diplomatic History* 9 (December 1985): 95–100; Rabe, *The Most Dangerous Area in the World: John F. Kennedy Confronts Communist Revolution in Latin America* (Chapel Hill: University of North Carolina, 1999); and David Schmitz, *Thank God They're on Our Side: The United States and Right-Wing Dictatorships, 1921–1965* (Chapel Hill: University of North Carolina Press, 1999). For the argument in favor of change, see Arthur Schlesinger, Jr., "The Lowering Hemisphere," *Atlantic Monthly* (January 1970): 79–88; and

John Daniel Coats, "A Matter of Perspective: U.S. Policy toward the Caribbean during the Kennedy and Johnson Administrations, 1961–1965" (Ph.D. diss., Texas A&M University, 1996).

17. Allen, "The Overseas Image of American Democracy," *Annals of the American Academy of Political and Social Science* 366 (July 1966): 62, 60; Smith interview.

18. Theodore Sorensen, *Kennedy* (New York: Harper and Row, 1965), p. 540.

19. *America,* 27 August 1966, p. 202; "Anti-Americanism Sweeps World," *U.S. News and World Report,* 8 April 1968, pp. 51–52; "Is Anti-Americanism Growing?" *U.S. News and World Report,* 5 August 1968, p. 8.

20. William Pfaff, "Yankees vs. Latins," *Commonweal,* 28 May 1965, p. 310; "The Anatomy of Anti-Americanism," *Senior Scholastic,* 11 February 1966, p. 7.

21. News conference, 11 October 2001, *Weekly Compilation of Presidential Documents,* 15 October 2001, 37 (Washington, D.C., GPO), pp. 1454–1462. One of the better articles with that title was Peter Ford, "'Why Do They Hate Us?'" *Christian Science Monitor,* 27 September 2001. Statistic on U.S. policies from Pew Research Center, "Global Attitudes Project."

22. Cited in James Saxon Childers, *The Nation on the Flying Trapeze: The United States as the People of the East See Us* (New York: David McKay, 1960), p. 81; Pew Research Center, "Global Attitudes Project"; Keith Richburg, "Divergent Views of U.S. Role in World," *Washington Post,* 20 December 2001, p. A34.

Selected Sources

Government Collections

Cuba

Fondo Ministerio de Estado, AGNC.
Fondo Minrex, AGNC.

Dominican Republic

Fondo Documental de la Presidencia, AGNDR.
Fondo Documental del Secretario de Estado de Interior y Policía, AGNDR.

Panama

Actas del Consejo Nacional de Relaciones Exteriores, PAMINREX.
Archivo de la Presidencia, ANRP.
Serie 9 de Enero 1964, PAMINREX.

United States

Administrative History File, LBJL.
Confidential File, LBJL.
Eisenhower Papers as President, DDEL.
Eisenhower Post-Presidential Papers, DDEL.
Handwriting File, LBJL.
Kennedy Papers, JFKL.
National Security File, JFKL.
National Security File, LBJL.
Office of the President File, LBJL.
President's Office File, JFKL.
Prints and Photographs, LCong.
Record Group 59, U.S. Department of State, NARA.

Record Group 84, Foreign Service Posts of the Department of State, NARA.
Record Group 111, Records of the Office of the Chief Signal Officer, NARA.
Record Group 185, Records of the Panama Canal, NARA.
Record Group 306, U.S. Information Agency, NARA.
Senate Papers, LBJL.
Vice-Presidential Security File, LBJL.
White House Central Files, DDEL.
White House Central Files, JFKL.
White House Central Files, LBJL.
White House Office, DDEL.
White House Series, Recordings and Transcripts of Conversations and Meetings,
    LBJL.

Private Collections

Ball, George, LBJL.
Bonsal, Philip, Manuscripts Division, LCong.
Califano, Joseph, LBJL.
Cassá, Roberto, ARC.
Dulles, John Foster, DDEL.
Eisenhower, Milton, DDEL.
Herter, Christian, DDEL.
Jorden, William, LBJL.
Mann, Thomas, DDEL.
Marks, Leonard, LBJL.
Martin, John Bartlow, Manuscripts Division, LCong.
De la Rosa, Diógenes, Biblioteca Nacional, Panama.
Schlesinger, Arthur, Jr., JFKL.
Sorensen, Theodore, JFKL.
Szulc, Tad, JFKL.
Tolentino Dipp, Hugo, AHT.
Waugh, Samuel, DDEL.

Interviews from Libraries

Aiken, George D. By Paige E. Mulhollan, 10 October 1968, Internet copy,
    LBJL.
Allen, George. By Ed Edwin, 7 March 1967, DDEL.
Bissell, Richard M., Jr. By Ed Edwin, 5 June 1967, DDEL.
————. By Richard D. Challener, 7 September 1966, Mudd Library, Princeton
    University.
Bosch, Juan. By Lloyd Cutler, Spring 1964, JFKL.

Briggs, Ellis. By John T. Mason, Jr., 15 October 1972, DDEL.

Bundy, McGeorge. By David Nunnerly, 30 January 1970, JFKL.

Cabot, John Moors. By William W. Moss, 27 January 1971, JFKL.

————. By Paige E. Mulhollan, 28 February 1969, LBJL.

————. By Philip A. Crowl, 15 November 1965, Mudd Library, Princeton University.

Califano, Joseph A., Jr. By Michael L. Gillette, 27 January 1988, LBJL.

Cushman, Robert E. By Thomas Soapes, 4 March 1977, DDEL.

Dulles, Allen. By Thomas Braden, 5–6 December 1964, JFKL.

Eisenhower, Dwight D. By Ed Edwin, 20 July 1967, DDEL.

Eisenhower, Milton S. By John Luter. 6 September 1967, DDEL.

————. By Philip A. Crowl, 6 March 1965, Mudd Library, Princeton University.

Fortas, Abe. By Joe B. Frantz, 14 August 1969, Internet copy, LBJL.

Goodpaster, Andrew J. By Ed Edwin, 2 August 1967, 26 June 1975, DDEL.

Hickenlooper, Bourke. By Paige E. Mulhollan, 19 September 1968, LBJL.

Linowitz, Sol. By Joe B. Frantz, 22 November 1968, LBJL.

Mankiewicz, Frank. By Stephen Goodell, 18 April 1969, LBJL.

Mann, Thomas C. By Maclyn P. Burg, 17 December 1975, DDEL.

————. By Larry Hackman, 13 March 1968, JFKL.

————. By Joe B. Frantz, 4 November 1968, LBJL.

————. By Philip A. Crowl, 24 May 1966, Mudd Library, Princeton University.

Martin, John Bartlow. By Paige E. Mulhollan, 30 January 1971, LBJL.

McCone, John A. By Joe B. Frantz, 19 August 1970, JFKL.

McElroy, Neil. By Columbia University, 9 May 1967, DDEL.

McPherson, Harry. Interview 1 by T. H. Baker, 5 December 1968, Internet copy, LBJL.

Muñoz Marin, Luis. By Lee White, 11 June 1965, JFKL.

Oliver, Covey T. By Paige E. Mulhollan, 2 and 12 December 1968, LBJL.

Paarlberg, Don. By Ed Edwin, 17 January 1968, DDEL.

Rostow, Walt W. By Richard Newstadt, 11 April 1964, JFKL.

Rubottom, Richard Roy, Jr. By John Luter, 22 December 1969, 11 August 1970, DDEL.

————. By Richard D. Challener, 12 June 1966, Mudd Library, Princeton University.

Rusk, Dean. Interview 1, 28 July 1969, and Interview 3, 2 January 1979, both by Paige E. Mulhollan, Internet copies, LBJL.

————. Vols. 1 and 2, 1969–1970, JFKL.

Schlesinger, Arthur, Jr. By Joe B. Frantz, 4 November 1971, LBJL.

Smathers, George A. By Donald Ritchie, 24 October 1989, JFKL.

Smith, Bromley. Interview 2 by Paige E. Mulhollan, 25 September 1969, Internet copy, LBJL.

Smith, Howard K. By John Luter, 19 January 1967, DDEL.

Vance, Cyrus. By Paige E. Mulhollan, 3 November 1969, LBJL.
Washburn, Mr. and Mrs. Abbott. By Ed Edwin, 5 January 1968, DDEL.

Interviews by Author

Ahumada, Adolfo. Tape recording, Panama City, Panama, 25 October 1999.
Alavez, Elena. Havana, Cuba, 25 June 1998.
Arias Chiari, Daira. Panama City, Panama, 3 November 1999.
Barnett, Deyanira. Tape recording, Panama City, Panama, 19 October 1999.
Boyd, Aquilino. Panama City, Panama, 27 October 1999.
Britton, Federico. Tape recording, Panama City, Panama, 20 October 1999.
Caamaño, Claudio. Tape recording, Santo Domingo, Dominican Republic, 2
    February 2000.
Cassá, Roberto. Santo Domingo, Dominican Republic, 27 January, 3 February,
    10 February, 17 February, 24 February, 3 March, 10 March, 14 April 1998.
Chaljub Mejía, Rafael. Tape recording, Santo Domingo, Dominican Republic, 12
    February 2000.
Cordero Michel, Emilio. Santo Domingo, Dominican Republic, 8 March 2000.
Cordero, Margarita. Tape recording, Santo Domingo, Dominican Republic, 17
    February 2000.
Cué, Daisy. Santiago, Cuba, 3 July 1998.
Cury, Jottin. Tape recording, Santo Domingo, Dominican Republic, 1 March 2000.
De Bernard, Napoleón. Tape recording, Panama City, Panama, 21 October 1999.
De Cruz, Porfirio. Tape recording, Panama City, Panama, 11 November 1999.
Despradel, Fidelio. Tape recording, Santo Domingo, Dominican Republic, 21
    February 2000.
Díaz, Gustavo. Tape recording, Santo Domingo, Dominican Republic, 11 Febru-
    ary 2000.
Eleta, Fernando. Tape recording, Panama City, Panama, 21 October 1999.
Figgins, Dan. Tape recording, Raleigh, North Carolina, 3 and 29 September
    1998.
Franco, Franklin. Tape recording, Santo Domingo, Dominican Republic, 18
    February 2000.
Galvá, Lorenzo. Santo Domingo, Dominican Republic, 19 February 2000.
Gastelú, Emilio. Tape recording, Panama City, Panama, 8 October 1999.
Gautreaux Pineyro, Bonaparte. Tape recording, Santo Domingo, Dominican Re-
    public, 15 March 2000.
González, Reymundo. Santo Domingo, Dominican Republic, 31 March 1998.
Guzmán, Leandro. Tape recording, Santo Domingo, Dominican Republic, 23
    February 2000.
Hermann, Hamlet. Tape recording, Santo Domingo, Dominican Republic, 18
    February 2000.

Hernando Ramírez, Miguel Ángel. Tape recording, Santo Domingo, Dominican Republic, 23 February 2000.

Illueca, Jorge. Tape recording, Panama City, Panama, 15 November 1999.

Isa Conde, Narciso. Tape recording, Santo Domingo, Dominican Republic, 28 February 2000.

Jakowska, Sophie. Santo Domingo, Dominican Republic, 2 March 2000.

Krebs, Max. Tape recording, Foxfire Village, North Carolina, 31 August, 9 September 1998.

Martínez, Padre José Ignacio. Tape recording, Panama City, Panama, 11 November 1999.

Matos, Húber. Tape recording, Chapel Hill, North Carolina, 24 February 1999.

Moreno, Miguel. Tape recording, Panama City, Panama, 11 October 1999.

Navas, Luis. Tape recording, Panama City, Panama, 12 October 1999.

Ortega, Julio. Tape recording, Panama City, Panama, 26 October 1999.

Ortega, Oydén. Tape recording, Panama City, Panama, 13 October 1999.

Pereira, Ramón. Tape recording, Panama City, Panama, 19 November 1999.

Pérez Terrero, Juan. Tape recording, Santo Domingo, Dominican Republic, 7 March 2000.

Plambeck, Arthur. Tape recording, Hillsborough, North Carolina, 1 September 1998.

Quinn, Bruce. Tape recording, Panama City, Panama, 11 October 1999.

Ricord, Humberto. Tape recording, Panama City, Panama, 14 December 1999.

Rostow, Walt W. Tape recording, Austin, Texas, 21 July 1999.

Sánchez, Mario. Tape recording, Santo Domingo, Dominican Republic, 14 February 2000.

Solís Palma, Manuel. Tape recording, Panama City, Panama, 28 October 1999.

Tabares del Real, José Antonio. Havana, Cuba, 18 June 1998.

Tolentino Dipp, Hugo. Tape recording, Santo Domingo, Dominican Republic, 11 March 2000.

Torres, Padre Rosendo. Tape recording, Panama City, Panama, 25 November 1999.

Veloz Maggiolo, Marcio. Tape recording, Santo Domingo, Dominican Republic, 29 February 2000.

Vergara, Luis. Tape recording, Panama City, Panama, 27 October 1999.

Villareal, César. Tape recording, Panama City, Panama, 15 October 1999.

Government and International-Organization Documents

Berle, Adolf A., Jr. *The Adolf A. Berle Diary.* Hyde Park, N.Y.: Franklin D. Roosevelt Library, 1978.

Bureau of Social Science Research, The American University. *Foreign Leaders' Reactions to the United States: An Interview Study.* Department of State, November 1954.

Caribbean Anti-Communist Research and Intelligence Bureau. *Invasion Report—Constanza Maimón Estero Hondo: Communist Aggression against the Dominican Republic.* 1959.

CIA Research Reports: Latin America, 1946–1976. Frederick, Md.: UPA, 1982.

Confidential U.S. State Department Central Files. Cuba 1955–1959. Frederick, Md.: UPA, 1987.

Council on Foreign Relations. *Documents on American Foreign Relations.* 1959 to 1964. New York: Harper, 1960–1965.

Crises in Panama and the Dominican Republic: National Security Files and NSC Histories, 1963–1969. Frederick, Md.: UPA, 1982.

Cuba, Ministerio de Estado, Departamento de Relaciones Públicas. *¡Cuba denuncia ante el mundo!* 1959.

———. *Una nueva diplomacia.* Havana: Ministerio de Estado, 1959.

Cuba, Ministerio de Trabajo. *Trabajo.* 1960–1961.

Dulles, John Foster. *Minutes of Telephone Conversations with Christian Herter, 1953–1961.* UPA, 1980.

Hearings of the Committee of the International Commission of Jurists in Panama, Republic of Panama. 6–13 March, 1964.

International Commission of Jurists. *Report on the Events in Panama, January 9–12, 1964.* Geneva, Switzerland, 1964.

OSS / State Department Intelligence and Research Reports, 15: Latin America: 1941–1961. Edited by Paul Kesaris. Washington, D.C.: UPA.

República de Panamá, Ministerio de Relaciones Exteriores. *Memoria que el ministro de Relaciones Exteriores presenta a la Honorable Asamblea Nacional en sus sesiones ordinarias.* 1958–1965.

The Anti-United States Riots of November 1959. Canal Zone: [1960?].

Transcript of the United States Oral Presentation on February 14 and 15, 1964, to the Committee Established under the Resolution of the OAS/OC, February 6, 1964.

U.S. Congress. *Congressional Record.* Washington, D.C.: GPO, 1959.

U.S. Department of State. *Foreign Relations of the United States.* Washington: GPO.

———. *Department of State Bulletin.*

U.S. Senate. *Communist Anti-American Riots: Mob Violence as an Instrument of Red Diplomacy.* Senate Internal Security Subcommittee, Judiciary Committee, 26 August 1960, Washington, D.C.: GPO, 1960.

———. Committee on Foreign Relations. *Report of Proceedings: Briefing by Secretary of State Dean Rusk on the World Situation.* Washington, D.C.: 16 January 1964.

———. *Top-Secret Hearings by the U.S. Senate Committee on Foreign Relations, 1959–1966.* Frederick, Md.: UPA, 1981.

Acknowledgments

This book on anti-Americanism is the result, appropriately enough, of a pan-American effort. From Canada to Panama, many people helped me to work in their country's archives and libraries, track down interviewees, and sometimes find shelter for the night. I am deeply grateful to the dozens of men and women whom I interviewed and whose names appear in the Selected Sources. Their thoughtful answers are, in many ways, the heart of this study.

The Social Sciences and Research Council of Canada, the U.S. Social Science Research Council, and the Duke-UNC Latin American Studies Program in collaboration with the U.S. Department of Education provided most of my funding. Thanks also to the Kennedy Library Foundation, the Lyndon Baines Johnson Foundation, and the Institute for Latin American Studies and the History Department at the University of North Carolina for additional grants. The Office of the Dean at Howard University's College of Arts and Sciences provided generous technical support.

Latin Americans often made special efforts to help make my trips pleasurable. In Cuba, I thank the staffs of the Archivo General de la Nación, the Archivo Fílmico del Instituto Cubano de Arte e Industria Cinematográficos, and the Biblioteca Nacional José Martí, all in Havana. Tomás Fernández of the Biblioteca became a friend in the process of introducing me to the scholars of Havana and Santiago. Ampáro Hernández and Belkis Quesada Guerra at the Instituto de Historia de Cuba eased my bureaucratic tasks. I also wish to acknowledge the hospitality offered, often at personal risk, by Juan and María, and especially by Daisy and her family, who nourished me with literary conversations and luscious El Caney mangoes.

In Panama, I benefited from the advice of historians Alfredo Castillero Calvo and Alfredo Figueroa Navarro, who have made important contributions to the scholarship in their country. Thanks also to Michael

Conniff, Aims McGuinness, Gloria Rudolf, Raúl Leis, Reymundo Gurdián Guerra, and Guillermo de Saint-Malo, and especially to Francisco López of the U.S. embassy for his friendship and expert chauffering in Panama City. Xiomara Sarmiento de Robletto, the director of the archives of the Foreign Ministry, was trusting and helpful with my inquiries, and the staffs of the Technical Resources Center, the Archivo Nacional, the Biblioteca Nacional, the Universidad de Panamá, the Organisación para Relaciones entre Estados Unidos y Panamá, and the Instituto Nacional were unfailingly courteous and professional during my two trips to the country. Most of all, I recall the good cheer and *jugo de tamarindo* of María Carazo and Hans Parisi, who have made a home for themselves and other expatriates in the heart of the Isthmus.

In the Dominican Republic, I received generous assistance from María Filomena González and Rubén Silié at FLACSO–Santo Domingo; Mu-Kien Sang and Ramonina Brea; Lynne Guitar and Severino "Jordan" Polanco; Eddy Jaquez and the staff of the Archivo General de la Nación; Kristine Jones and the Pontificia Universidad Católica Madre y Maestra; the men and women who enliven the Trinitaria bookstore; and the staffs of the Instituto Tecnológico de Santo Domingo, the Biblioteca Nacional, the Instituto Bonó, the Universidad Autónoma de Santo Domingo, and the Universidad Nacional Pedro Henríquez Ureña. The Sociedad Dominicana de Bibliófilos provided me with a room of my own; Juan Pérez Terrero let me reprint his photos and provided the story behind them. For opening their private archives, I thank Roberto Cassá and Hugo Tolentino Dipp. Cassá's generosity and integrity have been an inspiration to me and to countless Dominicans.

In the United States, many people helped me in my efforts to consult mountains of materials on a shoestring budget. I thank the archivists and librarians of the National Archives and Records Administration, the Library of Congress, the National Security Archive, and Howard University. The staffs of the Eisenhower, Kennedy, and Johnson libraries were always cheerful and cooperative. The Benson Latin American Collection in Austin and the Mudd Library at Princeton University likewise contained rare gems. For their hospitality, I am also grateful to John and Stephen in Austin, Claudio in Boston, Carol and Amy in Baltimore, and the Hages in Washington, D.C. In the course of shaping the manuscript, I benefited from the research assistance of Glenn Chambers at Howard University and from the guidance of editors and anonymous readers of Harvard University Press.

My most heartfelt thanks go to the people who surrounded me in Chapel Hill, where these stories of anti-Americanism came together as one. At Davis Library (University of North Carolina) and Perkins Library (Duke University), staff members were resourceful and patient. Steve Estes offered incisive observations on an early version of the manuscript. James Crawford, Xiaodong Wong, Matt Jacobs, and Christopher Endy responded to drafts with generous comments. Chris, especially, lifted my flagging spirits and offered constructive readings. John Chasteen, Peter Filene, Louis Pérez, Jr., and Lars Schoultz provided much wise counsel. And I will forever be grateful to Michael Hunt, one of the finest educators I have known. I share this book with him more than with anyone else, though I hold no one but myself responsible for its shortcomings.

Index